Italian

lonely planet

phrasebooks
and
Karina Coates & Pietro Iagnocco

Italian phrasebook
4th edition – February 2011

Published by Lonely Planet Publications Pty Ltd
ABN 36 005 607 983

Lonely Planet Offices
Australia Locked Bag 1, Footscray, Victoria 3011
USA 150 Linden St, Oakland CA 94607
UK 2nd fl, 186 City Rd, London, EC1V 2NT

Contact
talk2us@lonelyplanet.com.au
lonelyplanet.com/contact

Cover illustration Daniel New

ISBN 978 1 74179 334 5

text © Lonely Planet 2011
cover illustration © Lonely Planet 2011

10 9 8 7 6 5 4 3 2 1

Printed in China

MIX
Paper from
responsible sources
FSC™ C021741

acknowledgments

This 4th edition of Lonely Planet's *Italian* phrasebook is based on the previous three editions by the Lonely Planet Language Products team, Pietro Iagnocco, Karina Coates and Susie Walker for the Italian translations and pronunciation guides, and Mirna Cicioni who translated the Sustainable Travel section. For this edition, the new content was also added by Italian translator and language specialist Mirna Cicioni. *Grazie mille Mirna, Pietro, Karina e Susie!*

Thanks also to the others who contributed to the previous editions on which this one is based:

Jane Atkin, Francesca Coles, Adrienne Costanzo, Ben Handicott, Jim Jenkin, Piers Kelly, Emma Koch, Paul Piaia, Fabrice Rocher, Karin Vidstrup Monk, Meg Worby, and last but not least, Yukiyoshi Kamimura who created the inside illustrations.

Lonely Planet Language Products

Associate Publisher: Tali Budlender
Managing Editor: Annelies Mertens
Editor: Branislava Vladisavljevic
Managing Layout Designer: Celia Wood
Layout Designer: Wibowo Rusli
Cartographer: Wayne Murphy
Production Support: Yvonne Kirk, Glenn van der Knijff

make the most of this phrasebook ...

Anyone can speak another language! It's all about confidence. Don't worry if you can't remember your school language lessons or if you've never learnt a language before. Even if you learn the very basics (on the inside covers of this book), your travel experience will be the better for it. You have nothing to lose and everything to gain when the locals hear you making an effort.

finding things in this book

For easy navigation, this book is in sections. The Tools chapters are the ones you'll thumb through time and again. The Practical section covers basic travel situations like catching transport and finding accommodation. The Social section gives you conversational phrases, pick-up lines, the ability to express opinions – so you can get to know people. Food has a section all of its own: gourmets and vegetarians are covered and local dishes feature. Safe Travel equips you with health and police phrases, just in case. Remember the colours of each section and you'll find everything easily; or use the comprehensive Index. Otherwise, check the two-way traveller's Dictionary for the word you need.

being understood

Throughout this book you'll see coloured phrases on the right-hand side of each page. They're phonetic guides to help you pronounce the language. You don't even need to look at the language itself, but you'll get used to the way we've represented particular sounds. The pronunciation chapter in Tools will explain more, but you can feel confident that if you read the coloured phrase slowly, you'll be understood.

communication tips

Body language, ways of doing things, sense of humour – all have a role to play in every culture. 'Local talk' boxes show you common ways of saying things, or everyday language to drop into conversation. 'Listen for ...' boxes supply the phrases you may hear. They start with the phonetic guide (because you'll hear it before you know what's being said) and then lead in to the language and the English translation.

italian

Bern
Switzerland

Slovenia
Ljubljana
Zagreb

Croatia

San Marino

ITALY

Rome

Adriatic Sea

Tyrrhenian Sea

Sardinia

0 — 100 km
0 — 60 mi

MEDITERRANEAN SEA

Sicily

national language

official language

EUROPE

For more details see the **introduction**.

English-speakers will find Italian a beautiful language to listen to and an easy one to start speaking. The expressive rhythm and melody of the language, which has lent itself to the epic poetry of Dante and the grand operas of Verdi, has fascinated visitors for centuries. When even a simple sentence can sound like an aria you'll find it difficult to resist striking up a conversation.

Of all the Romance languages – which include French, Spanish, Portuguese and Romanian – Italian claims the closest family relationship to Latin. Because English has been heavily influenced by Latin (particularly through its contact with French), there are many basic resemblances between the two languages. Today, thanks to widespread migration and the enormous popularity of Italian culture and cuisine, most of us are also familiar with modern Italian words like *ciao*, *pasta*, and *bello*.

Outside Italy, Italian is spoken by minorities in Switzerland, Slovenia and France, and more recently by large communities of immigrants in Australia, Argentina and the US. Italian has official status in Croatia's Istrian peninsula where an Italian-speaking community has existed since the Venetians began colonising these parts of the Dalmatian coast during the 12th century.

at a glance ...

language name: Italian

name in language: *italiano*
ee·ta·*lya*·no

language family: Romance

key country: Italy

approximate number of speakers: 65 million

close relatives: French, Spanish, Portuguese

donations to English: Words to do with food, including *spaghetti*, *broccoli* and *macaroni;* musical words like *virtuoso*, *opera* and *viola;* architectural terms such as *studio* and *stucco;* artistic words such as *maestro* and *fresco*.

introduction

Another country where Italian is spoken is the African nation of Eritrea which remained a colony of Italy from 1880 until 1941. Today most Eritreans speak Italian only as a second language.

Around the world there are approximately 65 million Italian speakers, the majority of whom live in Italy. In Italy itself, most people also speak a local dialect. Dialects are spoken all over the country and some are so different from standard Italian as to be considered distinct languages in their own right. In fact, it wasn't until the nineteenth century that the Tuscan dialect – the language of Dante, Boccaccio, Petrarch and Macchiavelli – was chosen to become the standard language of the nation. Standard Italian is the official language of schools, media and administration, and is the form that will take you from the top of the boot to the very toe. All the language that we have provided here is in standard Italian.

This book gives you the words you need to get by, as well as all the fun, spontaneous phrases that lead to a better experience of Italy and its people. Need more encouragement? Remember, the contact you make through using Italian will make your travels unique. Local knowledge, new relationships and a sense of satisfaction are on the tip of your tongue, so don't just stand there, say something!

> **abbreviations used in this book**

f	feminine	**sg**	singular
inf	informal	**pl**	plural
m	masculine	**pol**	polite

pronuncia

The Italian sound system will be familiar to most English-speakers: almost all of the sounds you'll hear exist in English. You might notice some slight differences, particularly with the vowel sounds, but there's nothing to stop you from having a go and being understood. Standard Italian pronunciation is given in this book – the same form that's used in education and the media.

vowel sounds

symbol	english equivalent	italian example	transliteration
a	father	*pane*	*pa·ne*
e	red	*letto*	*le·to*
ee	bee	*vino*	*vee·no*
o	pot	*molto*	*mol·to*
oo	took	*frutta*	*froo·ta*

Italian vowel sounds are generally shorter than in English. They normally do not run together to form vowel sound combinations (diphthongs), though it can often sound that way to English-speakers. The following table presents four vowel sounds that roughly correspond to diphthongs in English:

symbol	english equivalent	italian example	transliteration
ai	aisle	*mai*	mai
ay	say	*vorrei*	vo·ray
ow	cow	*ciao, autobus*	chow, ow·to·boos
oy	boy	*poi*	poy

pronunciation

consonant sounds

symbol	english equivalent	italian example	transliteration
b	big	*bello*	*be·lo*
ch	chilli	*centro*	*chen·tro*
d	din	*denaro*	de·na·ro
dz	lids	*mezzo, zaino*	me·dzo, dzai·no
f	fun	*fare*	fa·re
g	go	*gomma*	go·ma
j	jam	*cugino*	koo·jee·no
k	kick	*cambio, quanto*	kam·byo, kwan·to
l	loud	*linea*	lee·ne·a
ly	million	*figlia*	fee·lya
m	man	*madre*	ma·dre
n	no	*numero*	noo·me·ro
ny	canyon	*bagno*	ba·nyo
p	pig	*pronto*	pron·to
r	run (strong and rolled)	*ristorante*	rees·to·ran·te
s	so	*sera*	se·ra
sh	show	*capisce*	ka·pee·she
t	tin	*teatro*	te·a·tro
ts	hits	*grazie, sicurezza*	gra·tsye
v	van	*viaggio*	vee·a·jo
w	win	*uomo*	wo·mo
y	yes	*italiano*	ee·ta·lya·no
z	zoo	*casa*	ka·za

As well as the pronunciation described above, Italian consonant sounds have an additional form: a stronger, almost emphatic pronunciation. The actual sounds are basically the same, though meaning can be altered between a normal consonant sound and this double consonant sound. It's referred to as a 'double consonant' because usually, if the word is written with a double letter, that's the cue to use the stronger form.

Here are some examples where this 'double consonant' effect can make a difference:

sonno	*son·no*	**sleep**
sono	*so·no*	**I am**
pappa	*pap·pa*	**baby food**
papa	*pa·pa*	**pope**

Unlike the above examples, the pronunciation guides in this book don't distinguish between the two forms. Refer to the written Italian beside each transliteration as the cue to making the consonant sounds a little stronger. Even if you never distinguish them, you'll always be understood in context – your audience will work out if you're talking about the pope or baby food!

word stress

In Italian, you generally emphasise the second-last syllable in a word. However, when a written word has an accent marked on a vowel, the stress is on that syllable. The characteristic sing-song quality of an Italian sentence is created by pronouncing the syllables evenly and rhythmically, then swinging down on the last word. The stressed syllable is always italicised in our pronunciation guides, so you can't go wrong!

reading & writing

italian alphabet					
A a	a	*B b*	bee	*C c*	chee
D d	dee	*E e*	e	*F f*	e·fe
G g	jee	*H h*	a·ka	*I i*	ee
L l	e·le	*M m*	e·me	*N n*	e·ne
O o	o	*P p*	pee	*Q q*	koo
R r	e·re	*S s*	e·se	*T t*	tee
U u	oo	*V v*	voo	*Z z*	*tse*·ta

spellbound

The relationship between Italian sounds and their spelling is straightforward and consistent. The following rules will help you read the Italian that you come across in your travels:

c, g, sc	• before *a*, *o*, *u* and *h* they sound hard like the 'k' in 'kick', 'g' in 'go' and 'sc' in 'scooter' respectively	*bianco, dischetto, gomma, fresco*
	• before *e* and *i* they sound soft like the 'ch' in 'chilli', 'j' in 'jam' and 'sh' in 'show' respectively	*centro, gelato, ascensore*
ci, gi, sci	before *a*, *o* and *u*, the *i* is not pronounced	*ciao, giallo, prosciutto*
h	never pronounced	*traghetto*
j, w, k, x, y	only found in foreign words that have been adopted by Italian	*jogging, weekend, kosher, fax, yogurt*
z	pronounced as 'dz' or as 'ts'	*zaino, grazie*
s	• pronounced as 'z' between vowels	*casa*
	• pronounced as 's' elsewhere	*sì, essere, scatola*
gli, gn	pronounced as the 'll' in 'million' and 'ny' in 'canyon' respectively	*figlia, bagno*

This chapter is designed to explain the main grammatical structures you need in order to make your own sentences. Look under each heading – listed in alphabetical order – for information on functions which these grammatical categories express in a sentence. For example, demonstratives are used for giving instructions, so you'll need them to tell the taxi driver where your hotel is, etc. A glossary of grammatical terms is included at the end of the chapter to help you.

adjectives & adverbs

describing people/things • doing things

Adjectives generally come after the noun in Italian. However, adjectives expressing quantity (eg 'much', 'few') always precede the noun.

black cat	*gatto nero*	ga·to ne·ro
	(lit: cat black-m-sg)	
many cats	*molti gatti*	mol·tee ga·tee
	(lit: many-m-pl cats)	

The adjective endings change depending on whether the noun is masculine or feminine, singular or plural (see **gender** and **plurals**).

	singular		plural	
m	*bello*	be·lo	*belli*	be·lee
f	*bella*	be·la	*belle*	be·le

Adjectives ending in -e in the singular, eg *felice* fe·lee·che (happy), take the ending -i in the plural, regardless of the noun's gender:

happy cats	*gatti felici*	ga·tee fe·lee·chee
	(lit: cats happy-m-pl)	

Many adverbs in Italian are derived from adjectives by adding the ending -*mente* ·*men*·te to the singular feminine form of the adjective (ie the form ending in -*a*), just like you add the ending '-ly' to the adjective in English. In Italian, adverbs are generally placed after the verb they refer to.

a slow train	*un treno lento*	oon *tre*·no *len*·to
	(lit: a-m-sg train slow-m-sg)	
to speak slowly	*parlare lentamente*	par·*la*·re len·ta·*men*·te
	(lit: to-speak slowly)	

articles

naming people/things

There are four words for the definite article (ie equivalents of 'the' in English) in Italian. Which one you use depends on the gender and the number of the noun (see **gender** and **plurals**).

definite articles			
m sg	the train	*il treno*	eel *tre*·no
m pl	the trains	*i treni*	ee *tre*·nee
f sg	the receipt	*la ricevuta*	la ree·che·*voo*·ta
f pl	the receipts	*le ricevute*	le ree·che·*voo*·te

Note that the forms *lo* lo and *gli* lyee are used before masculine nouns starting with *s* plus a consonant, or with *z*-, *gn*-, *pn*-, *ps*-, *x*- or *y*-. The form *l'* is used before masculine and feminine nouns starting with a vowel (joined in pronunciation with the noun).

the backpack	*lo zaino*	lo *dzai*·no
the backpacks	*gli zaini*	lyee *dzai*·nee
the exit	*l'uscita*	loo·*shee*·ta
the exits	*le uscite*	le oo·*shee*·te

The definite article in Italian is joined to some prepositions, when it's used after them, eg *di* dee (of) + *il* eel becomes *del* del, and *a* a (to) + *la* la becomes *alla* a·la. See also **prepositions**.

TOOLS

14

Italian has two words for the indefinite article (ie 'a/an'), depending on the noun's gender. Two other forms are used depending on the first letter of the next word: *uno* oo·no (for masculine nouns starting with *s* plus a consonant, or with *z-*, *gn-*, *pn-*, *ps-*, *x-* or *y-*) and *un'* oon (for feminine nouns starting with a vowel).

indefinite articles			
m sg	a sandwich	*un panino*	oon pa·*nee*·no
	a stadium	*uno stadio*	oo·no *sta*·dyo
f sg	an apple	*una mela*	oo·na *me*·la
	a friend	*un'amica*	oon·a·*mee*·ka

be

describing people/things • making statements

There are two equivalents of the English verb 'be' in Italian – *essere* e·se·re and *stare* sta·re – which are used depending on the context. For negative forms with 'be', see **negatives**.

use of *ESSERE* (to be)		
permanent characteristics of persons/things	*Sei molto bella.* say mol·to be·la	You're very beautiful.
occupations or nationality	*Sono dall'Inghilterra.* so·no da·leen·geel·te·ra	I am from Italy.
time or location of events	*È l'una.* e loo·na	It's one o'clock.
mood of a person	*Sei felice?* say fe·lee·che	Are you happy?
possession	*Non è mio.* non e mee·o	It's not mine.
use of *STARE* (to be)		
temporary characteristics of persons/things	*È malato.* e ma·la·to	He is sick.
time or location of events	*Stai a casa?* stai a ka·za	Are you at home?

ESSERE (to be) – present tense

I	am	io	sono	yo	so·no
you sg inf	are	tu	sei	too	say
you sg pol	are	Lei	è	lay	e
he/she/it	is	lui/lei	è	looy/lay	e
we	are	noi	siamo	noy	sya·mo
you pl inf	are	voi	siete	voy	sye·te
you pl pol	are	Loro	sono	lo·ro	so·no
they	are	loro	sono	lo·ro	so·no

STARE (to be) – present tense

I	am	io	sto	yo	sto
you sg inf	are	tu	stai	too	stai
you sg pol	are	Lei	sta	lay	sta
he/she/it	is	lui/lei	sta	looy/lay	sta
we	are	noi	stiamo	noy	stya·mo
you pl inf	are	voi	state	voy	sta·te
you pl pol	are	Loro	stanno	lo·ro	sta·no
they	are	loro	stanno	lo·ro	sta·no

demonstratives

giving instructions • indicating location • pointing things out

To point something out, just use the phrase *È ... e ...* (it-is ...):

It's a local custom.
È una tradizione locale.   e oo·na tra·dee·tsyo·ne lo·ka·le
(lit: it-is a-f-sg custom local-f-sg)

To refer to or to point out a person or object, use one of the following demonstratives before the noun. Each of these words changes form depending on the gender and number of the noun it refers to. See also **gender** and **plurals**.

demonstratives

	m sg			m pl	
this	*questo*	*kwe·sto*	these	*questi*	*kwe·stee*
that	*quel/ quello*	*kwel/ kwe·lo*	those	*quei/ quegli/ quelli*	*kway/ kwe·lyee/ kwe·lee*
	f sg			f pl	
this	*questa*	*kwe·sta*	these	*queste*	*kwe·ste*
that	*quella*	*kwe·la*	those	*quelle*	*kwe·le*

Demonstratives can also be used on their own:

How much is this?
   Quanto costa questo?   *kwan·to kos·ta kwe·sto*
   (lit: how-much costs this-m-sg)

gender

naming people/things

In Italian, all nouns are either masculine or feminine. You can recognise the noun's gender by the article, demonstrative, possessive or any other adjective used with the noun, as they all change form to agree with the noun's gender. The gender of words is also indicated in the dictionary, but here are some general rules:

- a word is masculine/feminine if it refers to a man/woman
- words ending in *-o, -ore* or a consonant are usually masculine
- words ending in *-a* or *-ione* are generally feminine

The masculine and feminine forms of words are indicated with m and f throughout this phrasebook where relevant. See also the box **mario or maria?**, page 117.

have

Possession can be indicated in various ways in Italian (see also **possessives**). One way is by using the verb *avere* a·ve·re (have). For negative forms with 'have', see **negatives**.

AVERE (to have) – present tense				
I	have	*io*	*ho*	yo	o
you sg inf	have	*tu*	*hai*	too	ai
you sg pol	have	*Lei*	*ha*	lay	a
he/she/it	has	*lui/lei*	*ha*	looy/lay	a
we	have	*noi*	*abbiamo*	noy	a·bya·mo
you pl inf	have	*voi*	*avete*	voy	a·ve·te
you pl pol	have	*Loro*	*hanno*	lo·ro	a·no
they	have	*loro*	*hanno*	lo·ro	a·no

You can also use the phrases *c'è* che (there is) and *ci sono* chee so·no (there are) to say or ask if something is available:

Is there hot water?   *C'è acqua calda?* che a·kwa kal·da
                          (lit: there-is water hot-f-sg)

negatives

To make a negative statement in Italian, just add the word *non* non (not) before the main verb of the sentence. Unlike English, Italian uses double negatives.

I don't understand.	*Non capisco.*	non ka·pee·sko
	(lit: not I-understand)	
I don't understand anything.	*Non capisco niente.*	non ka·pee·sko nyen·te
	(lit: not I-understand nothing)	

personal pronouns

making statements • naming people/things

Personal pronouns ('I', 'you' etc) change form in Italian depending on whether they're the subject or the object in a sentence. It's the same in English, which has 'I' and 'me' as the subject and object pronouns (eg 'I see her' and 'She sees me'). The subject pronoun is usually omitted in Italian as the subject is understood from the corresponding verb form.

I'm a student.   *Sono artista.*   *so·no ar·tees·ta*
(lit: I-am student)

subject pronouns					
I	*io*	yo	**we**	*noi*	noy
you sg inf	*tu*	too	**you** pl inf	*noi*	voy
you sg pol	*Lei*	lay	**you** pl pol	*Loro*	*lo·ro*
he/she/it	*lui/lei*	looy/lay	**they**	*loro*	*lo·ro*

When talking to people familiar to you or younger than you, it's usual to use the informal form of 'you', *tu* too, rather than the polite form, *Lei* lay. Phrases in this book use the form of 'you' that is appropriate to the situation. Where both forms are used, they are indicated by pol and inf. See also the box **getting friendly**, page 92.

object pronouns					
me	*mi*	mee	**us**	*ci*	chee
you sg inf	*ti*	tee	**you** pl inf	*vi*	vee
you sg pol	*La/Le*	la/le	**you** pl pol	*Li/Loro* m *Le/Loro* f	lee/*lo·ro* m le/*lo·ro* f
him **it**	*lo/gli*	lo/lyee	**them**	*li/loro* m *le/loro* f	lee/*lo·ro* m le/*lo·ro* f
her **it**	*la/le*	la/le			

*the forms separated by a slash are direct/indirect object pronouns

The direct and indirect object pronouns differ only for the third person ('he', 'she', 'it', 'they') and the polite 'you' form.

I've seen him.	*Lo ho visto.*	lo o *vee*·sto
	(lit: him I-have seen)	
I've talked to him.	*Gli ho parlato.*	lyee o par·*la*·to
	(lit: to-him I-have talked)	

The object pronouns generally come before the verb. The indirect object pronoun comes before the direct object pronoun.

I'll give it to you.	*Ti lo darò.*	tee lo da·*ro*
	(lit: to-you-sg-inf it I-will-give)	

plurals

naming people/things

General rules for forming plurals in Italian are pretty simple: words ending in *-a* in the singular end in *-e* in the plural, and words ending in *-o* or *-e* in the singular end in *-i* in the plural. See also the box **perplexing plurals**, page 124.

singular			plural		
a person	*una persona*	oo·na per·so·na	three people	*tre persone*	tre per·so·ne
a ticket	*un biglietto*	oon bee·*lye*·to	two tickets	*due biglietti*	*doo*·e bee·*lye*·tee
a country	*un paese*	oon pa·e·se	five countries	*cinque paesi*	*cheen*·kwe pa·e·see

possessives

possessing

A common way of indicating possession is by using possessive adjectives before the noun they refer to. Like other adjectives, they agree with the noun in number and gender, and they are preceded by the definite article (see **articles**).

It's my ticket.
> *È il mio biglietto.* e eel *mee*·o bee·*lye*·to
> (lit: it-is the-m-sg my-m-sg ticket)

In Italian, posessive adjectives (ie 'my', 'your' etc) and possessive pronouns (ie 'mine', 'yours' etc) are the same – if what is being talked about is clear from the context, the noun can be omitted:

It's mine.
> *È il mio.* e eel *mee*·o
> (lit: it-is the-m-sg mine-m-sg)

possessive adjectives & pronouns

my/ mine	*il mio*	eel *mee*·o	our/ ours	*il nostro*	eel *nos*·tro
	i miei	ee *mye*·ee		*i nostri*	ee *nos*·tree
	la mia	la *mee*·a		*la nostra*	la *nos*·tra
	le mie	le *mee*·e		*le nostre*	le *nos*·tre
your/ yours sg inf	*il tuo*	eel *too*·o	your/ yours pl inf	*il vostro*	eel *vos*·tro
	i tuoi	ee *two*·ee		*i vostri*	ee *vos*·tree
	la tua	la *too*·a		*la vostra*	la *vos*·tra
	le tue	le *too*·e		*le vostre*	le *vos*·tre
your/ yours sg pol	*il Suo*	eel *swo*·o	your/ yours pl pol	*il Loro*	eel *lo*·ro
	i Suoi	ee *swo*·ee		*i Loro*	ee *lo*·ro
	la Sua	la *soo*·a		*la Loro*	la *lo*·ro
	le Sue	le *soo*·e		*le Loro*	le *lo*·ro
his her(s) its	*il suo*	eel *soo*·o	their/ theirs	*il loro*	eel *lo*·ro
	i suoi	ee *swo*·ee		*i loro*	ee *lo*·ro
	la sua	la *soo*·a		*la loro*	la *lo*·ro
	le sue	le *soo*·e		*le loro*	le *lo*·ro

*the four alternatives are used with m sg, m pl, f sg and f pl nouns

Ownership can also be expressed with the verb *avere* a·*ve*·re (see **have**) or by using the construction '*di* dee (of) + noun/pronoun':

It's Lorenzo's backpack.
> *È lo zaino di Lorenzo.* e lo *dzai*·no dee lo·*ren*·dzo
> (lit: it-is the-m-sg backpack of Lorenzo)

Whose seat is this?
> *Di chi è questo posto?* dee kee e *kwe*·sto *pos*·to
> (lit: of who is this-m-sg place)

prepositions

giving instructions • indicating location •
pointing things out

Like English, Italian uses prepositions to explain where things are in time or space. Common prepositions are listed in the following table. More prepositions can be found in the **dictionary**.

When certain prepositions are followed by a definite article, they are contracted into a single word (see **articles**).

prepositions					
after	*dopo*	do·po	in (place)	*in*	een
at (time)	*a*	a	of	*di*	dee
before	*prima*	pree·ma	to	*a*	a
from	*da*	da	with	*con*	kon

questions

asking questions • negating

The easiest way of forming 'yes/no' questions in Italian is to add the phrase *è vero* e ve·ro (literally 'is it true') to the end of a statement, similar to 'isn't it?' in English.

This seat is free, isn't it?
  Questo posto è libero,   kwe·sto po·sto e lee·be·ro
  è vero?   e ve·ro
  (lit: this-m-sg seat is free-m-sg is-it true)

You can also turn a statement into a question by putting the verb before the subject of the sentence, just like in English.

Is this seat free?
  È libero questo posto?   e lee·be·ro kwe·sto po·sto
  (lit: is free-m-sg this-m-sg seat)

As in English, there are also question words for more specific questions. These words go at the start of the sentence.

question words					
how	*come*	*ko·*me	where	*dove*	*do·*ve
what	*che cosa*	ke *ko·*za	who	*chi*	kee
when	*quando*	*kwan·*do	why	*perché*	per·*ke*

verbs

doing things

There are three verb categories in Italian – those whose infinitive
(dictionary form) ends in *-are*, *-ere* or *-ire*, eg *parlare* par·*la·*re
(talk), *scrivere* skree·ve·re (write), *capire* ka·*pee·*re (understand).
Tenses are formed by adding various endings for each person to
the verb stem (the part of the verb that remains after removing
-are, *-ere* or *-ire* from the infinitive), and for most verbs these
endings follow regular patterns according to the verb category.
The verb endings for the present, past and future tenses are pre-
sented in the tables on the following pages.

As in any language, there are also irregular verbs in Italian. The
most important ones are *essere*, *stare* and *avere* (see **be** and
have). For negative forms of verbs, see **negatives**.

I speak, read and understand Italian.

Parlo, scrivo e   par·lo skree·vo e
capisco italiano.   ka·*pee·*sko ee·ta·*lya·*no
(lit: I-speak, I-write and I-understand Italian)

> ## present tense

Note that before the endings for the present tense, some verbs
ending in *-ire* (eg *capire*) also change their verb stem slightly.

present tense		*parlare*	*scrivere*	*capire*
I	*io*	parl**o**	scriv**o**	capis**co**
you sg inf	*tu*	parl**i**	scriv**i**	capis**ci**
you sg pol	*Lei*	parl**a**	scriv**e**	capis**ce**
he/she	*lui/lei*	parl**a**	scriv**e**	capis**ce**
we	*noi*	parl**iamo**	scriv**iamo**	cap**iamo**
you pl inf	*voi*	parl**ate**	scriv**ete**	cap**ite**
you pl pol	*Loro*	parl**ano**	scriv**ono**	capis**cono**
they	*loro*	parl**ano**	scriv**ono**	capis**cono**

> past tense

The main past tense in Italian, used for a completed action, is a compound tense, which means it is made up of an auxiliary verb – either *essere* e·se·re (be) or *avere* a·ve·re (have) – in the present tense, plus a form of the main verb, called 'past participle'. The past participle is formed by replacing the infinitive endings -are, -ere or -ire with -ato, -uto or -ito respectively. Some past participles are irregular. See also **be** and **have**.

	infinitive		past participle	
love	am**are**	a·ma·re	am**ato**	a·ma·to
believe	cred**ere**	kre·de·re	cred**uto**	kre·doo·to
follow	segu**ire**	se·gee·re	segu**ito**	se·gee·to

Past participles taking *essere* agree in gender and number with the subject, while those taking *avere* agree with the object.

I went there.
   Sono andato/andata là. m/f   so·no an·da·to/an·da·ta la
   (lit: I-am gone-m-sg/-f-sg there)

I saw her yesterday.
   La ho vista ieri.   la o vee·sta ye·ree
   (lit: her I-have seen-f-sg yesterday)

> future tense

future tense				
		parlare	*scrivere*	*capire*
I	*io*	*parler**ò***	*scriver**ò***	*capir**ò***
you sg inf	*tu*	*parler**ai***	*scriver**ai***	*capir**ai***
you sg pol	*Lei*	*parler**à***	*scriver**à***	*capir**à***
he/she	*lui/lei*	*parler**à***	*scriver**à***	*capir**à***
we	*noi*	*parler**emo***	*scriver**emo***	*capir**emo***
you pl inf	*voi*	*parler**ete***	*scriver**ete***	*capir**ete***
you pl pol	*Loro*	*parler**anno***	*scriver**anno***	*capir**anno***
they	*loro*	*parler**anno***	*scriver**anno***	*capir**anno***

You can also express future plans by using the present tense with
some indication of time referring to the future:

Tomorrow we're going to Rome.
> *Domani andiamo a Roma.*   do·ma·nee an·dya·mo a ro·ma
> (lit: tomorrow we-go to Rome)

word order

making statements

Italian has a basic word order of subject–verb–object, like English.
However, the subject pronoun (eg 'I' or 'you') is usually omitted
in Italian as the subject is understood from the corresponding
verb form (see **verbs**) – so the second example is more common:

We're waiting for the bus.
> *Noi aspettiamo l'autobus.*   noy as·pe·tya·mo low·to·boos
> (lit: we wait the-m-sg-bus)
> *Aspettiamo l'autobus.*   as·pe·tya·mo low·to·boos
> (lit: we-wait the-m-sg-bus)

See also **negatives** and **questions**.

grammar glossary

adjective	a word that describes something – '**gladiatorial** fighting originated as a form of **human** sacrifice'
adverb	a word that explains how an action is done – 'it became **increasingly** gruesome and exciting'
article	the words 'a', 'an' and 'the'
demonstrative	a word that means 'this' or 'that'
direct object	the thing or person in the sentence that has the action directed to it – 'and the crowds loved **it**'
gender	classification of *nouns* into classes (like masculine and feminine), requiring other words (eg *adjectives*) to belong to the same class
indirect object	the person or thing in the sentence that is the recipient of the action – 'Trajan once had 9000 gladiators perform for **him**'
infinitive	dictionary form of a *verb* – 'to **ensure** the greatest spectacle'
noun	a thing, person or idea – 'for the **emperor**'
number	whether a word is singular or plural – '**the combatants** (**prisoners** or **slaves**) were paired off'
personal pronoun	a word that means 'I', 'you' etc
possessive adjective	a word that means 'my', 'your' etc
possessive pronoun	a word that means 'mine', 'yours' etc
preposition	a word like 'for' or 'before' in English
subject	the thing or person in the sentence that does the action – '**fights** were not always to the death'
tense	form of a *verb* that tells you whether the action is in the present, past or future – eg 'dies' (present), 'died' (past), 'will die' (future)
verb	a word that tells you what action happened – 'as the defeated **could appeal** to the emperor'
verb stem	part of a *verb* that doesn't change – eg '**live**' in '**liv**ing' and '**liv**ed'

language difficulties
le difficoltà di lingua

Do you speak English?
Parla/Parli inglese? pol/inf · *par*·la/*par*·lee een·*gle*·ze

Does anyone speak English?
C'è qualcuno che parla inglese? · che kwal·*koo*·no ke *par*·la een·*gle*·ze

I need an interpreter who speaks English.
Ho bisogno di un interprete che parla l'inglese. · aw bee·*so*·nyo dee oon een·*ter*·pre·te ke *par*·la leen·*gle*·ze

Do you understand?
Capisce/Capisci? pol/inf · ka·*pee*·she/ka·*pee*·shee

I (don't) understand.
(Non) Capisco. · (non) ka·*pee*·sko

I speak Italian.
Parlo italiano. · *par*·lo ee·ta·*lya*·no

I don't speak Italian.
Non parlo italiano. · non *par*·lo ee·ta·*lya*·no

I speak English.
Parlo inglese. · *par*·lo een·*gle*·ze

I speak a little.
Parlo un po'. · *par*·lo oon po

I'd like to practise Italian.
Vorrei fare pratica con l'italiano. · vo·*ray* fa·re pra·tee·ka kon lee·ta·*lya*·no

What does 'vietato' mean?
Che cosa vuol dire 'vietato'? · ke *ko*·za vwol *dee*·re vye·*ta*·to

How do you ...?	*Come si ...?*	*ko*·me see ...
pronounce this	*pronuncia questo*	pro·*noon*·cha kwe·sto
write	*scrive*	skree·ve
'arrivederci'	*'arrivederci'*	a·ree·ve·*der*·chee

Could you please ...?	Può/Puoi ..., per favore? pol/inf	pwo/pwoy ... per fa·vo·re
repeat that	ripeterlo	ree·pe·ter·lo
speak more	parlare più	par·la·re pyoo
slowly	lentamente	len·ta·men·te
write it down	scriverlo	skree·ver·lo

tongue twisters

The sing-song music of the Italian language lends itself beautifully to tongue twisters or *scioglilingue* skee·o·lyee·*leen*·gwe. You can try to impress Italian acquaintances by casually slipping out one of these:

O schiavo con lo schiaccianoci che cosa schiacci? Schiaccio sei noci del vecchio noce con lo schiaccianoci.
o *skya*·vo kon lo skya·cha·*no*·chee ke *ko*·za *skya*·chee *skya*·cho say *no*·chee del *ve*·kyo *no*·che kon lo skya·cha·*no*·chee
('Oh, slave with the nutcracker what are you cracking? I am cracking six nuts from the old walnut tree with the nutcracker.')

Orrore, orrore, un ramarro verde su un muro marrone!
o·*ro*·re o·*ro*·re oon ra·*ma*·ro *ver*·de soo oon *moo*·ro ma·*ro*·ne
('Horror, horror, a green lizard on a brown wall!')

Trentatre Trentini entrarono a Trento, tutti e trentatre trotterelando.
tren·ta·*tre* tren·*tee*·nee en·*tra*·ro·no a *tren*·to *too*·tee e tren·ta·*tre* tro·te·re·*lan*·do
('Thirty-three Trentonians came into Trento, all thirty-three trotting.')

numbers & amounts

cardinal numbers

		i numeri cardinali
0	*zero*	*dze·*ro
1	*uno*	oo·no
2	*due*	doo·e
3	*tre*	tre
4	*quattro*	kwa·tro
5	*cinque*	cheen·kwe
6	*sei*	say
7	*sette*	se·te
8	*otto*	o·to
9	*nove*	no·ve
10	*dieci*	dye·chee
11	*undici*	oon·dee·chee
12	*dodici*	do·dee·chee
13	*tredici*	tre·dee·chee
14	*quattordici*	kwa·tor·dee·chee
15	*quindici*	kween·dee·chee
16	*sedici*	se·dee·chee
17	*diciassette*	dee·cha·se·te
18	*diciotto*	dee·cho·to
19	*diciannove*	dee·cha·no·ve
20	*venti*	ven·tee
21	*ventuno*	ven·too·no
22	*ventidue*	ven·tee·doo·e
30	*trenta*	tren·ta
40	*quaranta*	kwa·ran·ta
50	*cinquanta*	cheen·kwan·ta
60	*sessanta*	se·san·ta
70	*settanta*	se·tan·ta
80	*ottanta*	o·tan·ta
90	*novanta*	no·van·ta
100	*cento*	chen·to
200	*duecento*	doo·e·chen·to

1000	mille	mee·le
2000	duemila	doo·e·mee·la
1,000,000	un milione	oon mee·lyo·ne

ordinal numbers

1st	primo/a m/f	pree·mo/a
2nd	secondo/a m/f	se·kon·do/a
3rd	terzo/a m/f	ter·tso/a
4th	quarto/a m/f	kwar·to/a
5th	quinto/a m/f	kween·to/a

fractions

frazioni

a quarter	un quarto	oon kwar·to
a third	un terzo	oon ter·tso
a half	mezzo	me·dzo
three-quarters	tre quarti	tre kwar·tee
all	tutto/a m/f sg	too·to/a
	tutti/e m/f pl	too·tee/too·te
none	niente	nyen·te

useful amounts

quantità utili

How much?	Quanto/a? m/f	kwan·to/a
How many?	Quanti/e? m/f	kwan·tee/kwan·te
Please give me ...	Può darmi ..., per favore.	pwo dar·mee ... per fa·vo·re
(just) a little	(solo) un po'	(so·lo) oon po
some	alcuni/e m/f	al·koo·nee/al·koo·ne
much	molto/a m/f	mol·to/a
many	molti/e m/f	mol·tee/mol·te
less	di meno	(dee) me·no
more	di più	(dee) pyoo

For more amounts, see **self-catering**, page 156.

TOOLS

30

telling the time

When telling the time in Italian, 'It is ...' is expressed by *Sono le* so·no le, followed by a number. However, 'one o'clock' is *È l'una* e *loo*·na, and 'midday' is *È mezzogiorno* e me·dzo·*jor*·no. Note that in Italy the 24-hour clock is commonly used.

What time is it?	Che ora è?	ke o·ra e
It's one o'clock.	È l'una.	e *loo*·na
It's (two) o'clock.	Sono le (due).	so·no le (*doo*·e)
Five past (one).	(L'una) e cinque.	(*loo*·na) e *cheen*·kwe
Quarter past (one).	(L'una) e un quarto.	(*loo*·na) e oon *kwar*·to
Half past (one).	(L'una) e mezza.	(*loo*·na) e me·dza
Quarter to (eight).	(Le otto) meno un quarto.	(le o·to) me·no oon *kwar*·to
Twenty to (eight).	(Le otto) meno venti.	(le o·to) me·no ven·tee

am (in the morning)	di mattina	dee ma·*tee*·na
pm (in the afternoon)	di pomeriggio	dee po·me·*ree*·jo
in the evening	di sera	dee se·ra
at night	di notte	dee no·te
midday	mezzogiorno	me·dzo·*jor*·no
midnight	mezzanotte	me·dza·*no*·te
At what time ...?	A che ora ...?	a ke o·ra ...
At one.	All'una.	a·*loo*·na
At (six).	Alle (sei).	a·le (say)
At (7.57pm).	Alle (19.57).	a·le (dee·cha·*no*·ve e cheen·kwan·ta·*se*·te)

days of the week

Monday	*lunedì* m	loo·ne·*dee*
Tuesday	*martedì* m	mar·te·*dee*
Wednesday	*mercoledì* m	mer·ko·le·*dee*
Thursday	*giovedì* m	jo·ve·*dee*
Friday	*venerdì* m	ve·ner·*dee*
Saturday	*sabato* m	*sa*·ba·to
Sunday	*domenica* f	do·*me*·nee·ka

the calendar

il calendario

> months

January	*gennaio* m	je·*na*·yo
February	*febbraio* m	fe·*bra*·yo
March	*marzo* m	*mar*·tso
April	*aprile* m	a·*pree*·le
May	*maggio* m	*ma*·jo
June	*giugno* m	*joo*·nyo
July	*luglio* m	*loo*·lyo
August	*agosto* m	a·*gos*·to
September	*settembre* m	se·*tem*·bre
October	*ottobre* m	o·*to*·bre
November	*novembre* m	no·*vem*·bre
December	*dicembre* m	dee·*chem*·bre

> seasons

summer	*estate* f	es·*ta*·te
autumn	*autunno* m	ow·*too*·no
winter	*inverno* m	een·*ver*·no
spring	*primavera* f	pree·ma·ve·ra

dates

le date

| What date is it today? | *Che giorno è oggi?* | ke *jor*·no e o·jee |
| It's (3 March). | *È (il terzo) marzo.* | e (eel *ter*·tso *mar*·tso) |

present

now	*adesso*	a·de·so
this ...		
afternoon	*oggi pomeriggio*	o·jee po·me·ree·jo
morning	*stamattina*	sta·ma·tee·na
month	*questo mese*	kwe·sto me·ze
week	*questa settimana*	kwe·sta se·tee·ma·na
year	*quest'anno*	kwe·sta·no
weekend	*fine settimana*	fee·ne se·tee·ma·na
today	*oggi*	o·jee
tonight	*stasera*	sta·se·ra

past

il passato

day before yesterday	*l'altro ieri*	lal·tro ye·ree
last month	*il mese scorso*	eel me·ze skor·so
last night	*ieri notte*	ye·ree no·te
last week	*la settimana scorsa*	la se·tee·ma·na skor·sa
last year	*l'anno scorso*	la·no skor·so
since (May)	*da (maggio)*	da (ma·jo)
(three days) ago	*(tre giorni) fa*	(tre jor·nee) fa
yesterday ...	*ieri ...*	ye·ree ...
afternoon	*pomeriggio*	po·me·ree·jo
evening	*sera*	se·ra
morning	*mattina*	ma·tee·na

future

il futuro

day after tomorrow	*dopodomani*	do·po·do·ma·nee
in (six days)	*fra (sei giorni)*	fra (say jor·nee)
next month	*il mese prossimo*	eel me·ze pro·see·mo

next week	*la settimana*	la se·tee·*ma*·na
	prossima	*pro*·see·ma
next year	*l'anno prossimo*	*la*·no pro·see·mo
tomorrow	*domani*	do·*ma*·nee
tomorrow evening	*domani sera*	do·*ma*·nee se·ra
tomorrow	*domani*	do·*ma*·nee
afternoon	*pomeriggio*	po·me·*ree*·jo
tomorrow morning	*domani*	do·*ma*·nee
	mattina	ma·*tee*·na
until (June)	*fino a (giugno)*	*fee*·no a (*joo*·nyo)

during the day

durante il giorno

afternoon	*pomeriggio* m	po·me·*ree*·jo
dawn	*alba* f	*al*·ba
day	*giorno* m	*jor*·no
evening	*sera* f	*se*·ra
midday	*mezzogiorno* m	me·dzo·*jor*·no
midnight	*mezzanotte* f	me·dza·*no*·te
morning	*mattina* f	ma·*tee*·na
night	*notte* f	*no*·te
sunrise	*alba* f	*al*·ba
sunset	*tramonto* m	tra·*mon*·to

golden years

You'll often hear the centuries referred to as follows, particularly when talking about periods of history and art:

Il Duecento (lit: the 200)	
eel doo·e·*chen*·to	**13th century**
Il Trecento (lit: the 300)	
eel tre·*chen*·to	**14th century**
Il Quattrocento (lit: the 400)	
eel kwa·tro·*chen*·to	**15th century**
Il Cinquecento (lit: the 500)	
eel cheen·kwe·*chen*·to	**16th century**

How much is it?
Quant'è? kwan·*te*

How much is this?
Quanto costa questo? kwan·to kos·ta kwe·sto

It's free.
È gratuito. e gra·too·ee·to

It's ... euros.
È ... euro. e ... e·oo·ro

Can you write down the price?
Può scrivere il prezzo? pwo skree·ve·re eel *pre*·tso

Do you change money here?
Si cambiano i soldi qui? see kam·bya·no ee sol·dee kwee

I'd like to ...	*Vorrei ...*	vo·ray ...
arrange a transfer	*trasferire*	tras·fe·*ree*·re
	soldi	sol·dee
cash a cheque	*riscuotere*	ree·skwo·te·re
	un assegno	oo·na·se·nyo
change a travellers	*cambiare*	kam·bya·re
cheque	*un assegno*	oo·na·se·nyo
	di viaggio	dee vee·a·jo
change money	*cambiare*	kam·bya·re
	i soldi	ee sol·dee
get a cash	*prelevare con*	pre·le·va·re kon
advance	*carta di*	kar·ta dee
	credito	kre·dee·to
get change for	*cambiare questa*	kam·bya·re kwe·sta
this note	*banconota*	ban·ko·no·ta
withdraw money	*fare prelievi*	fa·re pre·lye·vee

Do you accept ...?	Accettate ...?	a·che·ta·te ...
credit cards	la carta di credito	la kar·ta dee kre·dee·to
debit cards	la carta di debito	la kar·ta dee de·bee·to
travellers cheques	gli assegni di viaggio	lyee a·se·nyee dee vee·a·jo

Where's the nearest ...?	Dov'è ... più vicino?	do·ve ... pyoo vee·chee·no
automatic teller machine	il Bancomat	eel ban·ko·mat
foreign exchange office	il cambio	eel kam·byo

What's the ...?	Quant'è ...?	kwan·te
commission	la commissione	la ko·mee·syo·ne
exchange rate	il cambio	eel kam·byo

I'd like ..., please.	Vorrei ..., per favore.	vo·ray ... per fa·vo·re
a receipt	una ricevuta	oo·na ree·che·voo·ta
a refund	un rimborso	oon reem·bor·so
my change	il mio resto	eel mee·o res·to

There's a mistake in the bill.

C'è un errore nel conto.   che oon e·ro·re nel kon·to

I don't want to pay the full price.

Non voglio pagare il prezzo intero.   non vo·lyo pa·ga·re eel pre·tso een·te·ro

Do I need to pay upfront?

Devo pagare in anticipo?   de·vo pa·ga·re ee·nan·tee·chee·po

For more money-related phrases, see **banking**, page 79.

---

listen for ...

vwo·le feer·ma·re o oo·sa·re eel soo·o peen

Vuole firmare o usare il suo PIN?   **Do you want to sign or use your PIN?**

getting around

andare in giro

At what time does the ... leave/arrive?	A che ora parte/arriva ...?	a ke o·ra par·te/a·ree·va ...
boat	la nave	la na·ve
bus	l'autobus	low·to·boos
ferry	il traghetto	eel tra·ge·to
hydrofoil	l'aliscafo	la·lees·ka·fo
metro	la metropolitana	la me·tro·po·lee·ta·na
plane	l'aereo	la·e·re·o
train	il treno	eel tre·no

At what time's the ... bus/boat?	A che ora passa ... autobus/nave? m/f	a ke o·ra pa·sa ... ow·to·boos/na·ve
first	il/la primo/a m/f	eel/la pree·mo/a
last	l'ultimo/a m/f	lool·tee·mo/a
next	il/la prossimo/a m/f	eel/la pro·see·mo/a

listen for ...

che oo·no sho·pe·ro
C'è uno sciopero.
There's a strike.

de·ve kam·bya·re a (par·ma)
Deve cambiare a (Parma).
You'll have to change at (Parma).

eel tre·no e kan·che·la·to
Il treno è cancellato.
The train is cancelled.

la·e·re·o e een ree·tar·do
L'aereo è in ritardo.
The plane is delayed.

la pro·see·ma fer·ma·ta e ...
La prossima fermata è ...
The next stop is ...

kwe·sta fer·ma·ta e ...
Questa fermata è ...
We're arriving at ...

transport

37

When's the next flight to (Cagliari)?
A che ora parte il   a ke o·ra par·te eel
prossimo volo per   pro·see·mo vo·lo per
(Cagliari)?   (ka·lya·ree)

Can you tell me when we get to (Taranto)?
Mi sa dire quando   mee sa dee·re kwan·do
arriviamo a (Taranto)?   a·ree·vya·mo a (ta·ran·to)

I want to get off here.
Voglio scendere qui.   vo·lyo shen·de·re kwee

Is this seat free?
È libero questo posto?   e lee·be·ro kwe·sto pos·to

That's my seat.
Quel posto è mio.   kwel pos·to e mee·o

For phrases on disabled access, see **senior & disabled travellers**, page 87.

buying tickets

acquisto di biglietti

Where can I buy a ticket?
Dove posso comprare   do·ve po·so kom·pra·re
un biglietto?   oon bee·lye·to

Do I need to book?
Bisogna prenotare   bee·zo·nya pre·no·ta·re
(un posto)?   (oon pos·to)

Can I get a stand-by ticket?
Posso essere messo/a in   po·so e·se·re me·so/a een
lista d'attesa? m/f   lee·sta da·te·sa

I'd like to ... my	*Vorrei ... il mio*	vo·ray ... eel mee·o
ticket, please.	*biglietto, per favore.*	bee·lye·to per fa·vo·re
cancel	*cancellare*	kan·che·la·re
change	*cambiare*	kam·bya·re
collect	*ritirare*	ree·tee·ra·re
confirm	*confermare*	kon·fer·ma·re

Two ... tickets (to Rome), please.	Due biglietti ... (per Roma), per favore.	doo·e bee·lye·tee ... (per ro·ma) per fa·vo·re
1st-class	di prima classe	dee pree·ma kla·se
2nd-class	di seconda classe	dee se·kon·da kla·se
child's	per bambini	per bam·bee·nee
one-way	di sola andata	dee so·la an·da·ta
return	di andata e ritorno	dee an·da·ta e ree·tor·no
student's	per studenti	per stoo·den·tee
I'd like a/an ... seat, please.	Vorrei un posto ..., per favore.	vo·ray oon pos·to ... per fa·vo·re
aisle	sul corridoio	sool ko·ree·do·yo
non-smoking	per non fumatori	per non foo·ma·to·ree
smoking	per fumatori	per foo·ma·to·ree
window	vicino al finestrino	vee·chee·no al fee·nes·tree·no
Is there (a) ...?	C'è ...?	che ...
air-conditioning	l'aria condizionata	la·rya kon·dee·tsyo·na·ta
blanket	una coperta	oo·na ko·per·ta
toilet	un gabinetto	oon ga·bee·ne·to
video	un video-registratore	oon vee·de·o·re·jee·stra·to·re

I'd like a sleeping berth.
Vorrei una cuccetta, per favore. vo·ray oo·na koo·che·ta per fa·vo·re

How much is it?
Quant'è? kwan·te

Do I need to pay a supplement?
Devo pagare un supplemento? de·vo pa·ga·re oon soo·ple·men·to

How long does the trip take?
Quanto ci vuole? kwan·to chee vwo·le

Is it a direct route?
È un itinerario diretto?   e oon ee·tee·ne·ra·ryo dee·re·to

What time do I have to check in?
A che ora devo presentarmi   a ke o·ra de·vo pre·zen·tar·mee
per l'accettazione?   per la·che·ta·tsyo·ne

For phrases about getting through customs and immigration,
see **border crossing**, page 49.

luggage

i bagagli

My luggage hasn't arrived.
Non è arrivato il mio   non e a·ree·va·to eel mee·o
bagaglio.   ba·ga·lyo

My luggage has been ...	*Il mio bagaglio è stato ...*	eel mee·o ba·ga·lyo e sta·to ...
damaged	*danneggiato*	da·ne·ja·to
lost	*perso*	per·so
stolen	*rubato*	roo·ba·to
I'd like ...	*Vorrei ...*	vo·ray ...
a luggage locker	*un armadietto per il bagaglio*	oon ar·ma·dye·to per eel ba·ga·lyo
some coins	*della moneta*	de·la mo·ne·ta
some tokens	*dei gettoni*	day je·to·nee

bus, tram & metro

autobus, tram & metrò

Which bus goes to (Rome)?
Quale autobus va a (Roma)?   kwa·le ow·to·boos va a (ro·ma)

Bus number (three).
Autobus numero (tre).   ow·to·boos noo·me·ro (tre)

Where's the bus stop?
Dov'è la fermata   do·ve la fer·ma·ta
dell'autobus?   del ow·to·boos

What's the next stop?
Qual'è la prossima fermata?   kwa·le la pro·see·ma fer·ma·ta

Fermata del Tram	fer·*ma*·ta del tram	**Tram Stop**
Fermata dell'autobus	fer·*ma*·ta de·*low*·to·boos	**Bus Stop**
Stazione della Metropolitana	sta·*tsyo*·ne de·la me·tro·po·lee·*ta*·na	**Metro Station**
Uscita	oo·*shee*·ta	**Way Out**

I'd like to get off at …

Vorrei scendere a …   vo·*ray* shen·*de*·re a …

How many stops to (the museum)?

Quante fermate   *kwan*·te fer·*ma*·te
mancano (al museo)?   *man*·ka·no (al moo·ze·o)

Please tell me when we get to (the market).

Mi dica per favore quando   mee *dee*·ka per fa·*vo*·re *kwan*·do
arriviamo (al mercato).   a·ree·*vya*·mo (al mer·*ka*·to)

For bus numbers, see **numbers & amounts**, page 29.

train

il treno

What station is this?
Che stazione è questa?   ke sta·*tsyo*·ne e *kwe*·sta

What's the next station?
Qual'è la prossima   kwa·*le* la *pro*·see·ma
stazione?   sta·*tsyo*·ne

Does this train stop at (Milan)?
Questo treno si ferma   *kwe*·sto *tre*·no see *fer*·ma
a (Milano)?   a (mee·*la*·no)

Do I need to change (trains)?
Devo cambiare (treno)?   *de*·vo kam·*bya*·re (*tre*·no)

Where's the dining car?
Dov'è il vagone ristorante?   do·*ve* eel va·*go*·ne rees·to·*ran*·te

Which carriage	*Quale carrozza*	kwa·*le* ka·*ro*·tsa
is ...?	*è ...?*	e ...
1st class	*di prima classe*	dee *pree*·ma *kla*·se
for (Rome)	*per (Roma)*	per (*ro*·ma)

---

trainspotting

diretto   dee·*re*·to
  indicates you don't need to change trains to reach
  your destination

espresso   es·*pre*·so
  stops only at major stations

Eurostar Italia (ES)   e·oo·ro·*star* ee·*ta*·lya
  very fast, Italy's answer to France's TGV

Inter City   een·ter see·tee
  runs between large cities

locale   lo·*ka*·le
  usually stops at all stations and can be very slow

rapido   ra·pee·do
  runs between large towns and cities; faster than the
  espresso

boat

la nave

Are there life jackets?
Ci sono giubbotti di salvataggio?
chee so·no joo·bo·tee dee sal·va·ta·jo

What's the sea like today?
Com'è il mare oggi?
ko·me eel ma·re o·jee

I feel seasick.
Ho il mal di mare.
o eel mal dee ma·re

taxi

il tassì

I'd like a taxi ...	*Vorrei un tassì ...*	vo·ray oon ta·see ...
at (9am)	*alle (nove di mattina)*	a·le (no·ve dee ma·tee·na)
tomorrow	*domani*	do·ma·nee

Where's the taxi stand?
Dov'è il posteggio dei tassì?
do·ve eel pos·te·jo day ta·see

Is this taxi free?
È libero questo tassì?
e lee·be·ro kwe·sto ta·see

How much is it to ...?
Quant'è per ...?
kwan·te per ...

How much is the flag fall/hiring charge?
Quanto costa la chiamata?
kwan·to kos·ta la kya·ma·ta

Please put the meter on.
Usi il tassametro, per favore.
oo·zee eel ta·sa·me·tro per fa·vo·re

Please take me to (this address).
Mi porti a (questo indirizzo), per piacere.
mee por·tee a (kwe·sto een·dee·ree·tso) per pya·che·re

Please ...	*..., per favore.*	... per fa·vo·re
slow down	*Rallenti*	ra·len·tee
stop here	*Si fermi qui*	see fer·mee kwee
wait here	*Mi aspetti qui*	mee as·pe·tee kwee

typical addresses

Borgo (B.go)	*bor·go*	district
Corso (C.so)	*kor·so*	main street/avenue
Largo (L.go)	*lar·go*	little square
Piazza (P.za)	*pya·tsa*	square
Strada (Str.)	*stra·da*	street
Via (V.)	*vee·a*	road/street
Viale (V.le)	*vee·a·le*	avenue/boulevard
Vicolo (V.lo)	*vee·ko·lo*	alley/lane

in Venice:		
Calle	*ka·le*	street
Campiello	*kam·pye·lo*	square without a church
Fondamenta	*fon·da·men·ta*	street
Riva	*ree·va*	street (lit: shore/bank)

in Genoa:		
Carrugio	*ka·roo·jo*	little street

in medieval cities:		
Contrà	*kon·tra*	street
Contrada	*kon·tra·da*	street

car & motorbike

la macchina & la moto

> car & motorbike hire

I'd like to hire a/an ...	*Vorrei noleggiare ...*	vo·ray no·le·ja·re ...
4WD	*un fuoristrada*	oon fwo·ree·stra·da
automatic (car)	*una macchina automatica*	oo·na ma·kee·na ow·to·ma·tee·ka
car	*una macchina*	oo·na ma·kee·na
manual (car)	*una macchina manuale*	oo·na ma·kee·na ma·noo·a·le
motorbike	*una moto*	oo·na mo·to

with/without ...	con/senza ...	kon/*sen*·tsa ...
air-conditioning	*aria*	a·rya
	condizionata	kon·dee·tsyo·*na*·ta
antifreeze	*anticongelante*	an·tee·kon·je·*lan*·te
a driver	*un'autista*	oo·now·*tee*·sta
snow chains	*le catene da neve*	le ka·*te*·ne da *ne*·ve

How much is it ...?	Quanto costa ...?	kwan·to kos·ta ...
daily	*al giorno*	al *jor*·no
hourly	*all'ora*	a·*lo*·ra
weekly	*alla settimana*	a·la se·tee·*ma*·na

Does that include insurance?
E' compresa
l'assicurazione?

e kom·*pre*·sa
la·see·koo·ra·*tsyo*·ne

Does that include mileage?
E' compreso il
chilometraggio?

e kom·*pre*·so eel
kee·lo·me·*tra*·jo

> on the road

What's the city/country speed limit?
Qual'è il limite di
velocità in
città/campagna?

kwa·*le* eel *lee*·mee·te dee
ve·lo·chee·*ta* een
chee·*ta*/kam·*pa*·nya

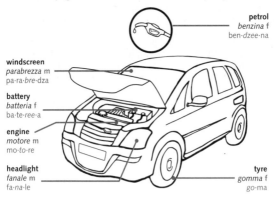

petrol
benzina f
ben·*dzee*·na

windscreen
parabrezza m
pa·ra·*bre*·dza

battery
batteria f
ba·te·*ree*·a

engine
motore m
mo·*to*·re

headlight
fanale m
fa·*na*·le

tyre
gomma f
go·ma

Is this the road to (Venice)?
Questa strada porta
a (Venezia)?
kwe·sta stra·da por·ta
a (ve·ne·tsya)

Where's a service station?
Dov'è una stazione
di servizio?
do·ve oo·na sta·tsyo·ne
dee ser·vee·tsyo

Please fill it up.
Il pieno, per favore.
eel pye·no per fa·vo·re

I'd like (30) litres.
Vorrei (trenta) litri.
vo·ray (tren·ta) lee·tree

diesel	gasolio/diesel m	ga·zo·lyo/dee·zel
leaded/unleaded petrol	benzina f con/ senza piombo	ben·dzee·na kon/ sen·tsa pyom·bo
LPG	gasauto m	ga·zow·to

road signs

Accesso Permanente	a·che·so per·ma·nen·te	24-Hour Access
Alt	alt	Stop
Attenzione	a·ten·tsyo·ne	Caution
Autostrada	ow·to·stra·da	Freeway
Dare la Precedenza	da·re la pre·che·den·tsa	Give Way
Deviazione	de·vya·tsyo·ne	Detour
Divieto di Accesso	dee·vye·to dee a·che·so	No Entry
Divieto di Sorpasso	dee·vye·to dee sor·pa·so	No Overtaking
Divieto di Sosta	dee·vye·to dee sos·ta	No Parking
Entrata	en·tra·ta	Entrance
Lavori in Corso	la·vo·ree een kor·so	Roadworks
Parcheggio	par·ke·jo	Parking
Passo Carrabile	pa·so ka·ra·bee·le	Keep Clear
Pedaggio	pe·da·jo	Toll
Pericolo	pe·ree·ko·lo	Danger
Rallentare	ra·len·ta·re	Slow Down
Rimozione Forzata	ree·mo·tsyo·ne for·tsa·ta	Tow-Away Zone
Senso Unico	sen·so oo·nee·ko	One Way
Uscita	oo·shee·ta	Exit

Please check the ...	Può controllare	pwo kon·tro·la·re
	..., per favore?	... per fa·vo·re
oil	l'olio	lo·lyo
tyre pressure	la pressione	la pre·syo·ne
	delle gomme	de·le go·me
water	l'acqua	la·kwa

(How long) Can I park here?
(Per quanto tempo) Posso   (per *kwan*·to *tem*·po) *po*·so
parcheggiare qui?   par·ke·*ja*·re kwee

Where do I pay?
Dove si paga?   do·ve see *pa*·ga

> problems

I need a mechanic.
Ho bisogno di un   o bee·zo·nyo dee oon
meccanico.   me·*ka*·nee·ko

The car/motorbike has broken down (at the intersection).
La macchina/moto si è   la ma·kee·na/mo·to see e
guastata (all'incrocio).   gwas·*ta*·ta (a·leen·*kro*·cho)

I had an accident.
Ho avuto un incidente.   o a·*voo*·to oon een·chee·*den*·te

The car/motorbike won't start.
La macchina/moto non parte.   la ma·kee·na/mo·to non *par*·te

I have a flat tyre.
Ho una gomma bucata.   o oo·na go·ma boo·*ka*·ta

I've lost my car keys.
Ho perso le chiavi della   o *per*·so le *kya*·vee de·la
macchina.   ma·kee·na

I've locked the keys inside the car.
Ho chiuso la macchina con   o *kyoo*·zo la ma·kee·na kon
le chiavi dentro.   le *kya*·vee *den*·tro

I've run out of petrol.
Ho esaurito la benzina.   o e·zow·*ree*·to la ben·*dzee*·na

Can you fix it (today)?
La può aggiustare (oggi)?   la pwo a·joo·*sta*·re (o·jee)

How long will it take?
Quanto ci vuole?   *kwan*·to chee *vwo*·le

bicycle

Where can I ...?	Dove posso ...?	do·ve po·so ...
hire a bicycle	noleggiare una bicicletta	no·le·ja·re oo·na bee·chee·kle·ta
buy a second-hand bike	comprare una bicicletta di seconda mano	kom·pra·re oo·na bee·chee·kle·ta dee se·kon·da ma·no

How much per ...?	Quanto costa ...?	kwan·to kos·ta ...
day	al giorno	al jor·no
hour	all'ora	a·lo·ra

I'd like to have my bicycle repaired.
Vorrei fare riparare la mia bicicletta.
vo·ray fa·re ree·pa·ra·re la mee·a bee·chee·kle·ta

I have a puncture.
Ho una gomma bucata.
o oo·na go·ma boo·ka·ta

Are there cycling paths?
Ci sono piste ciclabili?
chee so·no pee·ste chee·kla·bee·lee

Is there bicycle parking?
C'è un posteggio per le biciclette?
chay oon po·ste·jo per le bee·chee·kle·te

Can I take my bike on the train?
Posso portare la bicicletta in treno?
po·so por·ta·re la bee·chee·kle·ta een tre·no

bicycle path map	mappa f delle piste ciclabili	ma·pa de·le pee·ste chee·kla·bee·lee
bicycle pump	pompa f della bicicletta	pom·pa de·la bee·chee·kle·ta

listen for ...

de·vo or·dee·na·re eel pe·tso dee ree·kam·byo
Devo ordinare il pezzo di ricambio.
I have to order that part.

ke tee·po dee ma·kee·na/mo·to e
Che tipo di macchina/moto è?
What kind of car/motorbike is it?

passport control

controllo passaporti

I'm here ...	Sono qui ...	so·no kwee ...
in transit	in transito	een tran·see·to
on business	per affari	per a·fa·ree
on holiday	in vacanza	een va·kan·tsa
to study	per motivi di studio	per mo·tee·vee dee stoo·dyo
to visit relatives	per visitare parenti	per vee·zee·ta·re pa·ren·tee

I'm here for ...	Sono qui per ...	so·no kwee per ...
(21) days	(ventuno) giorni	(ven·too·no) jor·nee
(two) months	(due) mesi	(doo·e) me·zee
(three) weeks	(tre) settimane	(tre) se·tee·ma·ne

I have a residency/work permit.
Ho un permesso di soggiorno/lavoro.
o oon per·me·so dee so·jor·no/la·vo·ro

I'm going to (Perugia).
Vado a (Perugia).
va·do a (pe·roo·ja)

I'm staying at the ...
Alloggio al ...
a·lo·jo al ...

listen for ...

eel soo·o ... per fa·vo·re	Il Suo ..., per favore.	Your ..., please.
pa·sa·por·to	passaporto	**passport**
vee·sto	visto	**visa**
vee·a·ja ...	Viaggia ...?	Are you travelling ...?
da so·lo/a	da solo/a m/f	**on your own**
een groo·po	in gruppo	**in a group**
kon fa·mee·lya	con famiglia	**with a family**

at customs

I have nothing to declare.
*Non ho niente da
dichiarare.*
non o *nyen*·te da
dee·kya·*ra*·re

I have something to declare.
Ho delle cose da dichiarare.
o *de*·le *ko*·ze da dee·kya·*ra*·re

I didn't know I had to declare it.
*Non sapevo che dovevo
dichiararlo.*
non sa·*pe*·vo ke do·*ve*·vo
dee·kya·*rar*·lo

That's (not) mine.
(Non) È mio/mia. m/f
(non) e *mee*·o/*mee*·a

Do you have this form in English?
*Avete questo modulo
in inglese?*
a·*ve*·te *kwe*·sto *mo*·doo·lo
een een·*gle*·ze

signs

Controllo	kon·*tro*·lo	**Passport Control**
Passaporti	pa·sa·*por*·tee	
Dogana	do·*ga*·na	**Customs**
Immigrazione	ee·mee·gra·*tsyo*·ne	**Immigration**

finding accommodation

trovare alloggio

Where's a/an ...?	*Dov'è ...?*	*do·ve ...*
camping ground	*un campeggio*	oon kam·*pe*·jo
guesthouse	*una pensione*	oo·na pen·*syo*·ne
hotel	*un albergo*	oo·nal·*ber*·go
inn (budget hotel)	*una locanda*	oo·na lo·*kan*·da
youth hostel	*un ostello della gioventù*	oo·nos·*te*·lo *de*·la jo·ven·*too*

Can you recommend somewhere ...?	*Può consigliare qualche posto ...?*	pwo kon·see·*lya*·re *kwal*·ke *pos*·to ...
cheap	*economico*	e·ko·*no*·mee·ko
good	*buono*	*bwo*·no
luxurious	*di lusso*	dee *loo*·so
nearby	*vicino*	vee·*chee*·no
romantic	*romantico*	ro·*man*·tee·ko

farm stay	*agriturismo* m	a·gree·too·*reez*·mo
mountain hut	*rifugio* m	ree·*foo*·jo
ski resort	*stazione* f *sciistica*	sta·*tsyo*·ne shee·*ees*·tee·ka
spa	*terme* f pl	*ter*·me
wellness centre	*centro* m *benessere*	*chen*·tro be·*ne*·se·re

What's the address?
   Qual'è l'indirizzo?   kwa·*le* leen·dee·*ree*·tso

For more on how to get there, see **directions**, page 61.

local talk		
dive	*bettola* f	*be*·to·la
rat-infested	*infestato/a* m/f *da topi*	een·fes·*ta*·to/a da *to*·pee
top spot	*luogo* m *molto frequentato*	*lwo*·go *mol*·to fre·kwen·*ta*·to

booking ahead & checking in

Do you have a ... room?	Avete una camera ...?	a·ve·te oo·na ka·me·ra ...
double	doppia con letto matrimoniale	do·pya kon le·to ma·tree·mo·nya·le
single	singola	seen·go·la
twin	doppia a due letti	do·pya a doo·e le·tee

How much is it per ...?	Quanto costa per ...?	kwan·to kos·ta per ...
night	una notte	oo·na no·te
person	persona	per·so·na
week	una settimana	oo·na se·tee·ma·na

I'd like to book a room, please.
Vorrei prenotare una camera, per favore.
vo·ray pre·no·ta·re oo·na ka·me·ra per fa·vo·re

I have a reservation.
Ho una prenotazione.
o oo·na pre·no·ta·tsyo·ne

Do you offer (long-stay) discounts?
Fate sconti (per soggiorni lunghi)?
fa·te skon·tee (per so·jor·nee loon·gee)

Is breakfast included?
La colazione è compresa?
la ko·la·tsyo·ne e kom·pre·sa

Is there parking?
C'è il parcheggio?
chay eel par·ke·jo

For (three) nights/weeks.
Per (tre) notti/settimane.
per (tre) no·tee/se·tee·ma·ne

From (July 2) to (July 6).
Dal (due luglio) al (sei luglio).
dal (doo·e loo·lyo) al (say loo·lyo)

Can I see it?
Posso vederla?
po·so ve·der·la

It's fine. I'll take it.
Va bene. La prendo.
va be·ne la pren·do

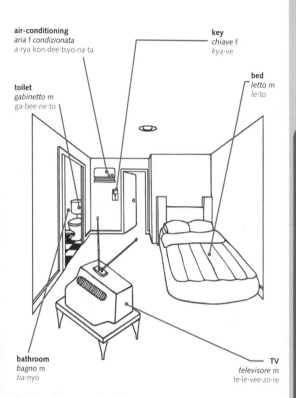

air-conditioning
aria f *condizionata*
a·rya kon·dee·tsyo·na·ta

key
chiave f
kya·ve

bed
letto m
le·to

toilet
gabinetto m
ga·bee·ne·to

bathroom
bagno m
ba·nyo

TV
televisore m
te·le·vee·zo·re

Do I need to pay upfront?
Devo pagare   de·vo pa·ga·re
in anticipo?   ee·nan·tee·chee·po

Can I pay by credit card?
Posso pagare con   po·so pa·ga·re kon
la carta di credito? la kar·ta dee kre·dee·to

For other methods of payment, see **money**, page 35.

requests & queries

When's breakfast served?
A che ora è la prima colazione?
a ke o·ra e la *pree*·ma ko·la·*tsyo*·ne

Where's breakfast served?
Dove si prende la prima colazione?
do·ve see *pren*·de la *pree*·ma ko·la·*tsyo*·ne

Please wake me at (seven).
Mi svegli (alle sette), per favore.
mee *sve*·lyee (a·le *se*·te) per fa·*vo*·re

Can I get another ...?
Può darmi un altro/a ... m/f
pwo *dar*·mee oo·*nal*·tro/a

Can I use the ...?	*Posso usare ...?*	*po*·so oo·za·re ...
Internet	*l'Internet*	*leen*·ter·net
kitchen	*la cucina*	la koo·*chee*·na
laundry	*la lavanderia*	la la·van·de·*ree*·a
telephone	*il telefono*	eel te·*le*·fo·no

Do you have a/an ...?	*C'è ...?*	che ...
elevator	*un ascensore*	oo·na·shen·*so*·re
laundry service	*il servizio lavanderia*	eel ser·*vee*·tsyo la·van·de·*ree*·a
message board	*una bacheca*	oo·na ba·*ke*·ka
safe	*una cassaforte*	oo·na ka·sa·*for*·te
swimming pool	*una piscina*	oo·na pee·*shee*·na

Do you ... here?	*Si ... qui?*	see ... kwee
arrange tours	*organizzano le gite*	or·ga·*nee*·dza·no le *jee*·te
change money	*cambiano i soldi*	*kam*·bya·no ee *sol*·dee

PRACTICAL

54

Can I leave a message for someone?

Posso lasciare un messaggio per qualcuno?

po·so la·*sha*·re oon me·*sa*·jo per kwal·*koo*·no

Is there a message for me?

C'è un messaggio per me?

che oon me·*sa*·jo per me

I'm locked out of my room.

Mi sono chiuso/a fuori dalla mia camera. m/f

mee *so*·no *kyoo*·zo/a *fwo*·ree *da*·la *mee*·a *ka*·me·ra

The (bathroom) door is locked.

La porta (del bagno) è chiusa a chiave.

la *por*·ta (del *ba*·nyo) e *kyoo*·za a *kya*·ve

listen for ...

a *oo*·na pre·no·ta·*tsyo*·ne
Ha una prenotazione? **Do you have a reservation?**

a oo·*za*·to eel *free*·go·bar
Ha usato il frigobar? **Did you use the mini-bar?**

kwa·*le* eel *soo*·o *noo*·me·ro dee *ka*·me·ra
Qual'è il Suo numero di camera? **What's your room number?**

la *kya*·ve e *a*·la ray·sep·*shon*
La chiave è alla reception. **The key is at reception.**

mee dees·*pya*·che e kom·*ple*·to
Mi dispiace, è completo. **I'm sorry, we're full.**

per kwan·te *no*·tee
Per quante notti? **For how many nights?**

accommodation

55

complaints

The room is	La camera è	la *ka*·me·ra e
too ...	troppo ...	*tro*·po ...
cold	*fredda*	*fre*·da
dark	*scura*	*skoo*·ra
expensive	*cara*	*ka*·ra
light/bright	*luminosa*	loo·mee·*no*·za
noisy	*rumorosa*	roo·mo·*ro*·za
small	*piccola*	*pee*·ko·la

The ... doesn't work.	... non funziona.	... non foon·*tsyo*·na
air-conditioning	*L'aria condizionata*	*la*·rya kon·dee·tsyo·*na*·ta
fan	*Il ventilatore*	eel ven·tee·la·*to*·re
heater	*La stufa*	la *stoo*·fa
toilet	*Il gabinetto*	eel ga·bee·*ne*·to

This ... isn't clean.
Questo/a ... non è pulito/a. m/f   *kwe*·sto/a ... *no*·ne poo·*lee*·to/a

There's no hot water.
Non c'è acqua calda.   non chay *ak*·wa *kal*·da

For more things you might see or want in your room, see the **dictionary**.

---

a knock at the door ...

Who is it?	Chi è?	kee e
Just a moment.	Un momento.	oon mo·*men*·to
Come in.	Avanti.	a·*van*·tee
Come back later, please.	Torni più tardi, per favore.	*tor*·nee pyoo *tar*·dee per fa·*vo*·re

checking out

What time is checkout?
A che ora si deve lasciar
libera la camera?
a ke o·ra see de·ve la·shar
lee·be·ra la ka·me·ra

Can I have a late checkout?
Posso liberare la
camera più tardi?
po·so lee·be·ra·re la
ka·me·ra pyoo tar·dee

Can I leave my luggage here?
Posso lasciare il mio
bagaglio qui?
po·so la·sha·re eel mee·o
ba·ga·lyo kwee

I'm leaving now.
Parto adesso.
par·to a·de·so

There's a mistake in the bill.
C'è un errore nel conto.
che oo·ne·ro·re nel kon·to

Can you call a taxi for me (for 11 o'clock)?
Può chiamarmi un tassì
(per le undici)?
pwo kya·mar·mee oon ta·see
(per le oon·dee·chee)

Could I have my ..., please?	*Posso avere ...,* *per favore?*	po·so a·ve·re ... per fa·vo·re
deposit	la caparra	la ka·pa·ra
passport	il mio passaporto	eel mee·o pa·sa·por·to
valuables	i miei oggetti di valore	ee myay o·je·tee dee va·lo·re
I'll be back ...	*Torno ...*	tor·no ...
in (three) days	fra (tre) giorni	fra (tre) jor·nee
on (Tuesday)	(martedì)	(mar·te·dee)

accommodation

57

I had a great stay, thank you.
Sono stato/a   so·no sta·to/a
benissimo/a, grazie. m/f   be·nee·see·mo/a gra·tsye

You've been terrific.
È stato/a bravissimo/a. m/f   e sta·to/a bra·vee·see·mo/a

I'll recommend it to my friends.
Lo consiglierò   lo kon·see·lye·ro
ai miei amici.   ai myay a·mee·chee

camping

il campeggio

Where's the nearest ...?	*Dov'è ... più vicino?*	do·ve ... pyoo vee·chee·no
campsite	*il campeggio*	eel kam·pe·jo
shop	*il negozio*	eel ne·go·tsyo
shower facility	*il servizio doccia*	eel ser·vee·tsyo do·cha
Do you have ...?	*Avete ...?*	a·ve·te ...
electricity	*la corrente*	la ko·ren·te
shower facilities	*servizio doccia*	ser·vee·tsyo do·cha
a site	*un sito*	oon see·to
tents for hire	*tende da noleggiare*	ten·de da no·le·ja·re
How much is it per ...?	*Quant'è per ...?*	kwan·te per ...
caravan	*roulotte*	roo·lot
person	*persona*	per·so·na
tent	*tenda*	ten·da
vehicle	*veicolo*	ve·ee·ko·lo
Can I ...?	*Si può ...?*	see pwo ...
camp here	*campeggiare qui*	kam·pe·ja·re kwee
park next to my tent	*parcheggiare accanto alla tenda*	par·ke·ja·re a·kan·to a·la ten·da
pitch the tent here	*piantare la tenda qui*	pyan·ta·re la ten·da kwee

Who do I ask to stay here?
A chi chiedo permesso per
stare qui?
a kee *kye*·do per·*me*·so per
sta·re kwee

Where's the nearest toilet block?
Dove sono i servizi
igienici più
vicini?
do·ve *so*·no ee ser·*vee*·tsee
ee·*je*·nee·chee pyoo
vee·*chee*·nee

Is it coin-operated?
Funziona a gettoni?
foon·*tsyo*·na a je·*to*·nee

Is the water drinkable?
L'acqua è potabile?
la·kwa e po·*ta*·bee·le

Could I borrow (a mallet)?
Potrei prendere in
prestito (un mazzuolo)?
po·*tray* pren·*de*·re een
pres·*tee*·to (oon ma·*tswo*·lo)

For more cooking utensils, see **self-catering**, page 158, and the **dictionary**.

renting

affittare

I'm here about the ... for rent.
Sono qui per il/la ... che
date in affitto. m/f
so·no kwee per eel/la ... ke
da·te een·a·*fee*·to

Do you have	*Avete ...*	a·*ve*·te ...
a/an ... for rent?	*d'affittare?*	da·fee·*ta*·re
apartment	*un appartamento*	oo·na·par·ta·*men*·to
cabin	*una cabina*	oo·na ka·*bee*·na
house	*una casa*	oo·na *ka*·za
room	*una camera*	oo·na *ka*·me·ra
villa	*una villa*	oo·na *vee*·la
(partly) furnished	*(in parte)*	(een *par*·te)
	ammobiliato/a m/f	a·mo·bee·*lya*·to/a
unfurnished	*non*	no·na·mo·bee·*lya*·to/a
	ammobiliato/a m/f	

How much is it for ...?	*Quant'è per ...?*	kwan·te per ...
(one) week	*(una) settimana*	(oo·na) se·tee·ma·na
(two) months	*(due) mesi*	(doo·e) me·zee

Are bills extra?
   Sono extra le bollette?   so·no ek·stra le bo·le·te

staying with locals

dalle persone del luogo

Can I stay at your place?
   Posso stare da Lei/te? pol/inf   po·so sta·re da lay/te

Is there anything I can do to help?

Posso aiutare in	po·so a·yoo·ta·re een
qualche modo?	kwal·ke mo·do

I have my	*Ho il mio*	o eel mee·o
own ...	*proprio ...*	pro·pryo ...
mattress	*materasso*	ma·te·ra·so
sleeping bag	*sacco a pelo*	sa·ko a pe·lo

Can I ...?	*Posso ...?*	po·so ...
bring anything	*portare qualcosa*	por·ta·re kwal·ko·za
for the meal	*per il pasto*	per eel pas·to
do the dishes	*lavare i piatti*	la·va·re ee pya·tee
set/clear the	*apparecchiare/*	a·pa·re·kya·re/
table	*sparecchiare*	spa·re·kya·re
take out the	*gettare la*	je·ta·re la
rubbish	*spazzatura*	spa·tsa·too·ra

Thanks for your hospitality.

Grazie per la Sua/tua	gra·tsye per la soo·a/too·a
ospitalità. pol/inf	os·pee·ta·lee·ta

For compliments to the chef, see **eating out**, page 149.

Where's (the bank)?
Dov'è (la banca)?   do·ve (la ban·ka)

I'm looking for (the public toilets).
Cerco (i servizi   cher·ko (ee ser·vee·tsee
igienici).   ee·je·nee·chee)

Which way's (the post office)?
Dove si trova (l'ufficio   do·ve see tro·va (loo·fee·cho
postale)?   pos·ta·le)

How do I get there?
Come ci si arriva?   ko·me chee see a·ree·va

How far is it?
Quant'è distante?   kwan·te dees·tan·te

Can you show me (on the map)?
Può mostrarmi   pwo mos·trar·mee
(sulla pianta)?   (soo·la pyan·ta)

What's the address?
Qual'è l'indirizzo?   kwa·le leen·dee·ree·tso

It's ...	È ...	e ...
behind ...	*dietro ...*	dye·tro ...
far away	*lontano*	lon·ta·no
here	*qui*	kwee
in front of ...	*davanti a ...*	da·van·tee a ...
left	*a sinistra*	a see·nee·stra
near (to ...)	*vicino (a ...)*	vee·chee·no (a ...)
next to ...	*accanto a ...*	a·kan·to a ...
on the corner	*all'angolo*	a lan·go·lo
opposite ...	*di fronte a ...*	dee fron·te a ...
right	*a destra*	a de·stra
straight ahead	*sempre diritto*	sem·pre dee·ree·to
there	*là*	la

Turn ...	Giri ...	jee·ree ...
at the corner	all'angolo	a·lan·go·lo
at the traffic lights	al semaforo	al se·ma·fo·ro
left	a sinistra	a see·nee·stra
right	a destra	a de·stra

It's ...	È a ...	e a ...
(100) metres	(cento) metri	(chen·to) me·tree
(30) minutes	(trenta) minuti	(tren·ta) mee·noo·tee

by bus	con l'autobus	kon low·to·boos
by taxi	con il tassì	ko·neel ta·see
by train	con il treno	ko·neel tre·no
on foot	a piedi	a pye·dee

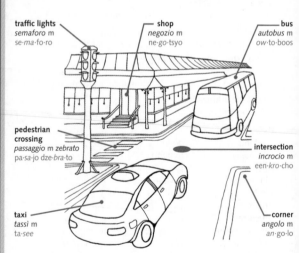

traffic lights
semaforo m
se·ma·fo·ro

shop
negozio m
ne·go·tsyo

bus
autobus m
ow·to·boos

pedestrian crossing
passaggio m *zebrato*
pa·sa·jo dze·bra·to

intersection
incrocio m
een·kro·cho

taxi
tassì m
ta·see

corner
angolo m
an·go·lo

looking for ...

Where's (a travel agency)?
Dov'è (un'agenzia di viaggi)?
do·ve (oo·na·jen·tsee·a dee vee·a·jee)

Where can I buy (bread)?
Dove posso comprare (pane)?
do·ve po·so kom·pra·re (pa·ne)

For more on shops and how to get there, see **directions**, page 61, and the **dictionary**.

signs		
Aperto	a·per·to	**Open**
Chiuso	kyoo·zo	**Closed**
Spingere	speen·je·re	**Push**
Tirare	tee·ra·re	**Pull**

making a purchase

I'd like to buy ...
Vorrei comprare ...
vo·ray kom·pra·re ...

I'm just looking.
Sto solo guardando.
sto so·lo gwar·dan·do

What is this made of?
Questo con che cosa è fatto?
kwe·sto kon ke ko·za e fa·to

How much is this?
Quanto costa questo?
kwan·to kos·ta kwe·sto

Can you write down the price?
Può scrivere il prezzo?
pwo skree·ve·re eel pre·tso

Do you have any others?
Ne avete altri?
ne a·ve·te al·tree

Can I look at it?
Posso dare un'occhiata? po·so da·re oo·no·kya·ta

Could I have it wrapped, please?
Può incartarlo, pwo een·kar·tar·lo
per favore? per fa·vo·re

I don't need a bag, thanks.
Non mi serve la busta, non mee ser·ve la boos·ta
grazie. gra·tsye

Does it have a guarantee?
Ha la garanzia? a la ga·ran·tsee·a

Can I have it sent overseas?
Può spedirlo all'estero? pwo spe·deer·lo a·les·te·ro

Can you order it for me?
Me lo può ordinare, me lo pwo or·dee·na·re
per favore? per fa·vo·re

Can I pick it up later?
Posso ritirarlo po·so ree·tee·rar·lo
più tardi? pyoo tar·dee

It's faulty.
È difettoso. e dee·fe·to·zo

It's broken.
È rotto. e ro·to

Do you accept ...?	*Accettate ...?*	a·che·ta·te ...
credit cards	*la carta di credito*	la kar·ta dee kre·dee·to
debit cards	*la carta di debito*	la kar·ta dee de·bee·to
travellers cheques	*gli assegni di viaggio*	lyee a·se·nyee dee vee·a·jo

old-fashioned manners

The plural polite form has become virtually obsolete in modern Italian. If you want to show respect to more than one person, use *voi* voy. See also **personal pronouns** in the **grammar** chapter, page 19.

Could I have a ..., please?	Può darmi ..., per favore?	pwo dar·mee ... per fa·vo·re
bag	un sacchetto	oon sa·ke·to
receipt	una ricevuta	oo·na ree·che·voo·ta

I'd like ..., please.	Vorrei ..., per favore.	vo·ray ... per fa·vo·re
my change	il mio resto	eel mee·o res·to
my money back	un rimborso	oon reem·bor·so
to change this	cambiare questo/a m/f	kam·bya·re kwe·sto/a
to return this	restituire questo/a m/f	res·tee·twee·re kwe·sto/a

bargaining

contrattare

That's too expensive.
È troppo caro/a. m/f — e tro·po ka·ro/a

The price is very high.
Il prezzo è molto alto. — eel pre·tso e mol·to al·to

Can you lower the price?
Può farmi lo sconto? — pwo far·mee lo skon·to

Do you have something cheaper?
Ha qualcosa di meno costoso? — a kwal·ko·za dee me·no kos·to·zo

I'll give you ...
Le offro ... — le o·fro ...

clothes

abbigliamento

Can I try it on?
Potrei provarmelo/a? m/f — po·tray pro·var·me·lo/a

It doesn't fit.
Non va bene. — non va be·ne

My size is ...	*Sono una taglia ...*	so·no oo·na ta·lya ...
large	*forte*	for·te
medium	*media*	me·dya
small	*piccola*	pee·ko·la

For clothing items see the **dictionary**, and for sizes see **numbers & amounts**, page 29.

repairs

le riparazioni

Can I have ... repaired here?	*Posso far aggiustare ... qui?*	po·so far a·joo·sta·re ... kwee
my backpack	*il mio zaino*	eel mee·o dzai·no
my camera	*la mia macchina fotografica*	la mee·a ma·kee·na fo·to·gra·fee·ka

When will my ... be ready?	*Quando saranno pronti/e ...?* m/f pl	kwan·do sa·ra·no pron·tee/e ...
(sun)glasses	*i miei occhiali* m pl *(da sole)*	ee myay o·kya·lee (da so·le)
shoes	*le mie scarpe* f pl	le mee·e skar·pe

don't touch!

In style-conscious Italy, though shop window displays may look good enough to eat, they're absolutely not to be touched. Disrupting a window display could jeopardise a shop's *bella figura* be·la fee·goo·ra – that all-important Italian preoccupation with creating a good impression.

hairdressing

I'd like (a) ...	Vorrei ...	vo·ray ...
blow wave	una messa in piega a fon	oo·na me·sa een pye·ga a fon
colour	farmi tingere i capelli	far·mee teen·je·re ee ka·pe·lee
haircut	un taglio	oon ta·lyo
highlights	i colpi di sole	ee kol·pee dee so·le
layers	un taglio scalato	oon ta·lyo ska·la·to
my beard trimmed	una spuntatina alla barba	oo·na spoon·ta·tee·na a·la bar·ba
perm	una permanente	oo·na per·ma·nen·te
shave	una rasatura	oo·na ra·za·too·ra
straightening	farmi stirare i capelli	far·mee stee·ra·re ee ka·pe·lee
streaks	le mèches	le mesh
tips	i colpi di sole	ee kol·pee dee so·le
trim	una spuntatina	oo·na spoon·ta·tee·na

Do you do ...?	Fate ...	fa·te ...
facials	i trattamenti di bellezza (al viso)	ee tra·ta·men·tee dee be·le·tsa (al vee·zo)
massage	i massaggi	ee ma·sa·jee
waxing	la depilazione	la de·pee·la·tsyo·ne

Don't cut it too short.
Non li tagli troppo corti. non lee ta·lyee tro·po kor·tee

Cut it all off!
Li tagli tutti! lee ta·lyee too·tee

Please use a new blade.
Usi una lametta nuova, per favore. oo·zee oo·na la·me·ta nwo·va per fa·vo·re

I should never have let you near me!
Non dovevo mai permetterLe di toccarmi! non do·ve·vo mai per·me·ter·le dee to·kar·mee

For colours, see the **dictionary**.

books & reading

Is there a/an (English-language) bookshop?
C'è una libreria   che oo·na lee·bre·*ree*·a
(specializzata in   (spe·cha·lee·*dza*·ta een
lingua inglese)?   *leen*·gwa een·*gle*·ze)

Is there an (English-language) entertainment guide?
C'è una guida agli   che oo·na gwee·da a·lyee
spettacoli (in inglese)?   spe·*ta*·ko·lee (ee·neen·*gle*·ze)

Do you have a book by (Alberto Moravia)?
C'è un libro di   che oon *lee*·bro dee
(Alberto Moravia)?   (al·*ber*·to mo·*ra*·vee·a)

Do you have Lonely Planet guidebooks?
Avete le guide del   a·ve·te le gwee·de del
Lonely Planet?   *lon*·lee pla·net

music & DVD

I'd like (a) ...	*Vorrei ...*	vo·*ray* ...
CD	*un CD*	oon chee·*dee*
DVD	*un DVD*	oon dee·voo·*dee*
headphones	*delle cuffia*	*de*·le koo·fya

I heard a band called (Marlene Kuntz).
Ho sentito un gruppo   o sen·*tee*·to oon groo·po
chiamato (Marlene Kuntz).   kya·*ma*·to (mar·*le*·ne koonts)

What's his/her best recording?
Qual'è la sua migliore   kwa·*le* la soo·a mee·*lyo*·re
incisione?   een·chee·zyo·ne

---

listen for ...

po·so a·yoo·*tar*·la
   Posso aiutarLa?   **Can I help you?**
no non ne a·*bya*·mo
   No, non ne abbiamo.   **No, we don't have any.**

Can I listen to this?
Potrei ascoltare questo?   po·*tray* as·kol·*ta*·re *kwe*·sto

Will this work on any DVD player?
Funzionerà con tutti   foon·tsyo·ne·*ra* kon *too*·tee
i lettori di DVD?   ee le·*to*·ree dee dee·voo·*dee*

What region is this DVD for?
Questo DVD a quale   *kwe*·sto dee·voo·*dee* a *kwa*·le
DVD Region appartiene?   dee·voo·*dee* re·jon a·par·*tye*·ne

video & photography

video & fotografia

I need a ...	*Vorrei un rullino*	vo·*ray* oon roo·*lee*·no
film for this	*... per questa*	... per *kwe*·sta
camera.	*macchina*	*ma*·kee·na
	fotografica.	fo·to·gra·*fee*·ka
B&W	*in bianco e nero*	een *byan*·ko e *ne*·ro
colour	*a colori*	a *ko*·lo·ree
slide	*per diapositive*	per dya·po·zee·*tee*·ve
(100) speed	*da (cento) ASA*	da (*chen*·to) *a*·za
Could you ...?	*Potrebbe ...?*	po·*tre*·be ...
develop this	*sviluppare*	svee·loo·*pa*·re
film	*questo rullino*	*kwe*·sto roo·*lee*·no
load my film	*inserire il*	een·se·*ree*·re eel
	mio rullino	*mee*·o roo·*lee*·no
Can you ...?	*Potete ...?*	po·*te*·te ...
print digital	*stampare foto*	stam·*pa*·re *fo*·to
photos	*digitali*	dee·jee·*ta*·lee
recharge the	*ricaricare la*	ree·ka·ree·*ka*·re la
battery for	*batteria della*	ba·te·*ree*·a *de*·la
my digital	*mia macchina*	*mee*·a *ma*·kee·na
camera	*fotografica*	fo·to·gra·*fee*·ka
	digitale	dee·jee·*ta*·le
transfer my	*trasferire le*	tra·sfe·*ree*·re le
photos from	*mie foto dalla*	*mee*·e *fo*·to *da*·la
camera	*macchina su*	*ma*·kee·na soo
to CD	*un CD*	oon chee·*dee*

Do you have (a) ... for this camera?	Avete ... per questa macchina fotografica?	a·ve·te ... per kwe·sta ma·kee·na fo·to·gra·fee·ka
batteries	batterie	ba·te·ree·e
flash (bulb)	una lampadina del flash	oo·na lam·pa·dee·na del flesh
light meter	un esposimetro	oon es·po·see·me·tro
memory cards	schede di memoria	ske·de dee me·mo·rya
zoom (lens)	uno zoom	oo·no zoom
... camera	macchina fotografica ...	ma·kee·na fo·to·gra·fee·ka ...
digital	digitale	dee·jee·ta·le
disposable	usa-e-getta	oo·sa·e·je·ta
underwater	subacquea	soo·ba·kwe·a

I need a cable to connect my camera to a computer.
Mi serve un cavo per collegare la mia macchina a un computer.
mee ser·ve oon ka·vo per ko·le·ga·re la mee·a ma·kee·na a oon komp·yoo·ter

I need a cable to recharge this battery.
Mi serve un cavo per ricaricare questa batteria.
mee ser·ve oon ka·vo per ree·ka·ree·ka·re kwe·sta ba·te·ree·a

I need a video cassette for this camera.
Mi serve una videocassetta per questa macchina.
mee ser·ve oo·na vee·de·o·ka·se·ta per kwe·sta ma·kee·na

How much is it to develop this film?
Quanto costa sviluppare questo rullino?
kwan·to kos·ta svee·loo·pa·re kwe·sto roo·lee·no

I need passport photos taken.
Vorrei delle foto tessera.
vo·ray de·le fo·to te·se·ra

When will it be ready?
Quando sarà pronto?
kwan·do sa·ra pron·to

I'm not happy with these photos.
Non mi piacciono queste foto.
non mee pya·cho·no kwe·ste fo·to

For more photographic equipment, see the **dictionary**.

post office

l'ufficio postale

I want to send a ...	Vorrei mandare un/una ... m/f	vo·ray man·da·re oon/oo·na ...
fax	fax m	faks
letter	lettera f	le·te·ra
parcel	pacchetto m	pa·ke·to
postcard	cartolina f	kar·to·lee·na

I want to buy ...	Vorrei comprare ...	vo·ray kom·pra·re ...
an aerogram	un aerogramma	oo·na·e·ro·gra·ma
an envelope	una busta	oo·na boo·sta
stamps	dei francobolli	day fran·ko·bo·lee

airmail	via f aerea	vee·a a·e·re·a
customs declaration	dichiarazione f doganale	dee·kya·ra·tsyo·ne do·ga·na·le
domestic	domestico/a m/f	do·mes·tee·ko/a
express mail	posta f prioritaria	pos·ta pryo·ree·ta·rya
fragile	fragile	fra·jee·le
glue	colla f	ko·la
international	internazionale	een·ter·na·tsyo·na·le
mail box	buca f delle lettere	boo·ka de·le le·te·re
PO box	casella f postale	ka·se·la po·sta·le
postal address	indirizzo m postale	een·dee·ree·tso po·sta·le
postcode	codice m postale	ko·dee·che pos·ta·le
registered mail	posta f raccomandata	pos·ta ra·ko·man·da·ta
regular mail	posta f ordinaria	pos·ta or·dee·na·rya
sea mail	via f mare	vee·a ma·re

Please send it by airmail (to Denmark).
Lo mandi via aerea   lo *man*·dee *vee*·a a·e·re·a
(in Danimarca),   (een da·nee·*mar*·ka)
per favore.   per fa·*vo*·re

Please send it by regular mail (to Rome).
Lo mandi per posta   lo *man*·dee per *pos*·ta
ordinaria (a Roma),   or·dee·*na*·rya (a *ro*·ma)
per favore.   per fa·*vo*·re

It contains ...
Contiene ...   kon·*tye*·ne ...

Where's the poste restante section?
Dov'è il fermo posta?   do·*ve* eel *fer*·mo *pos*·ta

Is there any mail for me?
C'è posta per me?   che *pos*·ta per me

---

listen for ...

do·ve lo spe·*dee*·she
Dove lo spedisce?   **Where are you sending it?**

per *pos*·ta pryo·ree·*ta*·rya o nor·*ma*·le
Per posta prioritaria   **By express post or regular**
o normale?   **post?**

---

phone

What's your phone number?
Qual'è il Suo/tuo   kwa·*le* eel soo·o/too·o
numero di telefono? pol/inf   *noo*·me·ro dee te·*le*·fo·no

Where's the nearest public phone?
Dov'è il telefono   do·*ve* eel te·*le*·fo·no
pubblico più vicino?   *poo*·blee·ko pyoo vee·*chee*·no

Can I look at a phone book?
Potrei guardare l'elenco   po·*tray* gwar·*da*·re le·*len*·ko
telefonico?   te·le·*fo*·nee·ko

I'd like to know the number for ...
Vorrei sapere il numero   vo·*ray* sa·*pe*·re eel *noo*·me·ro
di ...   dee ...

Do you have international prepaid phone cards?

Avete carte telefoniche internazionali prepagate?	a·ve·te *kar*·te te·le·*fo*·nee·ke een·ter·na·tsyo·*na*·lee pre·pa·*ga*·te	

I want to make a/an ...	*Vorrei fare una chiamata ...*	vo·*ray* fa·re oo·na kya·*ma*·ta ...
call to (Belgium)	*in (Belgio)*	een (*bel*·jo)
Internet call	*via Internet*	*vee*·a *een*·ter·net
local call	*urbana*	oor·*ba*·na
reverse-charge/ collect call	*a carico del destinatario*	a *ka*·ree·ko del des·tee·na·*ta*·ryo

I want to ...	*Vorrei ...*	vo·*ray* ...
buy a phone card	*comprare una scheda telefonica*	kom·*pra*·re oo·na *ske*·da te·le·*fo*·nee·ka
speak for (three) minutes	*parlare per (tre) minuti*	par·*la*·re per (tre) mee·*noo*·tee

How much does ... cost?	*Quanto costa ...?*	*kwan*·to *kos*·ta ...
a (three)-minute call	*una telefonata di (tre) minuti*	oo·na te·le·fo·*na*·ta dee (tre) mee·*noo*·tee
each extra minute	*ogni minuto in più*	*o*·nyee mee·*noo*·to een pyoo

The number is ...
Il numero è ...   eel *noo*·me·ro e ...

What's the area/country code for ...?
Qual'è il prefisso per ...?   kwa·*le* eel pre·*fee*·so per ...

It's engaged.
La linea è occupata.   la *lee*·ne·a e o·koo·*pa*·ta

I've been cut off.
È caduta la linea.   e ka·*doo*·ta la *lee*·ne·a

The connection's bad.
La linea non è buona.   la *lee*·ne·a no·ne *bwo*·na

Hello.	*Pronto!*	*pron*·to
It's ...	*Sono ...*	*so*·no ...

communications

73

Can I speak to …?
Posso parlare con …?   po·so par·*la*·re kon …

Can I leave a message?
Posso lasciare un messaggio?   po·so la·*sha*·re oon me·*sa*·jo

Please tell him/her I called.
Gli/Le dica che ho   lyee/le *dee*·ka ke o
telefonato, per favore.   te·le·fo·*na*·to per fa·*vo*·re

I'll call back later.
Richiamerò più tardi.   ree·kya·me·*ro* pyoo *tar*·dee

My number is …
Il mio numero è …   eel *mee*·o *noo*·me·ro e …

I don't have a contact number.
Non ho un numero fisso.   non o oon *noo*·me·ro *fee*·so

For telephone numbers, see **numbers & amounts**, page 29.

listen for ...

kon kee *par*·lo
Con chi parlo?   **Who's calling?**

kon kee *vwo*·le par·*la*·re
Con chi vuole   **Who do you want**
parlare?   **(to speak to)?**

lye·lo/*lye*·la *pa*·so
Glielo/Gliela passo.   **I'll put him/her on.**

mee dees·*pya*·che (*loo*·ee/lay) non che
Mi dispiace, (lui/lei)   **I'm sorry, he/she**
non c'è.   **is not here.**

mee dees·*pya*·che a sba·*lya*·to *noo*·me·ro
Mi dispiace, ha sbagliato   **Sorry, wrong number.**
numero.

see e *kwe*
Sì, è qui.   **Yes, he/she is here.**

mobile/cell phone

I'd like a/an ...	Vorrei ...	vo·ray ...
adaptor plug	un adattatore	oo·na·da·ta·to·re
charger for my	un	oon
phone	caricabatterie	ka·ree·ka·ba·te·ree·e
mobile/cell phone	un cellulare	oon che·loo·la·re
for hire	da noleggiare	da no·le·ja·re
prepaid mobile/	un cellulare	oon che·loo·la·re
cell phone	prepagato	pre·pa·ga·to
recharge card	una ricarica	oo·na re·ka·ree·ka
for ...	telefonica	te·le·fo·nee·ka
	per ...	per ...
SIM card for your	un SIM card	oon seem kard
network	per la vostra	per la vos·tra
	rete telefonica	re·te te·le·fo·nee·ka

What are the rates?
Quali sono le tariffe?   kwa·lee so·no le ta·ree·fe

the internet

Where's the local Internet cafe?
Dove si trova   do·ve see tro·va
l'Internet point?   leen·ter·net poynt

Do you have public Internet access here?
Qui c'è il collegamento   kwee chay eel ko·le·ga·men·to
a Internet?   a een·ter·net

Is there wireless Internet access here?
Qui c'è il collegamento   kwee chay eel ko·le·ga·men·to
Wi-Fi?   wai·fai

Can I connect my laptop here?
Posso collegare il mio   po·so ko·le·ga·re eel mee·o
portatile?   por·ta·tee·le

Do you have headphones (with a microphone)?
Avete una cuffia   a·ve·te oo·na koo·fya
(con microfono)?   (kon mee·kro·fo·no)

I'd like to buy a card/USB for prepaid mobile Internet.

Vorrei comprare una scheda/	vo·ray kom·*pra*·re oo·na *ske*·da/
chiavetta USB prepagata	kya·ve·ta oo·e·se·bee pre·pa·*ga*·ta
per internet mobile.	per *een*·ter·net mo·*bee*·le

I'd like to ...	Vorrei ...	vo·ray ...
burn a CD	*masterizzare*	mas·te·ree·*tsa*·re
	un CD	oon chee·*dee*
check my email	*controllare il*	kon·tro·*la*·re eel
	mio email	*mee*·e e·mayl
download my	*scaricare le*	ska·ree·*ka*·re le
photos	*mie foto*	*mee*·e *fo*·to
get Internet access	*usare Internet*	oo·*za*·re *een*·ter·net
use a printer	*usare una*	oo·*za*·re oo·na
	stampante	stam·*pan*·te
use a scanner	*scandire*	skan·*dee*·re
use Skype	*usare Skype*	oo·*za*·re skaip

How much per ...?	Quanto costa ...?	*kwan*·to *kos*·ta ...
hour	*all'ora*	a·*lo*·ra
page	*a pagina*	a *pa*·jee·na

How do I log on?	Come posso	*ko*·me *po*·so
	accedere?	a·*che*·de·re
It's crashed.	*Si è bloccato.*	see e blo·*ka*·to
I've finished.	*Ho finito.*	o fee·*nee*·to

Can I connect	Posso collegare	*po*·so ko·le·*ga*·re
my ... to this	*... a questo*	... a *kwe*·sto
computer?	*computer?*	kom·*pyoo*·ter
camera	*la mia macchina*	la *mee*·a *ma*·kee·na
	fotografica	fo·to·*gra*·fee·ka
iPod	*il mio iPod*	eel *mee*·o *ai*·pod
media player	*il mio lettore*	eel *mee*·o le·*to*·re
(MP3)	*MP3*	e·me·pee·*tre*
portable hard	*il mio hard*	eel *mee*·o hard
drive	*drive portatile*	draiv por·*ta*·tee·le
PSP	*la mia consolle*	la *mee*·a kon·*so*·le
	PSP portatile	pee·e·se·pee
		por·*ta*·tee·le
USB flash drive	*la mia chiavetta*	la *mee*·a kya·*ve*·ta
(memory stick)	*USB*	oo·e·se·bee

I'm attending a ...	Sono qui per ...	so·no kwee per ...
conference	una conferenza	oo·na kon·fe·ren·tsa
course	un corso	oon kor·so
meeting	una riunione	oo·na ree·oo·nyo·ne
trade fair	una fiera	oo·na fye·ra
	commerciale	ko·mer·cha·le

I'm here with ...	Sono qui con ...	so·no kwee kon ...
my company	la mia azienda	la mee·a a·dzyen·da
my colleague	il mio collega m	eel mee·o ko·le·ga
	la mia collega f	la mee·a ko·le·ga
(two) others	(due) altri	(doo·e) al·tree

I'm staying at the ..., room ...
Alloggio al ..., camera ...   a·lo·jo al ... ka·me·ra ...

I'm alone.
Sono solo/a. m/f   so·no so·lo/a

I'm here for (two) days/weeks.
Sono qui per (due)   so·no kwee per (doo·e)
giorni/settimane.   jor·nee/se·tee·ma·ne

Here's my business card.
Ecco il mio biglietto   e·ko eel mee·o bee·lye·to
da visita.   da vee·zee·ta

Can I have your business card?
Potrei avere il suo   po·tray a·ve·re eel soo·o
biglietto da visita?   bee·lye·to da vee·zee·ta

I have an appointment with ...
Ho un appuntamento   o oo·na·poon·ta·men·to
con ...   kon ...

That went very well.
È andato bene.   e an·da·to be·ne

Thank you for your time.
Grazie della sua   gra·tsye de·la soo·a
disponibilità.   dees·po·nee·bee·lee·ta

Shall we go for a drink/meal?

Andiamo a bere/   an·*dya*·mo a *be*·re/
mangiare qualcosa?   man·*ja*·re kwal·*ko*·za

Where's the conference/meeting?

Dov'è la conferenza/   do·ve la kon·fe·*ren*·tsa/
riunione?   ree·oo·*nyo*·ne

I need ...	*Ho bisogno di ...*	o bee·*zo*·nyo dee ...
a computer	*un computer*	oon kom·*pyoo*·ter
a connection to	*una connessione*	oo·na ko·ne·*syo*·ne
the Internet	*Internet*	*een*·ter·net
an interpreter	*un/un'interprete* m/f	oo·neen·*ter*·pre·te
more business	*più biglietti*	pyoo bee·*lye*·tee
cards	*da visita*	da *vee*·zee·ta
some space to	*un posto dove*	oon *pos*·to *do*·ve
set up	*sistemare*	sees·te·*ma*·re
to send an	*mandare un*	man·*da*·re oon
email/fax	*email/fax*	ee·*mayl*/faks

I'm expecting a ...	*Aspetto ...*	a·*spet*·o ...
call	*una telefonata*	oo·na te·le·fo·*na*·ta
fax	*un fax*	oon faks

data projector	*proiettore* m	pro·ye·*to*·re
flip chart	*lavagna* f *con fogli*	la·*va*·nya kon *fo*·lyee
overhead	*lavagna* f	la·*va*·nya
projector	*luminosa*	loo·mee·*no*·sa
whiteboard	*lavagna* f *bianca*	la·*va*·nya *byan*·ka

the language of italian business

Italian business culture is formal and hierarchical. First names aren't used between executives and subordinates, and using the right personal or professional titles (see page 93) may help you clinch that deal. Business isn't usually discussed over a meal, and if you dine with Italian colleagues or business partners, wait for them to initiate any discussions about business. As a visitor you'll be expected to be *in orario* een o·*ra*·ryo (on time), but don't get touchy about being kept waiting.

banking

Where can I ...?	*Dove posso ...?*	*do·ve po·so ...*
I'd like to ...	*Vorrei ...*	*vo·ray ...*
arrange a transfer	*trasferire soldi*	tras·fe·ree·re sol·dee
cash a cheque	*riscuotere*	ree·skwo·te·re
	un assegno	oo·na·se·nyo
change a travellers cheque	*cambiare un assegno di viaggio*	kam·bya·re oo·na·se·nyo dee vee·a·jo
change money	*cambiare denaro*	kam·bya·re de·na·ro
get a cash advance	*prelevare con carta di credito*	pre·le·va·re kon kar·ta dee kre·dee·to
get change for this note	*cambiare questa banconota*	kam·bya·re kwe·sta ban·ko·no·ta
withdraw money	*fare un prelievo*	fa·re oon pre·lye·vo
Where's the nearest ...?	*Dov'è ... più vicino?*	do·ve ... pyoo vee·chee·no
automatic teller machine	*il Bancomat*	eel ban·ko·mat
foreign exchange office	*il cambio*	eel kam·byo

What time does the bank open?
A che ora apre la banca?   a ke o·ra a·pre la ban·ka

The automatic teller machine took my card.
Il Bancomat ha trattenuto la mia carta di credito.
eel ban·ko·mat a tra·te·noo·to la mee·a kar·ta dee kre·dee·to

I've forgotten my PIN.
Ho dimenticato il mio codice PIN.
o dee·men·tee·ka·to eel mee·o ko·dee·che peen

Can I use my credit card to withdraw money?
Si può usare la carta di credito per fare prelievi?
see pwo oo·za·re la kar·ta dee kre·dee·to per fa·re pre·lye·vee

What's the exchange rate?
    Quant'è il cambio?   kwan·*te* eel *kam*·byo

What's the commission?
    Quant'è la commissione?   kwan·*te* la ko·mee·*syo*·ne

What's the charge for that?
    Quanto costa?   kwan·to kos·ta

Can I have smaller notes?
    Mi può dare banconote   mee pwo *da*·re ban·ko·*no*·te
    più piccole?   pyoo *pee*·ko·le

Has my money arrived yet?
    È arrivato il mio denaro?   e a·ree·*va*·to eel *mee*·o de·*na*·ro

How long will it take to arrive?
    Quanto tempo ci vorrà   kwan·to *tem*·po chee vo·*ra*
    per il trasferimento?   per eel tras·fe·ree·*men*·to

For other useful phrases, see **money**, page 35.

For other useful phrases, see **money**, page 35.

---

listen for ...

eel *soo*·o ...	*il Suo ...*	**your ...**
do·koo·*men*·to	*documento*	
dee·den·tee·*ta*	*d'identità*	**ID**
pa·sa·*por*·to	*passaporto*	**passport**
fra ...	*Fra ...*	**In ...**
(*kwa*·tro) *jor*·nee	*(quattro) giorni*	**(four)**
la·vo·ra·*tee*·vee	*lavorativi*	**working days**
oo·na se·tee·*ma*·na	*una settimana*	**one week**
pwo ... per	*Può ..., per*	**Please ...**
fa·*vo*·re	*favore?*	
feer·*ma*·re kwee	*firmare qui*	**sign here**
skree·*ver*·lo	*scriverlo*	**write it down**

che oon pro·*ble*·ma ko·neel *soo*·o *kon*·to
  C'è un problema con il   **There's a problem**
  Suo conto.   **with your account.**

non po·*sya*·mo *far*·lo
  Non possiamo farlo.   **We can't do that.**

sightseeing
giri turistici

I'd like a/an ...	Vorrei ...	vo·ray ...
audio set	un auricolare	oo·now·ree·ko·la·re
catalogue	un catalogo	oon ka·ta·lo·go
guide (person)	una guida	oo·na gwee·da
guidebook in English	una guida in inglese	oo·na gwee·da ee·neen·gle·ze
local map	una cartina della zona	oo·na kar·tee·na de·la dzo·na

Do you have information on ... sights?	Avete delle informazioni su posti ...?	a·ve·te de·le een·for·ma·tsyo·nee soo pos·tee ...
architectural	architettonici	ar·kee·te·to·nee·chee
cultural	culturali	kool·too·ra·lee
historical	storici	sto·ree·chee
local	locali	lo·ka·lee
natural	di bellezza naturale	dee be·le·tsa na·too·ra·le
religious	religiosi	re·lee·jo·zee
unique	particolari	par·tee·ko·la·ree

I'd like to see ...
Vorrei vedere ...   vo·ray ve·de·re ...

I'd like to hire a local guide.
Vorrei ingaggiare una   vo·ray een·ga·ja·re oo·na
guida del posto.   gwee·da del po·sto

What's that?
Cos'è?   ko·ze

Who made it?
Chi l'ha fatto?   kee la fa·to

How old is it?
Quanti anni ha?   kwan·tee a·nee a

Could you take a photograph of me?
Può farmi una foto?   pwo far·mee oo·na fo·to

Can I take a photograph (of you)?
 Posso fare una foto   *po*·so fa·re oo·na *fo*·to
 (di Lei/tu)? pol/inf   (dee lay/too)

I'll send you the photograph.
 Le spedirò la foto.   le spe·dee·*ro* la *fo*·to

signs

Entrata	en·*tra*·ta	**Entrance**
Gabinetti	ga·bee·*ne*·tee	**Toilets**
Informazioni	een·for·ma·*tsyo*·nee	**Information**
Ingresso	een·*gre*·so	**Entrance**
Ingresso	een·*gre*·so	**Free Admission**
Gratuito	gra·*too*·ee·to	
Messa in	*me*·sa een	**Service in**
Corso	*kor*·so	**Progress**
Non Calpestare	non kal·pe·*sta*·re	**Keep Off the**
l'Erba	*ler*·ba	**Grass**
Non Entrare	no·nen·*tra*·re	**No Entry**
Proibito	pro·ee·*bee*·to	**Prohibited**
Servizi	ser·vee·tsee	**Public**
Pubblici	*poo*·blee·chee	**Toilets**
Uscita	oo·*shee*·ta	**Exit**
Uscita di	oo·*shee*·ta dee	**Emergency**
Sicurezza	see·koo·*re*·tsa	**Exit**
Vietato	vye·*ta*·to	**Prohibited**
Vietato	vye·*ta*·to	**No Eating or**
Consumare	kon·soo·*ma*·re	**Drinking**
Cibi o Bevande	*chee*·bee o be·*van*·de	**Allowed**
Vietato Entrare	vye·*ta*·to en·*tra*·re	**No Entry**
Vietato	vye·*ta*·to	**Do Not Take**
Fotografare	fo·to·gra·*fa*·re	**Photographs**
Vietato Fumare	vye·*ta*·to foo·*ma*·re	**No Smoking**
Vietato l'Ingresso	vye·*ta*·to leen·*gre*·so	**No Admittance**
Vietato Toccare	vye·*ta*·to to·*ka*·re	**Do Not Touch**
Vietato Usare	vye·*ta*·to oo·*za*·re	**Do Not Use**
Flash	flesh	**Flash**

getting in

What time does it open/close?
A che ora apre/chiude?   a ke o·ra a·pre/kyoo·de

What's the admission charge?
Quant'è il prezzo d'ingresso?   kwan·te eel pre·tso deen·gre·so

It costs (seven euros).
Costa (sette euro).   kos·ta (se·te e·oo·ro)

Is there a	C'è uno	che oo·no
discount for ...?	sconto per ...?	skon·to per ...
children	bambini	bam·bee·nee
families	famiglie	fa·mee·lye
groups	gruppi	groo·pee
older people	persone	per·so·ne
	anziane	an·tsya·ne
pensioners	pensionati	pen·syo·na·tee
students	studenti	stoo·den·tee

tours

Can you	Può consigliare	pwo kon·see·lya·re
recommend a ...?	una ...?	oo·na ...
boat-trip	gita in barca	jee·ta een bar·ka
tour	gita	jee·ta
	turistica	too·ree·stee·ka

When's the	A che ora parte la	a ke o·ra par·te la
next ...?	prossima ...?	pro·see·ma ...
day trip	escursione in	es·koor·syo·ne een
	giornata	jor·na·ta
excursion	escursione	es·koor·syo·ne

Is ... included?	È incluso ...?	e een·kloo·zo ...
accommodation	l'alloggio	la·lo·jo
food	il vitto	eel vee·to
transport	il trasporto	eel tras·por·to

Are there organised walking tours?
Ci sono visite — chee so·no vee·zee·te
guidate a piedi? — gwee·da·te a pye·dee

I'd like to do cooking/language classes.
Vorrei fare un corso di — vo·ray fa·re oon kor·so dee
cucina/lingua. — koo·chee·na/leen·gwa

Do I need to take ... with me?
Devo portare ... con me? — de·vo por·ta·re ... kon me

The guide will pay.
La guida pagherà. — la gwee·da pa·ge·ra

The guide has paid.
La guida ha pagato. — la gwee·da a pa·ga·to

How long is the tour?
Quanto dura la gita? — kwan·to doo·ra la jee·ta

What time should we be back?
A che ora dovremmo — a ke o·ra dov·re·mo
ritornare? — ree·tor·na·re

I'm with them.
Sono con loro. — so·no kon lo·ro

I've lost my group.
Ho perso il mio gruppo. — o per·so eel mee·o groo·po

---

local talk

What's (Rome) like?
Com'è (Roma)? — ko·me (ro·ma)

There's (not) ...	(Non) C'è ...	(non) che ...
fabulous nightlife	una vita notturna favolosa	oo·na vee·ta no·toor·na fa·vo·lo·sa
a great restaurant/ hotel	un buon ristorante/ albergo	oon bwon rees·to·ran·te/ al·ber·go
a lot to see	molto da vedere	mol·to da ve·de·re
lots of culture	molta cultura	mol·ta kool·too·ra

While a knowledge of Italian will help you in your travels through the Italy of today, it's a knowledge of Latin that will help you to understand the Italy of the past. Here are a few common words and phrases that will help you make sense of some inscriptions and dedications you'll come across while sightseeing:

AED	*aedilis*	aedile (magistrate)
ANN	*annos/anni*	years
COL	*colonia*	colony
COS	*consul*	consul
COSS	*consules*	consuls
C R	*cives Romani*	Roman citizens
CVR	*curavit*	attended to/took care of
D	*dat/dedit*	he gives/he gave
DEC	*decreto*	by decree
DED	*dedit*	gave
D M	*dis manibus*	to the spirits of the dead
EX S C	*ex senatus consulto*	by a decree of the Senate
F	*feci/faciundum/ filius/filia*	did/to be done/ son/daughter
FID	*fidelis*	faithful
IMP	*imperator*	general/emperor
I O M	*Iuppiter Optimus Maximus*	Jupiter Best (and) Greatest
P C	*Patres conscripti*	senators
P(ONT) M(AX)	*Pontifex Maximus*	chief priest
P R	*Populus Romanus*	the People of Rome
R	*Romanus*	Roman
REST	*restituit*	restored
R P	*res publica*	state/republic
S C	*senatus consulto*	by decree of the Senate
S P Q R	*Senatus Populusque Romanus*	the Senate and the People of Rome

traveller's latin

some common names:

AVG	*Augustus*	SP	*Spurius*
L	*Lucius*	CN	*Gnaeus*
Q	*Quintus*	MAM	*Mamius*
A	*Aulus*	T	*Titus*
M	*Marcus*	D	*Decimus*
S	*Servius*	P	*Publius*
C	*Gaius*	TI	*Tiberius*
M'	*Manius*		

numbers:

I	1	VI	6	L	50
II	2	VII	7	C	100
III	3	VIII	8	D	500
IV or IIII	4	IX	9	M	1000
V	5	X	10		

Here are some rules to help you work out the bigger numbers. In general, a smaller number to the left of a larger number should be subtracted from that number (eg IX = 9 and XL = 40), whereas a smaller number to the right of a larger number should be added to that number (eg XI = 11 and LX = 60):

MDCCCCLXXXV	1985
DCCCCXXV or **CMXXV**	925
MMIV	2004

senior & disabled travellers
viaggiatori anziani & disabili

I'm deaf.
Sono sordo/a. m/f   so·no sor·do/a

I'm hard of hearing.
Non ci sento bene.   non chee sen·to be·ne

I have a hearing aid.
Ho un apparecchio   o oo·na·pa·re·kyo
acustico.   a·koos·tee·ko

My companion is blind.
Il mio compagno è cieco. m   eel mee·o kom·pa·nyo e che·ko
La mia compagna è cieca. f   la mee·a kom·pa·nya e che·ka

I'm disabled.
Sono disabile.   so·no dee·za·bee·le

I need assistance.
Ho bisogno di assistenza.   o bee·zo·nyo dee a·sees·ten·tsa

What services do you have for people with a disability?
Di quali servizi   dee kwa·lee ser·vee·tsee
disponete per i   dees·po·ne·te per ee
disabili?   dee·za·bee·lee

Are guide dogs permitted?
Sono ammessi i cani   so·no a·me·see ee ka·nee
guida?   gwee·da

Is there wheelchair access?
C'è un'entrata per   che oo·nen·tra·ta per
sedie a rotelle?   se·dye a ro·te·le

How many steps are there?
Quanti gradini ci sono?   kwan·tee gra·dee·nee chee so·no

How wide is the entrance?
Quant'è larga l'entrata?   kwan·te lar·ga len·tra·ta

signs

Riservato	ree·ser·va·to	**Reserved for**
ai Disabili	ai dee·za·bee·lee	**People with a**
		Disability

Is there a lift?
C'è un ascensore?   che oo·na·shen·so·re

Is there somewhere I can sit down?
C'è un posto dove sedersi?   che oon pos·to do·ve se·der·see

Are there any toilets for the disabled?
Ci sono gabinetti   chee so·no ga·bee·ne·tee
per disabili?   per dee·za·bee·lee

Are there rails in the bathroom?
Ci sono corrimani   chee so·no ko·ree·ma·nee
nel bagno?   nel ba·nyo

Are there parking spaces for the disabled?
Ci sono parcheggi per   chee so·no par·ke·jee per
disabili?   dee·za·bee·lee

Could you call me a taxi for the disabled?
Può chiamarmi un tassì   pwo kya·mar·mee oon ta·see
per i disabili?   per ee dee·za·bee·lee

Could you help me cross the street?
Può aiutarmi   pwo a·yoo·tar·mee
ad attraversare la strada?   a·da·tra·ver·sa·re la stra·da

access for people with a disability	*accesso* m *per i disabili*	a·che·so per ee dee·za·bee·lee
Braille library	*biblioteca* f *braille*	bee·blyo·te·ka bray
crutches	*stampelle* f pl	stam·pe·le
guide dog	*cane* m *guida*	ka·ne gwee·da
person with a disability	*disabile* m&f	dee·za·bee·le
ramp	*rampa* f	ram·pa
senior person	*persona* f *anziana*	per·so·na an·tsya·na
space (to move around)	*spazio* m	spa·tsyo
walking frame	*deambulatore* m	de·am·boo·la·to·re
walking stick	*bastone* m	ba·sto·ne
wheelchair	*sedia* f *a rotelle*	se·dya a ro·te·le

Is there a/an ...?	C'è ...?	che ...
baby change room	un bagno con fasciatoio	oon *ba*·nyo kon fa·sha·*to*·yo
(English-speaking) babysitter	un/una baby-sitter (che parli inglese) m/f	oon/*oo*·na be·bee·*see*·ter (ke *par*·lee een·*gle*·ze)
child discount	uno sconto per bambini	*oo*·no *skon*·to per bam·*bee*·nee
child-minding service	un servizio di babysitter	oon ser·*vee*·tsyo dee be·bee·*see*·ter
children's menu	un menù per bambini	oon me·*noo* per bam·*bee*·nee
family discount	uno sconto per famiglia	*oo*·no *skon*·to per fa·*mee*·lya
park	un parco	oon *par*·ko
playground	un parco giochi	oon *par*·ko *jo*·kee
nearby	da queste parti	da *kwe*·ste *par*·tee
toyshop	un negozio di giocattoli	oon ne·*go*·tsyo dee jo·*ka*·to·lee

I need a ...	Ho bisogno di ...	o bee·*zo*·nyo dee ...
child seat	un seggiolino per bambini	oon se·jo·*lee*·no per bam·*bee*·nee
cot	una culla	*oo*·na *koo*·la
potty	un vasino	oon va·*zee*·no
stroller	un passeggino	oon pa·se·*jee*·no

Do you sell ...?	Vendete ...?	ven·*de*·te ...
baby wipes	salviettine detergenti per bambini	sal·vye·*tee*·ne de·ter·*jen*·tee per bam·*bee*·nee
disposable nappies/diapers	pannolini usa-e-getta	pa·no·*lee*·nee *oo*·sa·e·*je*·ta
milk formula	latte in polvere	*la*·te een *pol*·ve·re
painkillers for infants	anti-dolorifici per bambini	an·tee·do·lo·*ree*·fee·chee per bam·*bee*·nee

Do you mind if I breast-feed here?
Le dispiace se allatto
il/la bimbo/a qui? m/f

le dees·*pya*·che se a·*la*·to
eel/la *beem*·bo/a kwee

Are children allowed?
I bambini sono ammessi?

ee bam·*bee*·nee *so*·no a·*me*·see

Is this suitable for (two)-year-old children?
Questo è adatto per
bambini di (due) anni?

kwe·sto e a·*da*·to per
bam·*bee*·nee dee (*doo*·e) a·nee

If your child is sick, see **health**, page 183.

kids' talk

What's your name?
Come ti chiami?

ko·me tee *kya*·mee

How old are you?
Quanti anni hai?

kwan·tee a·nee ai

When's your birthday?
Quand'è il tuo
compleanno?

kwan·*de* eel *too*·o
kom·ple·a·no

What grade are you in?
Quale classe fai?

kwa·le *kla*·se fai

Do you like school?
Ti piace la scuola?

tee *pya*·che la *skwo*·la

Do you like sport?
Ti piace lo sport?

tee *pya*·che lo sport

What do you do after school?
Cosa fai dopo la scuola?

ko·za fai *do*·po la *skwo*·la

Do you learn English?
Stai imparando l'inglese?

stai eem·pa·*ran*·do leen·*gle*·ze

Do you have a pet at home?
Hai un animale
domestico a casa?

ai oon a·nee·*ma*·le
do·*mes*·tee·ko a *ka*·za

Do you want to play a game?
Vuoi giocare?

vwoy jo·*ka*·re

You're good at this game!
Sei bravo/a in questo
gioco! m/f

say *bra*·vo/a een *kwe*·sto
jo·ko

SOCIAL > meeting people
fare conoscenze

basics

l'essenziale

Yes.	*Sì.*	see
No.	*No.*	no
Please.	*Per favore.*	per fa·*vo*·re
Thank you. (very much)	*Grazie (mille).*	*gra*·tsye (*mee*·le)
You're welcome.	*Prego.*	*pre*·go
Sorry.	*Mi dispiace.*	mee dees·*pya*·che
Excuse me. (for attention/ apology)	*Mi scusi.* pol	mee *skoo*·zee
	Scusami. inf	*skoo*·za·mee
Excuse me. (if going past)	*Permesso.*	per·*me*·so

greetings

i saluti

Although *ciao* is a common greeting, it's best not to use it when addressing strangers. Also note that in Italy the word *buonasera* bwo·na·*se*·ra (good evening) may be heard any time from early afternoon onwards.

Hello.	*Buongiorno/Salve.* pol	bwon·*jor*·no/*sal*·ve
Hi.	*Ciao.* inf	chow
Good day.	*Buongiorno.*	bwon·*jor*·no
Good morning.	*Buongiorno.*	bwon·*jor*·no
Good afternoon.	*Buongiorno.*	bwon·*jor*·no
Good evening.	*Buonasera.*	bwo·na·*se*·ra
Good night.	*Buonanotte.*	bwo·na·*no*·te
See you.	*Ci vediamo.*	chee ve·*dya*·mo
See you later.	*A più tardi.*	a pyoo *tar*·dee
Goodbye.	*Arrivederci.* pol	a·ree·ve·*der*·chee
Bye.	*Ciao.* inf	chow

How are you?
>*Come sta?* pol .... *ko·me sta*
>*Come stai?* inf .... *ko·me stai*
>*Come state?* pl pol&inf ... *ko·me sta·te*

Fine.
>*Bene.* .... *be·ne*

And you?
>*E Lei/tu?* pol/inf .... e lay/too

What's your name?
>*Come si chiama?* pol .... *ko·me see kya·ma*
>*Come ti chiami?* inf .... *ko·me tee kya·mee*

My name is ...
>*Mi chiamo ...* .... mee *kya·mo ...*

I'd like to introduce you to ...
>*Le/Ti presento ...* pol/inf .... le/tee pre·*zen·to ...*

I'm pleased to meet you.
>*Piacere.* .... pya·*che·re*

getting friendly

Italian has two forms for the singular 'you'. With family, friends, children or peers use the informal form *tu* too. When addressing strangers, older people, or people whom you've just met, use the polite form *Lei* lay. When your newly-made friends feel it's time to swap to the more informal forms, they might suggest:

Let's use the *tu* form.
>*Diamoci del tu.* .... dya·mo·chee del too

See also **personal pronouns** in the **grammar** chapter, page 19.

titles & addressing people

Italians will greatly appreciate your efforts to try to speak their language and you'll leave an even better impression if you use the correct titles and forms of address. So when in Rome ...

Mr/Sir	*Signore*	see·*nyo*·re
Mrs/Madam	*Signora*	see·*nyo*·ra
Miss/Ms	*Signorina*	see·nyo·*ree*·na

Doctor (anyone with a university degree)
  Dottore/Dottoressa m/f   do·*to*·re/do·to·*re*·sa

Professor (high-school teacher or university lecturer)
  Professore/Professoressa m/f   pro·fe·*so*·re/pro·fe·so·*re*·sa

Director or Manager (anybody that runs anything)
  Direttore/Direttrice m/f   dee·re·*to*·re/dee·re·*tree*·che

making conversation

Nice weather, isn't it?
  Fa bel tempo, no?   fa bel *tem*·po no

How did (Juventus) go?
  Cos'ha fatto (la Juve)?   ko·za fa·to (la yoo·ve)

Do you live here?
  Lei è di qui? pol   lay e dee kwee
  Tu sei di qui? inf   too say dee kwee

Where are you going?
  Dove va/vai? pol/inf   *do*·ve va/vai

What are you doing?
  Che fa/fai? pol/inf   ke fa/fai

Are you waiting (for a bus)?
  Aspetta/Aspetti   as·*pe*·ta/as·*pe*·tee
  (un autobus)? pol/inf   (oo·*now*·to·boos)

What's this called?

Come si chiama questo?   ko·me see kya·ma kwe·sto

That's (beautiful), isn't it!

È (bello/a), no? m/f   e (be·lo/a) no

This is my ...	*Le/Ti*	le/tee
	presento ... pol/inf	pre·zen·to ...
colleague	*il mio collega* m	eel mee·o ko·le·ga
	la mia collega f	la mee·a ko·le·ga
friend	*il mio amico* m	eel mee·o a·mee·ko
	la mia amica f	la mee·a a·mee·ka
husband	*mio marito*	mee·o ma·ree·to
partner	*il mio compagno* m	eel mee·o kom·pa·nyo
	la mia compagna f	la mee·a kom·pa·nya
wife	*mia moglie*	mee·a mo·lye

Are you here on holiday?

È/Sei qui in vacanza? pol/inf   e/say kwee een va·kan·tsa

How long are you here for?

Quanto tempo si   kwan·to tem·po see
fermerà? pol   fer·me·ra
Quanto tempo ti   kwan·to tem·po tee
fermerai? inf   fer·me·rai

---

local talk

Hey!	*Uei!*	way
What's up?	*Cosa mi racconta/*	ko·za mee ra·kon·ta/
	racconti? pol/inf	ra·kon·tee
What's the matter?	*Cosa c'è?*	ko·za che
Everything OK?	*Tutto a posto?*	too·ta pos·to
It's/I'm OK.	*Va/Sto bene.*	va/sto be·ne
Great!	*Fantastico!*	fan·tas·tee·ko
No problem.	*Non c'è problema.*	non che pro·ble·ma
Sure.	*Certo.*	cher·to
Maybe.	*Forse.*	for·se
No way!	*Assolutamente no!*	a·so·loo·ta·men·te no
Congratulations!	*Congratulazioni!*	kon·gra·too·la·tsyo·nee

I'm here ...	*Sono qui ...*	*so*·no kwee ...
for a holiday	*in vacanza*	een va·*kan*·tsa
on business	*per affari*	per a·*fa*·ree
to study	*per motivi di studio*	per mo·*tee*·vee dee *stoo*·dyo
with my family	*con la mia famiglia*	kon la *mee*·a fa·*mee*·lya
with my partner	*con il mio compagno* m	kon eel *mee*·o kom·*pa*·nyo
	con la mia compagna f	kon la *mee*·a kom·*pa*·nya

nationalities

le nazionalità

Where are you from?
Da dove viene/vieni? pol/inf   da *do*·ve *vye*·ne/*vye*·nee

I'm from ...	*Vengo ...*	*ven*·go ...
Australia	*dall'Australia*	dal·ow·*stra*·lya
Canada	*dal Canada*	dal *ka*·na·da
England	*dall'Inghilterra*	da·leen·geel·*te*·ra
New Zealand	*dalla Nuova Zelanda*	*da*·la *nwo*·va ze·*lan*·da
the USA	*dagli Stati Uniti*	*da*·lyee *sta*·tee oo·*nee*·tee

For more countries, see the **dictionary**.

age

How old ...?	Quanti anni ...?	kwan·tee a·nee ...
are you	ha/hai pol/inf	a/ai
is your son	ha Suo/tuo	a soo·o/too·o
	figlio pol/inf	fee·lyo
is your	ha Sua/tua	a soo·a/too·a
daughter	figlia pol/inf	fee·lya

I'm ... years old.
Ho ... anni.   o ... a·nee

He's/She's ... years old.
Ha ... anni.   a ... a·nee

For your age, see **numbers & amounts**, page 29.

occupations & studies

What's your occupation?
Che lavoro fa/fai? pol/inf   ke la·vo·ro fa/fai

I'm a/an ...	Sono ...	so·no ...
manual worker	manovale m&f	ma·no·va·le
office worker	impiegato/a m/f	eem·pye·ga·to/a
tradesperson	operaio/a m/f	o·pe·ra·yo/a

I work in ...	Lavoro nel campo ...	la·vo·ro nel kam·po ...
administration	dell'amministra-zione	de·la·mee·nee·stra·tsyo·ne
public relations	delle relazioni pubbliche	de·le re·la·tsyo·nee poo·blee·ke
retail	della vendità al minuto	de·la ven·dee·ta al mee·noo·to

I'm ...	Sono ...	so·no ...
retired	pensionato/a m/f	pen·syo·na·to/a
unemployed	disoccupato/a m/f	dee·zo·koo·pa·to/a

Che vuoi?
ke vwoy
What do you want?

Chi se ne frega?
kee se ne *fre*·ga
Who gives a damn?

Va' al diavolo!
va al *dya*·vo·lo
Go to hell!

Disgraziato!
dees·gra·tsee·a·to
You're a disgrace!

È delizioso!
e de·lee·*tsyo*·zo
It's delicious!

Che rottura di palle!
ke ro·*too*·ra dee *pa*·le
You're breaking my balls!

I'm self-employed.
Lavoro in proprio.   la·*vo*·ro een *pro*·pryo

What are you studying?
Cosa studia/studi? pol/inf   ko·za stoo·*dya*/stoo·dee

I'm studying ...	*Sto studiando ...*	sto stoo·*dyan*·do ...
arts/humanities	*lettere*	*le*·te·re
business	*commercio*	ko·*mer*·cho
engineering	*ingegneria*	een·je·nye·*ree*·a

For more occupations and studies, see the **dictionary**.

family

la famiglia

Do you have (children)?
Ha/Hai (bambini)? pol/inf   a/ai (bam·*bee*·nee)

I have (a partner).
Ho (un/una compagno/a). m/f   o (oon/oo·na kom·*pa*·nyo/a)

This is (my mother).
Le/Ti presento   le/tee pre·*zen*·to
(mia madre). pol/inf   (*mee*·a ma·dre)

---

in the mouth of the wolf

An Italian will typically wish you good luck with the expression *In bocca al lupo!*, which is literally translated as 'In the mouth of the wolf!'. Make sure your answer is *Crepi!* (literally 'Die!'), to ward off bad luck.

Break a leg!
In bocca al lupo!   een *bo*·ka·*loo*·po

Response:
Crepi!   *kre*·pee

Do you live with (your family)?

Abita con (la Sua famiglia)? pol	a·bee·ta kon (la *soo·*a fa·*mee·*lya)
Abiti con (la tua famiglia)? inf	a·bee·tee kon (la *too·*a fa·*mee·*lya)

I live with (my parents).

Abito con (i miei genitori).	a·bee·to kon (ee myay je·nee·*to·*ree)

Are you married?

È sposato/a? m/f pol	e spo·*za·*to/a
Sei sposato/a? m/f inf	say spo·*za·*to/a

I live with someone.

Convivo.	kon·*vee·*vo

For more kinship terms, see the **dictionary**.

---

body language

Italians are emotionally demonstrative so expect to see lots of cheek kissing among acquaintances, embraces between men who are good friends and lingering handshakes. Italian men may walk along arm-in-arm too, as may Italian women. Pushing and shoving in busy places is not considered rude, so don't be offended by it. Try to hold your ground amidst the scrimmage.

If you don't want to tread on any toes, be aware that respectful behaviour is expected in churches. Women should ideally cover their heads and avoid exposing too much flesh – wearing shorts or skimpy tops is considered disrespectful.

I'm ...	*Sono ...*	so·no ...
married	*sposato/a* m/f	spo·*za·*to/a
separated	*separato/a* m/f	se·pa·*ra·*to/a
single		
(man)	*celibe* m&f	*che·*lee·be
(woman)	*nubile* m&f	*noo·*bee·le

farewells

Tomorrow is my last day here.

Domani è il mio — do·*ma*·nee e eel *mee*·o
ultimo giorno qui. — *ool*·tee·mo *jor*·no kwee

Here's my ...	*Ecco il mio ...*	e·ko eel *mee*·o ...
What's your ...?	*Qual'è il*	kwa·*le* eel
	Suo/tuo ...? pol/inf	*soo*·o/*too*·o ...
(email) address	*indirizzo*	een·dee·*ree*·tso
	(di email)	(dee e·mayl)
fax number	*numero di fax*	*noo*·me·ro dee faks
mobile number	*numero di*	*noo*·me·ro dee
	cellulare	che·loo·*la*·re
work number	*numero di*	*noo*·me·ro dee
	lavoro	la·*vo*·ro

If you ever visit	*Caso mai venissi*	*ka*·zo mai ve·*nee*·see
(Scotland), ...	*in (Scozia), ...*	een (*sko*·tsya) ...
come and visit us	*vieni a trovarci*	*vye*·ne a tro·*var*·chee
you can stay	*puoi stare da me*	pwoy *sta*·re da me
with me		

It's been great meeting you.

È stato veramente un — e *sta*·to ve·ra·*men*·te oon
piacere conoscerti. — pya·*che*·re ko·*no*·sher·tee

Are you on Facebook?

Lei è su Facebook? pol — lay e soo *fays*·book
Sei su Facebook? inf — say soo *fays*·book

Keep in touch!

Teniamoci in contatto! — te·*nya*·mo·chee een kon·*ta*·to

For more on addresses, see **directions**, page 61.

common interests

interessi comuni

What do you do in your spare time?
Cosa fai nel tuo   *ko·*za fai nel *too·*o
tempo libero?   *tem·*po *lee·*be·ro

Do you like ...?	*Ti piace/ piacciono ...?* sg/pl	tee *pya·*che/ *pya·*cho·no ...
I (don't) like ...	*(Non) Mi piace/ piacciono ...* sg/pl	(non) mee *pya·*che/ *pya·*cho·no ...
art	*l'arte* sg	*lar·*te
card games	*i giochi* pl *di carte*	ee *jo·*kee dee *kar·*te
cooking	*cucinare* sg	koo·chee·*na·*re
drawing	*disegnare* sg	dee·se·*nya·*re
films	*i film* pl	ee feelm
socialising	*socializzare* sg	so·cha·lee·*dza·*re
travelling	*viaggiare* sg	vee·*a·ja·*re

For more hobbies and sporting interests, see **sports**, page 127, and the **dictionary**.

---

like it or not

In Italian, in order to say you like something, you say *mi piace* mee *pya·*che (lit: me it-pleases). If it's in plural, use *mi piacciono* mee *pya·*cho·no (lit: me they-please):

I like this band.
Mi piace questo   mee *pya·*che *kwe·*sto
gruppo.   *groo·*po

I like soap operas.
Mi piacciono   mee *pya·*cho·no
le telenovelle.   le te·le·no·*ve·*le

music

Do you like to ...?	*Ti piace ...?*	tee *pya*·che ...
dance	*ballare*	ba·*la*·re
go to concerts	*andare ai concerti*	an·*da*·re ai kon·*cher*·tee
listen to music	*ascoltare la musica*	as·kol·*ta*·re la moo·zee·ka
play an instrument	*suonare uno strumento*	swo·*na*·re oo·no stroo·*men*·to
sing	*cantare*	kan·*ta*·re

What bands do you like?
Quali gruppi ti piacciono?
kwa·lee groo·pee tee *pya*·cho·no

What music do you like?
Quale tipo di musica ti piace?
kwa·le *tee*·po dee moo·zee·ka tee *pya*·che

... music	*musica ...*	moo·zee·ka ...
classical	*classica*	*kla*·see·ka
electronic	*elettronica*	e·le·*tro*·nee·ka
jazz	*jazz*	jaz
metal	*heavy metal*	*he*·vee *me*·tal
pop	*pop*	pop
punk	*punk*	punk
rock	*rock*	rok
traditional	*tradizionale*	tra·dee·tsyo·*na*·le
world	*etnica*	*et*·nee·ka

Planning to go to a concert? See **buying tickets**, page 38, and **going out**, page 109.

cinema & theatre

I feel like going	Ho voglia	o vo·lya
to a ...	d'andare a ...	dan·da·re a ...
ballet	un balletto	oon ba·le·to
comedy	una commedia	oo·na ko·me·dya
	comica	ko·mee·ka
film	vedere un film	ve·de·re oon feelm
play	teatro	te·a·tro

What's showing at the cinema/theatre tonight?
Cosa danno al cinema/   ko·za da·no al chee·ne·ma/
teatro stasera?   te·a·tro sta·se·ra

Is it in English/Italian?
È in inglese/italiano?   e een een·gle·ze/ee·ta·lya·no

Is it dubbed?
E' doppiato?   e do·pya·to

Does it have subtitles?
Ci sono i sottotitoli?   chee so·no ee so·to·tee·to·lee

Have you seen ...?
Hai visto ...?   ai vee·sto ...

Who's in it?
Chi sono i   kee so·no ee
protagonisti?   pro·ta·go·nee·stee

It stars ...
Il/La protagonista   eel/la pro·ta·go·nee·sta
principale è ... m/f   preen·chee·pa·le e ...

Did you like (the film)?
Ti è piaciuto (il film)?   tee e pya·choo·to (eel feelm)

I thought	L'ho trovato/a ... m/f	lo tro·va·to/a ...
it was ...		
excellent	ottimo/a m/f	o·tee·mo/a
long	lungo/a m/f	loon·go/a
OK	passabile m&f	pa·sa·bee·le

I (don't) like ...	(Non) Mi piacciono ...	(non) mee pya·cho·no ...
action movies	i film d'azione	ee feelm da·tsyo·ne
animated films	i film animati	ee feelm a·nee·ma·tee
black comedy	i film tragicomici	ee feelm tra·jee·ko·mee·chee
comedies	le commedie comiche	le ko·me·dye ko·mee·ke
documentaries	i documentari	ee do·koo·men·ta·ree
drama	i film drammatici	ee feelm dra·ma·tee·chee
film noir	i film noir	ee feelm nwar
horror movies	i film d'orrore	ee feelm do·ro·re
period dramas	i drammi d'ambiente	ee dra·mee dam·byen·te
sci-fi	i film di fantascienza	ee feelm dee fan·ta·shen·tsa
short films	i film corti	ee feelm kor·tee
thrillers	i gialli	ee ja·lee
war movies	i film di guerra	ee feelm dee gwe·ra

local talk

No way!	Per niente!	per nyen·te
Shut up!	Taci!	ta·chee
That's (not) true!	(Non) È vero!	(non) e ve·ro
Unbelievable!	Incredibile!	een·kre·dee·bee·le
Yeah, right!	Figuriamoci!	fee·goo·rya·mo·chee
You're kidding!	Scherzi!	sker·tsee
If only!	Magari!	ma·ga·ree

feelings

i sentimenti

Feelings are described with nouns or adjectives: nouns use 'have' (eg, 'I have hunger') and adjectives use 'be' (like in English).

I'm (not) ...	(Non) Sono ...	(non) so·no ...
Are you ...?	È/Sei ...? pol/inf	e/say ...
happy	felice m&f	fe·lee·che
sad	triste m&f	tree·ste
worried	preoccupato/a m/f	pre·o·koo·pa·to/a

I'm (not) ...	(Non) Ho ...	(non) o ...
Are you ...?	Ha/Hai ...? pol/inf	a/ai ...
cold	freddo	fre·do
hungry	fame	fa·me
sleepy	sonno	so·no

If you're not feeling well, see **health**, page 187.

opinions

le opinioni

Did you like it?
   Ti è piaciuto/a? m/f   tee e pya·choo·to/a

What did you think of it?
   Che cosa ne pensi?   ke ko·za ne pen·see

I thought	Pensavo che	pen·sa·vo ke
it was ...	fosse ...	fo·se ...
It's ...	È ...	e ...
boring	noioso/a m/f	no·yo·zo/a
great	ottimo/a m/f	o·tee·mo/a
interesting	interessante m&f	een·te·re·san·te
OK	passabile m&f	pa·sa·bee·le
weird	strano/a m/f	stra·no/a

mixed emotions

a little
  un po'   oon po
I'm a little sad.
  Sono un po' triste.   so·no oon po *tree*·ste

very
  molto   *mol*·to
I'm very content.
  Sono molto contento/a. m/f   so·no *mol*·to kon·*ten*·to/a

extremely
  -issimo/a m/f   ·ee·see·mo/a
I feel extremely lucky.
  Mi sento   mee *sen*·to
  fortunatissimo/a. m/f   for·too·na·*tee*·see·mo/a

politics & social issues

le questioni politiche & sociali

Italians don't shy away from discussing political and social issues and might be interested in knowing your opinion on all kinds of topics. Even *il campionato* eel kam·pyo·*na*·to, 'the soccer', takes on the dimensions of a serious political issue.

Who do you vote for?
  Per chi vota Lei? pol   per kee *vo*·ta lay
  Per chi voti? inf   per kee *vo*·tee

I support	*Sono per*	so·no per
the ... party.	*il partito ...*	eel par·*tee*·to ...
I'm a member	*Sono iscritto/a*	so·no ees·*kree*·to/a
of the ... party.	*al partito ...* m/f	al par·*tee*·to ...
communist	*comunista*	ko·moo·*nee*·sta
conservative	*conservatore*	kon·ser·va·*to*·re
green	*verde*	*ver*·de
liberal (progressive)	*liberale*	lee·be·*ra*·le
labour	*laburista*	la·boo·*ree*·sta
socialist	*socialista*	so·cha·*lee*·sta

Do you agree with it?
È/Sei d'accordo con ...? pol/inf   e/say da·*kor*·do kon ...

I (don't) agree with ...
(Non) Sono d'accordo con ...   (non) *so*·no da·*kor*·do kon ...

Are you against ... ?
È/Sei contro ...? pol/inf   e/say *kon*·tro ...

Are you in favour of ...?
È/Sei a favore di ...? pol/inf   e/say a fa·*vo*·re dee ...

How do people feel about ...?
Cosa pensa la gente di ...?   ko·za *pen*·sa la *jen*·te dee ...

abortion	*aborto* m	a·*bor*·to
corruption	*corruzione* f	ko·roo·*tsyo*·ne
crime	*criminalità* f	kree·mee·na·lee·*ta*
discrimination	*discriminazione* f	dees·kree·mee·na·*tsyo*·ne
drugs	*droghe* f pl	*dro*·ge
the economy	*economia* f	e·ko·no·*mee*·a
education	*istruzione* f	ees·troo·*tsyo*·ne
equal opportunity	*pari opportunità* f	pa·ree o·por·too·nee·*ta*
EU expansion	*espansione* f	es·pan·*syo*·ne
	dell'Unione	de·loo·*nyo*·ne
	Europea	e·oo·ro·*pe*·a
euthanasia	*eutanasia* f	e·oo·ta·na·*zee*·a
globalisation	*globalizzazione* f	glo·ba·lee·dza·*tsyo*·ne
health care	*servizi* m pl *sanitari*	ser·*vee*·tsee sa·nee·*ta*·ree
human rights	*diritti* m pl *umani*	dee·*ree*·tee oo·*ma*·nee
immigration	*immigrazione* f	ee·mee·gra·*tsyo*·ne
inequality	*ineguaglianza* f	ee·ne·gwa·*lyan*·tsa
living with your	*vivere con i*	*vee*·ve·re kon ee
parents	*genitori*	je·nee·*to*·ree
party politics	*politica* f *di partito*	po·*lee*·tee·ka dee par·*tee*·to
privatisation	*privatizzazione* f	pree·va·tee·dza·*tsyo*·ne
racism	*razzismo* m	ra·*tseez*·mo
refugees	*profughi* m pl	*pro*·foo·gee
sexism	*sessismo* m	se·*seez*·mo
social welfare	*assistenza* f *sociale*	a·sees·*ten*·tsa so·*cha*·le
taxes	*tasse* f pl	*ta*·se
terrorism	*terrorismo* m	te·ro·*reez*·mo
unemployment	*disoccupazione* f	dee·zo·koo·pa·*tsyo*·ne
war in ...	*guerra* f *in ...*	*gwe*·ra een ...

feelings & opinions

the environment

l'ambiente

Is there a/an (environmental) problem here?
C'è un problema che oon pro·*ble*·ma
(ambientale) qui? (am·byen·*ta*·le) kwee

alternative energy sources	*fonti* f pl *alternative di energia*	*fon*·tee al·ter·na·*tee*·ve dee e·ner·*jee*·a
animal rights	*diritti* m pl *animali*	dee·*ree*·tee a·*nee*·*ma*·lee
biodegradable	*biodegradabile*	bee·o·de·gra·*da*·bee·le
carbon dioxide emissions	*emissioni* f pl *di anidride carbonica*	e·mee·*syo*·nee dee a·nee·*dree*·de kar·*bo*·nee·ka
climate change	*cambiamento* m *del clima*	kam·bya·*men*·to del *klee*·ma
conservation	*conservazione* f	kon·ser·va·*tsyo*·ne
deforestation	*disboscamento* m	dees·bos·ka·*men*·to
drought	*siccità* f	see·chee·*ta*
the environment	*ambiente* m	am·*byen*·te
flood risk	*rischio* m *di alluvioni*	*ree*·skee·o dee a·loo·*vyo*·nee
global warming	*riscaldamento* m *globale*	rees·kal·da·*men*·to glo·*ba*·le
hydroelectricity	*energia* f *idroelettrica*	e·ner·*jee*·a ee·dro·e·*le*·tree·ka
irrigation	*irrigazione* f	ee·ree·ga·*tsyo*·ne
ozone layer	*strato* m *d'ozono*	*stra*·to do·*dzo*·no
pesticides	*pesticidi* m pl	pes·tee·*chee*·dee
pollution	*inquinamento* m	een·kwee·na·*men*·to
recycling programme	*programma* m *di riciclaggio*	pro·*gra*·ma dee ree·chee·*kla*·jo
sustainable energy	*energia* f *sostenibile*	e·ner·*jee*·a sos·te·*nee*·bee·le
toxic waste	*rifiuti* m pl *tossici*	ree·*fyoo*·tee *to*·see·chee

Is this a protected ...? *m/f* *È ... protetto/a questo/a?* m/f e ... pro·*te*·to/a *kwe*·sto/a

forest	*una foresta* f	*oo*·na fo·*res*·ta
park	*un parco* m	oon *par*·ko
species	*una specie* f	*oo*·na *spe*·che

where to go

dove andare

What's there to do in the evenings?
Cosa si fa di sera? ko·za see fa dee se·ra

What's on ...?	*Che c'è in programma ...?*	ke che een pro·gra·ma ...
locally	*in zona*	een dzo·na
this weekend	*questo finesettimana*	kwe·sto fee·ne·se·tee·ma·na
today	*oggi*	o·jee
tonight	*stasera*	sta·se·ra

Where are the ...?	*Dove sono ...?*	do·ve so·no ...
bars	*dei locali*	day lo·ka·lee
cafes	*dei bar*	day bar
clubs	*dei clubs*	day kloobs
gay venues	*dei locali gay*	day lo·ka·lee ge
places to eat	*posti in cui mangiare*	pos·tee een koo·ee man·ja·re
pubs	*dei pub*	day pab

Is there a local ... guide?	*C'è una guida ... in questa città?*	che oo·na gwee·da ... een kwe·sta chee·ta
entertainment	*agli spettacoli*	a·lyee spe·ta·ko·lee
film	*ai film*	ai feelm

What's the cover charge?
   Quant'è l'ingresso?   kwan·*te* leen·*gre*·so

It's free.
   È gratuito.   e gra·*too*·ee·to

it's not what it seems

Looking for a place to go in the wee hours? While you can have a *Nastro Azzurro* in a *birreria* and show off your moves in a *discoteca*, you'll be hard-pressed finding an Italian *bar* open after midnight:

bar m bar – is more like a snack bar where you can get coffee, tea and soft drinks but also alcoholic drinks, along with croissants, rolls and sandwiches. They open early in the morning and close somewhere between 10pm and midnight, depending on their location. They're mainly used by people dropping in for a quick coffee, consumed while standing at the counter – it costs more to sit down. Office workers tend to pop out or send out for a coffee from a *bar*.

osteria f os·te·*ree*·a – this is more of a sit-down eating place where people have wine with their meal

pub m pab – a new and popular addition to the Italian night scene, inspired by English and Irish pubs; they usually stay open until around 3am

birreria f bee·re·*ree*·a – has a pub-like atmosphere but specialises in beer

nite m nait – denotes a more elegant nightclub

nightclub m – this English term is used and will be readily understood, but *il nite* eel nait is more common

locale notturno m lo·*ka*·le no·*toor*·no – this is the generic term for every type of night spot

discoteca m dees·ko·*te*·ka – the most commonly frequented night spot for the under-30 age group

I feel like going to ...	Ho voglia d'andare ...	o vo·lya dan·da·re ...
a bar	a un locale	a oon lo·ka·le
a cafe	a un bar	a oon bar
a coffee bar	a un caffè	a oon ka·fe
a concert	a un concerto	a oon kon·cher·to
the movies	al cinema	al chee·nee·ma
a nightclub	in un locale notturno	een oon lo·ka·le no·toor·no
a party	a una festa	a oo·na fes·ta
a pub	a un pub	a oon pab
a restaurant	in un ristorante	een oon rees·to·ran·te
the theatre	al teatro	al te·a·tro

For more on bars, drinks and partying, see **eating out**, page 150.

invitations

What are you doing ...?	Cosa fai/ fate ...? sg/pl	ko·za fai/ fa·te ...
right now	proprio adesso	pro·pryo a·de·so
this evening	stasera	sta·se·ra
this weekend	questo fine settimana	kwe·sto fee·ne se·tee·ma·na

Would you like to go (for a) ...?	Vuoi/Volete andare a ...? sg/pl	vwoy/vo·le·te an·da·re a ...
I feel like going (for a) ...	Ho voglia d'andare a ...	o vo·lya dan·da·re a ...
coffee	prendere un caffè	pren·de·re oon ka·fe
dancing	ballare	ba·la·re
drink	bere qualcosa	be·re kwal·ko·za
meal	mangiare qualcosa	man·ja·re kwal·ko·za
out somewhere	spasso	spa·so
walk	fare una passeggiata	fa·re oo·na pa·se·ja·ta

My round.
  Offro io.   o·fro ee·o

Do you know a good restaurant?
  Conosci/Conoscete un   ko·no·shee/ko·no·she·te oon
  buon ristorante? sg/pl   bwon rees·to·ran·te

Do you want to come to a (jazz) concert with me?
  Vuoi/Volete venire a   vwoy/vo·le·te ve·nee·re a
  un concerto (di   oon kon·cher·to (dee
  musica jazz)? sg/pl   moo·zee·ka jaz)

We're having a party.
  Facciamo una festa.   fa·chya·mo oo·na fes·ta

You should come.
  Dovresti/Dovreste   dov·res·tee/dov·res·te
  venire. sg/pl   ve·nee·re

responding to invitations

Sure!
  Certo!   cher·to

Yes, I'd love to.
  Sì, mi piacerebbe.   see mee pya·che·re·be

Where shall we go?
  Dove andiamo?   do·ve an·dya·mo

No, I'm afraid I can't.
  No, temo di no.   no te·mo dee no

What about tomorrow?
  Domani che ne   do·ma·nee ke ne
  dici/dite? sg/pl   dee·chee/dee·te

Sorry, I can't sing/dance.
  Scusa. Non so   skoo·za. non so
  cantare/ballare.   kan·ta·re/ba·la·re

arranging to meet

fissare un appuntamento

What time shall we meet?
A che ora ci vediamo? — a ke o·ra chee ve·*dya*·mo

Where will we meet?
Dove ci vediamo? — *do*·ve chee ve·*dya*·mo

I'll pick you up.
Ti/Vi vengo a prendere. sg/pl — tee/vee *ven*·go a *pren*·de·re

I'll be coming later.
Verrò più tardi. — ve·*ro* pyoo *tar*·dee

Where will you be?
Dove ti troverai? sg — *do*·ve tee tro·ve·*rai*
Dove vi troverete? pl — *do*·ve vee tro·ve·*re*·te

If I'm not there by (nine), don't wait for me.
Se non ci sono entro — se non chee *so*·no *en*·tro
(le nove), non aspettarmi. — (le *no*·ve) non as·pe·*tar*·mee

Let's meet at ...   *Incontriamoci ...*   een·kon·*trya*·mo·chee ...
  (eight) o'clock   *alle (otto)*   *a*·le (*o*·to)
  the entrance   *all'entrata*   a·len·*tra*·ta

OK!
D'accordo!   da·*kor*·do

I'll see you then.
Ci vediamo allora.   chee ve·*dya*·mo a·*lo*·ra

See you later.
A più tardi.   a pyoo *tar*·dee

See you tomorrow.
A domani.   a do·*ma*·nee

I'm looking forward to it.
Non vedo l'ora.   non ve·do *lo*·ra

Sorry I'm late.
Scusa, sono in ritardo.   *skoo*·za *so*·no een ree·*tar*·do

Never mind.
Non importa.   non eem·*por*·ta

drugs

le droghe

I don't take drugs.
Non mi drogo.   non mee *dro*·go

I have ... occasionally.
Prendo ... ogni tanto.   *pren*·do ... o·nyee *tan*·to

Do you want to have a smoke?
Lo vuoi uno spinello?   lo vwoy *oo*·no spee·*ne*·lo

Do you have a light?
Hai d'accendere?   ai da·*chen*·de·re

If the police are talking to you about drugs, see **police**, page 181, for useful phrases.

asking someone out

darsi appuntamenti

Would you like to do something (tonight)?
Vuoi fare qualcosa   vwoy *fa·*re kwal·*ko·*za
(stasera)?   (sta·*se·*ra)

Yes, I'd love to.
Sì, mi piacerebbe molto.   see mee pya·che·re·be *mol·*to

No, I'm afraid I can't.
No, temo di no.   no *te·*mo dee no

Not if you were the last person on Earth!
Neanche se tu fossi   ne·*an·*ke se too *fo·*see
l'ultima persona   *lool·*tee·ma per·*so·*na
sulla terra!   *soo·*la *te·*ra

local talk

He/She gets around.
Si dà da fare.   see da da *fa·*re

Did you check out that guy/girl?
Hai adocchiato quello/a?   ai a·do·*kya·*to kwe·lo/a

He's/She's a ...	*È ...*	e ...
babe	*un bel figo* m	oon bel *fee·*go
	una bella figa f	oo·na *be·*la *fee·*ga
bastard	*un bastardo* m	oon bas·*tar·*do
bitch	*una cagna* f	oo·na *ka·*nya
prick	*uno stronzo* m	oo·no *stron·*dzo
	una stronza f	oo·na *stron·*dza

romance

115

pick-up lines

Would you like a drink?
Prendi qualcosa da bere?   pren·dee kwal·ko·za da be·re

Do you have a light?
Hai d'accendere?   ai da·chen·de·re

You're a fantastic dancer.
Balli benissimo.   ba·lee be·nee·see·mo

Shall we get some fresh air?
Andiamo a prendere un   an·dya·mo a pren·de·re oon
po' d'aria fresca?   po da·rya fres·ka

Can I take you for a ride (on my bike)?
Ti posso portare a fare   tee po·so por·ta·re a fa·re
un giro (in moto)?   oon jee·ro (een mo·to)

You have	Hai ...	ai ...
(a) beautiful ...		
body	*un bel fisico*	oon bel fee·zee·ko
eyes	*gli occhi belli*	lyee o·kee be·lee
hands	*le mani belle*	le ma·nee be·le
laugh	*un bel riso*	oon bel ree·zo
personality	*una bella*	oo·na be·la
	personalità	per·so·na·lee·ta
smile	*un bel sorriso*	oon bel so·ree·zo
Can I ...?	Posso ...?	po·so ...
dance with you	*ballare con te*	ba·la·re kon te
sit here	*sedermi qui*	se·der·mee kwee
take you home	*accompagnarti*	a·kom·pa·nyar·tee
	a casa	a ka·za

rejections

il rifiuto

I'm here with my boyfriend.
Sono qui con il mio ragazzo.
so·no kwee kon eel *mee·*o ra·*ga·*tso

I'm here with my girlfriend.
Sono qui con la mia ragazza.
so·no kwee kon la *mee·*a ra·*ga·*tsa

Excuse me, I have to go now.
Scusa, adesso devo andare.
skoo·za a·*de·*so *de·*vo an·*da·*re

I'm sorry, but I don't feel like it.
Mi dispiace ma non ne ho voglia.
mee dees·*pya·*che ma non ne o *vo·*lya

Your ego is out of control.
Il tuo ego è fuori controllo.
eel *too·*o e·go e *fwo·*ree kon·*tro·*lo

I'm not interested.
Non mi interessa.
non mee een·te·*re·*sa

Leave me alone!
Lasciami in pace!
la·sha·mee een *pa·*che

Don't touch me!
Non mi toccare!
non mee to·*ka·*re

Let me through!
Lasciami passare!
la·sha·mee pa·*sa·*re

Get out of my face!
Levati dai piedi!
*le·*va·tee dai *pye·*dee

mario or maria?

Throughout this book we have used the abbreviations m and f to indicate whether a word is masculine or feminine. Where a word can be either masculine or feminine, the feminine ending is added after a slash. For example, the two forms of the word for 'beautiful' are written as *bello/a* be·lo/a m/f. See also **gender** in the **grammar** chapter, page 17.

getting closer

You're very nice.
Sei molto simpatico/a. m/f   say *mol*·to seem·*pa*·tee·ko/a

You're great.
Sei fantastico/a. m/f   say fan·*tas*·tee·ko/a

Can I kiss you?
Ti posso baciare?   tee *po*·so ba·*cha*·re

Will you take me home?
Mi porti a casa?   mee *por*·tee a *ka*·za

Do you want to come inside for a while?
Vuoi entrare per un po'?   vwoy en·*tra*·re per oon po

sex

I want to make love to you.
Voglio fare l'amore con te.   *vo*·lyo *fa*·re la·*mo*·re kon te

Do you have a condom?
Hai un preservativo?   ai oon pre·ser·va·*tee*·vo

I won't do it without protection.
Non lo farò senza   non lo fa·*ro* sen·tsa
protezione.   pro·te·*tsyo*·ne

I think we should stop now.
Penso che dovremmo   *pen*·so ke dov·*re*·mo
fermarci adesso.   fer·*mar*·chee a·*de*·so

Let's go to bed!
Andiamo a letto!   an·*dya*·mo a *le*·to

---

the birds & the bees

Be mindful of the word *finocchio* fee·*no*·kyo, which means both 'fennel' and 'queer' (homosexual). Likewise, keep in mind that *uccello* oo·*che*·lo can mean either 'bird' or 'dick'.

Kiss me.
Baciami.   ba·cha·mee

I want you.
Ti desidero.   tee de·see·de·ro

Touch me here.
Toccami qui.   to·ka·mee kwee

Do you like this?
Ti piace questo?   tee pya·che kwe·sto

I (don't) like that.
(Non) Mi piace quello.   (non) mee pya·che kwe·lo

Oh yeah!	*Ah sì!*	a see
Oh my god!	*Oh dio mio!*	o dee·o mee·o
Easy tiger!	*Calma!*	kal·ma
Come on!	*Dai!*	dai

That was amazing.
È stato stupendo.   e sta·to stoo·pen·do

Can I stay over?
Posso restare la notte?   po·so res·ta·re la no·te

When can I see you again?
Quando possiamo   kwan·do po·sya·mo
rivederci?   ree·ve·der·chee

endearments

delicious one	*delizia*	de·lee·tsya
honey/sugar	*dolcezza*	dol·che·tsa
my darling	*caro/a*	ka·ro/a
	mio/a m/f	mee·o/a
my joy	*gioia mia*	jo·ya mee·a
my little chook	*pollastrello/a*	po·la·stre·lo/a
	mio/a m/f	mee·o/a
my little fleshy	*ciccino/a*	chee·chee·no/a
thing	*mio/a* m/f	mee·o/a
my love	*amore mio*	a·mo·re mee·o
my treasure	*tesoro mio*	te·zo·ro mee·o

love

l'amore

I'm in love with you.
Sono innamorato/a di te. m/f so·no ee·na·mo·ra·to/a dee te

I love you.
Ti amo. tee a·mo

Do you love me?
Mi ami? mee a·mee

I think we're good together.
Penso che stiamo pen·so ke stya·mo
bene insieme. be·ne een·sye·me

I want us to stay in touch.
Voglio che ci teniamo vo·lyo ke chee te·nya·mo
in contatto. een kon·ta·to

problems

i problemi

Are you seeing someone else?
Frequenti fre·kwen·tee
qualcun'altro/a? m/f kwal·koo·nal·tro/a

He's just a friend.
È solo un amico. e so·lo oo·na·mee·ko

She's just a friend.
È solo un'amica. e so·lo oo·na·mee·ka

I don't think it's working out.
Non credo che stia non kre·do ke stee·a
funzionando fra noi due. foon·tsyo·nan·do fra noy doo·e

We'll work it out.
Troveremo una soluzione. tro·ve·re·mo oo·na so·loo·tsyo·ne

I never want to see you again.
Non voglio vederti mai più. non vo·lyo ve·der·tee mai pyoo

I want to stay friends.
Voglio che restiamo amici. vo·lyo ke res·tya·mo a·mee·chee

Italy is a paradise for art lovers and Italians are proud of the many treasures the country harbours. If art is your thing, you'll find plenty of people to talk to or to share your impressions with.

When's the gallery open?
Quando è aperta
la galleria?
kwan·do e a·*per*·ta
la ga·le·*ree*·a

When's the museum open?
Quando è aperto
il museo?
kwan·do e a·*per*·to
eel moo·ze·o

What kind of art are you interested in?
Che tipo di arte Le/ti
interessa? pol/inf
ke *tee*·po dee *ar*·te le/tee
een·te·*re*·sa

What do you think of ...?
Cosa ne pensa/
pensi di ...? pol/inf
ko·za ne *pen*·sa/
pen·see dee ...

It's a/an (futurist art) exhibition.
È una mostra di
(arte futurista).
e *oo*·na *mos*·tra dee
(*ar*·te foo·too·*ree*·sta)

I'm interested in ... art/ architecture.	Mi interessa l'arte/ l'architettura ...	mee een·te·*re*·sa *lar*·te/ lar·kee·te·*too*·ra ...
baroque	barocca	ba·*ro*·ka
byzantine	bizantina	bee·dzan·*tee*·na
Gothic	gotica	*go*·tee·ka
graphic	grafica	*gra*·fee·ka
impressionist	impressionista	eem·pre·syo·*nee*·sta
modernist	modernista	mo·der·*nee*·sta
performance	d'esibizione	de·zee·bee·*tsyo*·ne
Renaissance	rinascimentale	ree·na·shee·men·*ta*·le
Romanesque	romanica	ro·*ma*·nee·ka

affresco m	a·*fres*·ko	fresco
arcata f	ar·*ka*·ta	series of arches
architrave m	ar·kee·*tra*·ve	lintel
arco m	*ar*·ko	arch
badia f	ba·*dee*·a	abbey
baldacchino m	bal·da·*kee*·no	canopy supported by columns over an altar
basilica f	ba·*zee*·lee·ka	in ancient Rome, an administration building • later a Christian church in the same style
battistero m	ba·tees·*te*·ro	baptistry
bottega f	bo·*te*·ga	(work)shop
contrafforte m	kon·tra·*for*·te	buttress
campanile m	kam·pa·*nee*·le	bell tower
cappella f	ka·*pe*·la	chapel • small room or altarpiece in a church
cattedrale f	ka·te·*dra*·le	cathedral
cenacolo m	che·*na*·ko·lo	supper room or refectory
chiesa f	*kye*·za	church
chiostro m	*kyos*·tro	cloister • covered walkway around a quadrangle
circo m	*cheer*·ko	oval or circular arena
cofano m	*ko*·fa·no	coffer • recessed panel in ceiling or vault
colonna f	ko·*lo*·na	column
colonnato m	ko·lo·*na*·to	a row of columns
cortile m	kor·*tee*·le	courtyard
cupola f	*koo*·po·la	dome (of cathedral)
cupolone m	koo·po·*lo*·ne	big dome
curia f	*koo*·rya	arcade of columns in a Venetian Byzantine palace
duomo m	*dwo*·mo	dome • cathedral
fascia f	*fa*·sha	frieze
fontana f	fon·*ta*·na	fountain
foro m	*fo*·ro	forum

architectural terms

fresco m	*fres*·ko	fresco
gargolla m	gar·*go*·la	gargoyle (carved creature, often a watersprout)
guglia f	*goo*·lya	spire
intarsio m	een·*tar*·syo	inlaid wood, marble or metal
intonaco m	een·*to*·na·ko	plaster surfacing of a wall
liagò m	lya·*go*	roofed terrace or enclosed balcony
loggia f	*lo*·ja	covered area on the side of a building • porch • small cottage garden
maestà f	ma·es·*ta*	Madonna and Child on a throne
navata f	na·*va*·ta	nave
centrale	chen·*tra*·le	
pala f **d'altare**	*pa*·la dal·*ta*·re	altarpiece
palazzo m	pa·*la*·tso	large building
persiane f pl	per·*sya*·ne	louvre shutters
piazza f	*pya*·tsa	square
piazzale m	pya·*tsa*·le	large open square
pietà f	pye·*ta*	Virgin with dead Christ
ponte m	*pon*·te	bridge
portico m	por·*tee*·ko	covered walkway
putti m pl	*poo*·tee	cherubs
rilievo m	ree·*lye*·vo	relief
rocca f	*ro*·ka	fortress
sala f	*sa*·la	room or hall
sassi m pl	*sa*·see	houses carved out of rock
scale f pl	*ska*·le	stairs
scalinata f	ska·lee·*na*·ta	stairway
scavi m pl	*ska*·vee	excavations
terrazzo m	te·*ra*·tso	terrace • balcony
tondo m	*ton*·do	round painting
torre m	*to*·re	tower
trittico m	*tree*·tee·ko	triptych
vetrata f	ve·*tra*·ta	stained-glass window

artwork	opera f d'arte	o·pe·ra dar·te
curator	conservatore/	kon·ser·va·to·re/
	conservatrice m/f	kon·ser·va·tree·che
design	disegno m	dee·ze·nyo
engraving	incisione f	een·chee·zyo·ne
etching	acquaforte f	a·kwa·for·te
exhibition hall	salone m	sa·lo·ne
	d'esposizione	des·po·zee·tsyo·ne
installation	installazione f	een·sta·la·tsyo·ne
opening	apertura f	a·per·too·ra
painter	pittore/	pee·to·re/
	pittrice m/f	pee·tree·che
painting (the art)	pittura f	pee·too·ra
painting (canvas)	quadro m	kwa·dro
period	periodo m	pe·ree·o·do
permanent	collezione f	ko·le·tsyo·ne
collection	permanente	per·ma·nen·te
print	riproduzione f	ree·pro·doo·tsyo·ne
sculptor	scultore/	skool·to·re/
	scultrice m/f	skool·tree·che
sculpture	scultura f	skool·too·ra
statue	statua f	sta·too·a
studio	studio m	stoo·dee·o
style	stile m	stee·le
tapestry	tappezzeria f	ta·pe·tse·ree·a
technique	tecnica f	tek·nee·ka

perplexing plurals

Italian has some irregular plural forms – here are a couple:

il dio	eel dee·o m sg	the god
i dei	ee day m pl	the gods
la ala	la a·la f sg	the wing
le ali	le a·lee f pl	the wings

Furthermore, some words change gender in the plural:

il labbro	eel la·bro m sg	the lip
le labbra	le la·bra f pl	the lips

See also **plurals** in the **grammar** chapter, page 20.

beliefs & cultural differences

i fedi & le differenze culturali

religion

la religione

What's your religion?
Di che religione è Lei? pol   dee ke re·lee·jo·ne e lay
Di che religione sei tu? inf   dee ke re·lee·jo·ne say too

I (don't) believe in God.
(Non) Credo in Dio.   (non) kre·do een dee·o

I'm (not) ...	*(Non) Sono ...*	(non) so·no ...
agnostic	*agnostico/a* m/f	a·nyos·tee·ko/a
atheist	*ateo/a* m/f	a·te·o/a
Buddhist	*buddista* m&f	boo·dee·sta
Catholic	*cattolico/a* m/f	ka·to·lee·ko/a
Christian	*cristiano/a* m/f	krees·tya·no/a
Hindu	*indù* m&f	een·doo
Jewish	*ebreo/a* m/f	e·bre·o/a
Muslim	*musulmano/a* m/f	moo·sool·ma·no/a
(Eastern) Orthodox	*ortodosso/a* m/f	or·to·do·so/a
practising	*praticante* m&f	pra·tee·kan·te
religious	*religioso/a* m/f	re·lee·jo·zo/a

I'd like to go to (the) ...	*Vorrei andare ...*	vo·ray an·da·re ...
church	*alla chiesa*	a·la kye·za
mosque	*alla moschea*	a·la mos·ke·a
synagogue	*alla sinagoga*	a·la see·na·go·ga
temple	*al tempio*	a·la tem·pyo

Can I ... here?	Posso ... qui?	po·so ... kwee
Where can I ...?	Dove posso ...?	do·ve po·so ...
attend mass	andare a messa	an·da·re a me·sa
go to church	andare in chiesa	an·da·re een kye·za
make confession	confessarmi	kon·fe·sar·mee
(in English)	(in inglese)	(een en·gle·ze)
pray	pregare	pre·ga·re
receive	ricevere la	ree·che·ve·re la
communion	comunione	ko·moo·nyo·ne

cultural differences

le differenze culturali

Is this a local or national custom?
> È una tradizione
> locale o nazionale?

e oo·na tra·dee·tsyo·ne
lo·ka·le o na·tsyo·na·le

I don't mind watching, but I'd rather not join in.
> Non mi dispiace
> guardare ma preferisco
> non partecipare.

non mee dees·pya·che
gwar·da·re ma pre·fe·rees·ko
non par·te·chee·pa·re

I'm not used to this.
> Non ci sono abituato/a. m/f

non chee so·no a·bee·twa·to/a

I'll try it.
> Lo proverò.

lo pro·ve·ro

I'm sorry, I didn't mean to do/say anything wrong.
> Mi dispiace, non
> volevo dire/fare
> qualcosa di sbagliato.

mee dees·pya·che non
vo·le·vo dee·re/fa·re
kwal·ko·za dee sba·lya·to

I'm sorry, it's against my ...	Mi dispiace, non è permesso dalla mia ...	mee dees·pya·che non e per·me·so da·la me·a ...
beliefs	fede	fe·de
culture	cultura	kool·too·ra
religion	religione	re·lee·jo·ne

sporting interests

gli interessi sportivi

Do you like (sport)?
Ti piace (lo sport)? tee *pya*·che (lo sport)

Yes, very much.
Sì, moltissimo. see mol·*tee*·see·mo

Not really.
Non molto. non *mol*·to

I like watching it.
Mi piace assistere. mee *pya*·che a·*see*·ste·re

What sport do you play?
Quale sport pratichi? *kwa*·le sport *pra*·tee·kee

I play (soccer).
Pratico (il calcio). *pra*·tee·ko (eel *kal*·cho)

I follow (car racing).
Seguo (l'automobilismo). *se*·gwo (low·to·mo·bee·*leez*·mo)

For more sports, see the **dictionary**.

Who's your favourite sportsman?
Chi è il tuo sportivo kee e eel *too*·o spor·*tee*·vo
preferito? pre·fe·*ree*·to

Who's your favourite sportswoman?
Chi è la tua sportiva kee e la *too*·a spor·*tee*·va
preferita? pre·fe·*ree*·ta

Who's your favourite team?
Qual'è la tua squadra kwa·*le* la *too*·a *skwa*·dra
preferita? pre·fe·*ree*·ta

going to a game

Would you like to go to a game?
*Ti piacerebbe andare
ad una partita?*
tee pya·che·re·be an·da·re
a·doo·na par·tee·ta

Who are you supporting?
Per chi fai il tifo?
per kee fai eel tee·fo

Who's playing?
Chi gioca?
kee jo·ka

Who's winning?
Chi vince?
kee veen·che

How much time is left?
Quanto tempo manca?
kwan·to tem·po man·ka

What's the score?
Qual'è il punteggio?
kwa·le eel poon·te·jo

It's a draw.
Hanno pareggiato.
a·no pa·re·ja·to

The referee has disallowed it.
*L'arbitro non l'ha
permesso.*
lar·bee·tro non la
per·me·so

That was a … game!	*Che partita …!*	ke par·tee·ta …
bad	*brutta*	broo·ta
boring	*noiosa*	no·yo·za
great	*fantastica*	fan·tas·tee·ka

sports talk

What a …!	*Che …!*	ke …
goal	*gol*	gol
hit	*colpo*	kol·po
kick	*calcio*	kal·cho
pass	*passaggio*	pa·sa·jo
performance	*esecuzione*	e·se·koo·tsyo·ne

playing sport

Do you want to play?
Vuoi giocare? — vwoy jo·ka·re

Can I join in?
Posso giocare anch'io? — po·so jo·ka·re an·kee·o

Yes, that'd be great.
Sì, sarebbe bello. — see sa·re·be be·lo

I'm sorry, I can't.
Mi dispiace, non posso. — mee dees·pya·che non po·so

I have an injury.
Sono infortunato/a. m/f — so·no een·for·too·na·to/a

Where's the best place to jog around here?
Qual'è il miglior posto — kwa·le eel mee·lyor pos·to
per fare il footing — per fa·re eel foo·teeng
qui intorno? — kwee een·tor·no

Where's the nearest ...?	*Dov'è ...?*	do·ve ...
gym	*la palestra più vicina*	la pa·le·stra pyoo vee·chee·na
swimming pool	*la piscina più vicina*	la pee·shee·na pyoo vee·chee·na
tennis court	*il campo da tennis più vicino*	eel kam·po da te·nees pyoo vee·chee·no

What's the charge per ...?	*Qual'è il prezzo richiesto ...?*	kwa·le eel pre·tso ree·kye·sto ...
day	*per la giornata*	per la jor·na·ta
game	*per una partita*	per oo·na par·tee·ta
hour	*all'ora*	a·lo·ra
visit	*a visita*	a vee·see·ta

Can I hire a ...?	*Posso noleggiare ...?*	po·so no·le·ja·re ...
ball	*una palla*	oo·na pa·la
court	*un campo*	oon kam·po
racquet	*una racchetta*	oo·na ra·ke·ta

e·ra fwo·ree	Era fuori.	That was out.
eem·bro·lyo·ne/a	Imbroglione/a! m/f	Cheat!
gra·tsye de·la par·tee·ta	Grazie della partita.	Thanks for the game.
jo·kee be·ne	Giochi bene.	You're a good player.
pa·sa·la a me	Passala a me!	Kick/Pass it to me!
poon·to a me/te	Punto a me/te.	Your/My point.

Do I have to be a member to attend?
    È necessario essere soci?   e ne·che·sa·ryo e·se·re so·chee

Is there a women-only session?
    Ci sono i corsi per   chee so·no ee kor·see per
    sole donne?   so·le do·ne

Where are the changing rooms?
    Dove sono gli spogliatoi?   do·ve so·no lyee spo·lya·to·ee

cycling

il ciclismo

Where does the race finish?
    Dove finisce la gara?   do·ve fee·nee·she la ga·ra

Where does it pass through?
    Dove passa?   do·ve pa·sa

Who's winning?
    Chi vince?   kee veen·che

How many kilometres is today's (leg)?
    (La tappa) di oggi è di   (la ta·pa) dee o·jee e dee
    quanti chilometri?   kwan·tee kee·lo·me·tree

My favourite cyclist is ...
    Il mio ciclista   eel mee·o chee·klee·sta
    preferito è ...   pre·fe·ree·to e ...

cyclist	*ciclista* m/f	chee·*klee*·sta
the (yellow) jersey	*la maglia* f *(gialla)*	ma·lya *(ja*·la)
leg (in race)	*tappa* f	*ta*·pa
mountain stage	*tappa* f *in salita*	*ta*·pa een sa·*lee*·ta
race	*gara*	*ga*·ra
the tour of Italy	*il giro* m *d'Italia*	eel *jee*·ro dee·*ta*·lya
time trial	*prova* f	*pro*·va
	a cronometro	a kro·*no*·me·tro
winner (of a leg)	*vincitore/*	veen·chee·*to*·re/
	vincitrice m/f	veen·chee·*tree*·che
	(di tappa)	(dee *ta*·pa)

For phrases on getting around by bike, see **transport**, page 48.

diving

fare immersioni

I'd like to ...	*Vorrei ...*	vo·*ray* ...
explore wrecks	*esplorare relitti*	es·plo·*ra*·re re·*lee*·tee
go scuba diving	*fare immersioni*	*fa*·re ee·mer·*syo*·nee
	subacquee	soo·ba·*kwe*·e
go snorkelling	*fare immersioni*	*fa*·re ee·mer·*syo*·nee
	in apnea	ee·nap·*ne*·a
hire diving gear	*noleggiare*	no·le·*ja*·re
	l'attrezzatura per	la·tre·tsa·*too*·ra per
	immersioni	ee·mer·*syo*·nee
	subacquee	soo·ba·*kwe*·e
hire snorkelling	*noleggiare*	no·le·*ja*·re
gear	*l'attrezzatura*	la·tre·tsa·*too*·ra per
	per immersioni	ee·mer·*syo*·nee
	in apnea	ee·nap·*ne*·a
join a diving tour	*partecipare*	par·te·chee·*pa*·re
	ad una gita	a·*doo*·na *jee*·ta
	d'immersione	dee·mer·*syo*·ne
learn to dive	*imparare a fare*	eem·pa·*ra*·re a *fa*·re
	immersioni	ee·mer·*syo*·nee
	subacquee	soo·ba·*kwe*·e

Where are some good diving sites?
Dove sono dei buoni   do·ve so·no day bwo·nee
posti per fare immersioni?   pos·tee per fa·re ee·mer·syo·nee

Are there jellyfish?
Ci sono meduse?   chee so·no me·doo·ze

Where can I hire (flippers)?
Dove posso noleggiare   do·ve po·so no·le·ja·re
(pinne)?   (pee·ne)

extreme sports

gli sport estremi

Are you sure this is safe?
Sei sicuro che questo   say see·koo·ro ke kwe·sto
sia sicuro?   see·a see·koo·ro

Is the equipment secure?
È sicura l'attrezzatura?   e see·koo·ra la·tre·tsa·too·ra

This is insane.
Questa è roba da matti.   kwe·sta e ro·ba da ma·tee

abseiling	*discesa* f *a corda doppia*	dee·she·sa a kor·da do·pya
caving	*esplorazione* f *di caverne*	es·plo·ra·tsyo·ne dee ka·ver·ne
canoeing/rowing	*canottaggio* m	ka·no·ta·jo
canyoning	*torrentismo* m	to·ren·teez·mo
game fishing	*pesca* f *ai pesci selvatici*	pes·ka ai pe·shee sel·va·tee·chee
paragliding	*parapendio* m	pa·ra·pen·dyo
rock-climbing	*andare su roccia* f	an·da·re soo ro·cha
skydiving	*paracadutismo* m *acrobatico*	pa·ra·ka·doo·teez·mo ak·ro·ba·tee·ko
snowboarding	*surf* m *da neve*	soorf da ne·ve
trekking	*escursionismo* m *a piedi*	es·koor·syo·neez·mo a pye·dee
white-water rafting	*rafting* m	raf·teeng

For phrases on hiking, see **outdoors**, page 137, and **camping**, page 58.

soccer/football

Who plays for (Sampdoria)?
*Chi gioca per
(la Sampdoria)?*
kee *jo*·ka per
(la samp·do·*ree*·a)

He's a great (player).
È un bravo (giocatore).
e oon *bra*·vo (jo·ka·*to*·re)

He played brilliantly in the match against (England).
*Ha fatto un'ottima
partita contro
(l'Inghilterra).*
a *fa*·to oo·*no*·tee·ma
par·*tee*·ta *kon*·tro
(leen·geel·*te*·ra)

Which team is at the top of the league?
*Quale squadra è in
testa alla classifica?*
kwa·le *skwa*·dra e een
tes·ta *a*·la kla·*see*·fee·ka

What a terrible team!
Che squadra schifosa!
ke *skwa*·dra skee·*fo*·za

ball	*pallone* m	pa·*lo*·ne
coach	*allenatore/*	a·le·na·*to*·re/
	allenatrice m/f	a·le·na·*tree*·che
corner	*angolo* m	*an*·go·lo
corner kick	*calcio* m *d'angolo*	*kal*·cho *dan*·go·lo
defensive player	*giocatore/*	jo·ka·*to*·re/
	giocatrice m/f	jo·ka·*tree*·che
	difensivo/a	de·fen·*see*·vo/a
expulsion	*espulsione* f	es·pool·*syo*·ne
fans	*tifosi* m pl	tee·*fo*·zee
foul	*fallo* m	*fa*·lo
free kick	*calcio* m	*kal*·cho
	di punizione	dee poo·nee·*tsyo*·ne
goal	*gol* m	gol

goal (place)	porta f	por·ta
goalkeeper	portiere m&f	por·tye·re
goal-scorer	cannoniere m	ka·no·nye·re
kick-off	calcio m d'inizio	kal·cho dee·nee·tsyo
league	serie f	se·rye
manager	manager m&f	me·na·je
mid-fielder	centrocampista m&f	chen·tro·kam·pee·sta
offside	fuorigioco m	fwo·ree·jo·ko
penalty (kick)	rigore m	ree·go·re
penalty area	area f di rigore	a·re·a dee ree·go·re
player	giocatore/	jo·ka·to·re/
	giocatrice m/f	jo·ka·tree·che
red card	cartellino m rosso	kar·te·lee·no ro·so
to score	segnare	se·nya·re
soccer player	calciatore/	kal·cha·to·re/
	calciatrice m/f	kal·cha·tree·che
striker	attaccante/avanti m	a·ta·kan·te/a·van·tee
supporters	tifosi m pl	tee·fo·zee
throw-in	rimessa f laterale	ree·me·sa la·te·ra·le
warning	ammonizione f	a·mo·nee·tsyo·ne
yellow card	cartellino m giallo	kar·te·lee·no ja·lo

listen for ...

a·le	Alé!	Come on!
for·tsa a·dzoo·ree	Forza Azzurri!	Come on 'blues'!
for·tsa ra·ga·tsee	Forza ragazzi!	Come on boys!

skiing

sci

I'd like to hire ...	Vorrei noleggiare ...	vo·ray no·le·ja·re ...
boots	gli scarponi	lyee skar·po·nee
goggles	gli occhiali di	lyee o·kya·lee dee
	protezione	pro·te·tsyo·ne
poles	i bastoncini	ee bas·ton·chee·nee
skis	gli sci	lyee shee
a ski suit	una tuta da sci	oo·na too·ta da shee

SOCIAL

134

Is it possible to go ... here/there?	Si può ... qui/là?	see pwo ... kwee/la
Alpine skiing	fare lo sci alpino	fa·re lo shee al·pee·no
cross-country skiing	fare lo sci di fondo	fa·re lo shee dee fon·do
snowboarding	fare il surf da neve	fa·re eel soorf da ne·ve
tobogganing	andare in slitta	an·da·re een slee·ta

How much is a pass?
Quant'è una tessera? kwan·te oo·na te·se·ra

Can I take lessons?
Posso prendere lezioni? po·so pren·de·re le·tsyo·nee

What level is that slope?
Qual'è il livello di quella pista? kwa·le eel lee·ve·lo dee kwe·la pee·sta

Which are the ... slopes?	Quali sono le piste per ...?	kwa·lee so·no le pee·ste per ...
advanced	avanzati	a·van·tsa·tee
beginner	principianti	preen·chee·pyan·tee
intermediate	intermedi	een·ter·me·dee

What are the skiing conditions like ...?	In quali condizioni sono le piste ...?	een kwa·lee kon·dee·tsyo·nee so·no le pee·ste ...
at (Cortina d'Ampezzo)	a (Cortina d'Ampezzo)	a (kor·tee·na dam·pe·tso)
higher up	più in alto	pyoo ee·nal·to
on that run	su quella pista	soo kwe·la pee·sta

cable car	*funivia* f	foo·nee·*vee*·a
chairlift	*seggiovia* f	se·jo·*vee*·a
instructor	*maestro/a* m/f	ma·*es*·tro/a
	di sci	dee shee
resort	*località* f	lo·ka·lee·*ta*
	sciistica	shee·*ee*·stee·ka
ski-lift	*sciovia* f	shee·o·*vee*·a
sled	*slittino* m	slee·*tee*·no
'white week'	*settimana* f	se·tee·*ma*·na
(skiing holiday)	*bianca*	*byan*·ka

swearing

God!	*Dio!*	*dee*·o
Christ!	*Cristo!*	*kree*·sto
Jesus!	*Gesù!*	je·*soo*
Goodness!	*Madonna!*	ma·*do*·na
Shit!	*Merda!*	*mer*·da
Damn!	*Maledizione!*	ma·le·dee·*tsyo*·ne

hiking

escursionismo a piedi

Where can I ...?	*Dove posso ...?*	do·ve po·so ...
buy supplies	*comprare delle provviste*	kom·pra·re de·le pro·vee·ste
find out about hiking trails	*informarmi sulle piste per l'escursionismo a piedi*	een·for·mar·mee soo·le pee·ste per les·koor·syo·neez·mo a pye·dee
find someone who knows this area	*trovare qualcuno che conosca la zona*	tro·va·re kwal·koo·no ke ko·no·ska la dzo·na
get a map	*trovare una carta*	tro·va·re oo·na kar·ta
hire hiking gear	*noleggiare l'attrezzatura per l'escursionismo a piedi*	no·le·ja·re la·tre·tsa·too·ra per les·koor·syo·neez·mo a pye·dee

Do we need to take ...?	*Dobbiamo portare ...?*	do·bya·mo por·ta·re ...
bedding	*qualcosa per dormire*	kwal·ko·za per dor·mee·re
food	*del cibo*	del chee·bo
water	*dell'acqua*	de·la·kwa
How ...?	*Quant'è ...?*	kwan·te ...
high is the climb	*alta la salita*	al·ta la sa·lee·ta
long is the hike	*lunga l'escursione*	loon·ga les·koor·syo·ne
long is the trail	*lungo il sentiero*	loon·go eel sen·tye·ro

Is the track ...?	*La pista è ...?*	la *pee*·sta e ...
(well-)marked	*(ben) segnata*	(ben) se·*nya*·ta
open	*aperta*	a·*per*·ta
scenic	*panoramica*	pa·no·ra·*mee*·ka

Which is the ... route?	*Qual'è il percorso più ...?*	kwa·*le* eel per·*kor*·so pyoo ...
easiest	*facile*	*fa*·chee·le
most interesting	*interessante*	een·te·re·*san*·te
shortest	*corto*	*kor*·to

Where's a ...?	*Dov'è ...?*	do·*ve* ...
a camping site	*un campeggio*	oon kam·*pe*·jo
the nearest village	*il villaggio più vicino*	eel vee·*la*·jo pyoo vee·*chee*·no

Where are the ...?	*Dove sono ...?*	*do*·ve so·no ...
showers	*le docce*	le *do*·che
toilets	*i servizi igienici*	ee ser·*vee*·tsee ee·*je*·nee·chee

Do we need a guide?
Occorre una guida?   o·*ko*·re oo·na *gwee*·da

Are there guided treks?
Ci sono delle escursioni guidate?   chee *so*·no *de*·le es·koor·*syo*·nee gwee·*da*·te

Is it safe?
È sicuro?   e see·*koo*·ro

Is there a hut there?
C'è un rifugio là?   che oon re·*foo*·jo la

When does it get dark?
Quando fa buio?   *kwan*·do fa *boo*·yo

Where have you come from?
Da dove è venuto/a? m/f pol   da *do*·ve e ve·*noo*·to/a
Da dove sei venuto/a? m/f inf   da *do*·ve say ve·*noo*·to/a

How long did it take?
  Quanto ci è voluto? — kwan·to chee e vo·loo·to

Does this path go to (Ginostra)?
  Questo sentiero va verso (Ginostra)? — kwe·sto sen·tye·ro va ver·so (jee·nos·tra)

Can we go through here?
  Possiamo passare da qui? — po·sya·mo pa·sa·re da kwee

Is the water OK to drink?
  Si può bere l'acqua? — see pwo be·re la·kwa

I'm lost.
  Mi sono perso/a. m/f — mee so·no per·so/a

at the beach

alla spiaggia

Where's the ...	*Dov'è la*	do·ve la
beach?	*spiaggia ...?*	spya·ja ...
best	*migliore*	mee·lyo·re
nearest	*più vicina*	pyoo vee·chee·na
nudist	*nudista*	noo·dee·sta
public	*pubblica*	poo·blee·ka
Is it safe to ...	*Si può ... senza*	see pwo ... sen·tsa
here?	*pericolo?*	pe·ree·ko·lo
dive	*fare i tuffi*	fa·re ee too·fee
scuba dive	*fare le immersioni*	fa·re le ee·mer·syo·nee
swim	*nuotare*	nwo·ta·re

<table>
<tr><td colspan="3">signs</td></tr>
<tr><td>Vietato Nuotare</td><td>vye·ta·to noo·o·ta·re</td><td>No Swimming</td></tr>
</table>

What time is	A che ora è ...	a ke o·ra e ...
... tide?	marea?	ma·re·a
high	l'alta	lal·ta
low	la bassa	la ba·sa
How much for a/an ...?	Quanto costa ...?	kwan·to ko·sta ...
deckchair	una sedia a sdraio	oo·na se·dya a zdra·yo
hut	una capanna	oo·na ka·pa·na
umbrella	un ombrello	oo·nom·bre·lo

listen for ...

de·ve pa·ga·re
 Deve pagare. **You have to pay.**

e pe·ree·ko·lo·zo
 È pericoloso! **It's dangerous!**

fa a·ten·tsyo·ne al ree·soo·kyo
 Fa attenzione al risucchio! **Be careful of the undertow!**

weather

il tempo

What's the weather like?
 Che tempo fa? ke *tem*·po fa

What's the weather forecast?
 Cosa dicono le previsioni del tempo? ko·za dee·ko·no le pre·vee·zyo·nee del *tem*·po

(Today) It's ...	(Oggi) È ...	(o·jee) e ...
Will it be ... tomorrow?	Domani sarà ...?	do·ma·nee sa·ra ...
cloudy	nuvoloso	noo·vo·lo·zo
fine	sereno	se·re·no
sunny	soleggiato	so·le·ja·to

(Today) It's ...	(Oggi) Fa ...	(o·jee) fa ...
Will it be ... tomorrow?	Domani farà ...?	do·ma·nee fa·ra ...
cold	freddo	fre·do
hot	caldo	kal·do
warm	bel tempo	bel tem·po

It's freezing.	Si gela.	see je·la
It's raining.	Piove.	pyo·ve
It's snowing.	Nevica.	ne·vee·ka
It's windy.	Tira vento.	tee·ra ven·to

Will it be ... tomorrow?	Domani ...?	do·ma·nee ...
raining	pioverà	pyo·ve·ra
snowing	nevicherà	ne·vee·ke·ra
windy	ci sarà vento	chee sa·ra ven·to

flora & fauna

la flora & la fauna

What (kind of) ... is that?	Che (tipo di) ... è quello?	ke (tee·po dee) ... e kwe·lo?
animal	animale	a·nee·ma·le
bird	uccello	oo·che·lo
flower	fiore	fyo·re
plant	pianta	pyan·ta
tree	albero	al·be·ro

Is it ...?	È ...?	e ...
common	comune	ko·moo·ne
dangerous	pericoloso/a m/f	pe·ree·ko·lo·zo/a
endangered	in pericolo d'estinzione	een pe·ree·ko·lo des·teen·tsyo·ne
poisonous	velenoso/a m/f	ve·le·no·zo/a
protected	protetto/a m/f	pro·te·to/a

What's it used for?
A che cosa serve?   a ke *ko*·za *ser*·ve

Can you eat it?
Si può mangiarlo?   see pwo man·*jar*·lo

For geographical and agricultural terms, and names of animals
and plants, see the **dictionary**.

souvenirs		
antiques	*pezzi* m	pe·tsee
	d'antiquariato	dan·tee·kwa·*rya*·to
blown glass	*vetro* m *soffiato*	*ve*·tro so·*fya*·to
Carnevale	*maschere* f pl *di*	*ma*·ske·re dee
masks	*Carnevale*	kar·ne·*va*·le
ceramics	*ceramiche* f pl	che·*ra*·mee·ke
embroidery	*ricamo* m	ree·*ka*·mo
glassware	*vetrame* m	ve·*tra*·me
handicrafts	*ogetti* m pl	o·*je*·tee
	d'artigianato	dar·tee·ja·*na*·to
jewellery	*gioielli* m pl	jo·*ye*·lee
lace	*merletto* m	mer·*le*·to
leather goods	*pelletterie* f pl	pe·le·te·*ree*·e
marbled paper	*carta* f	*kar*·ta
	marmorizzata	mar·mo·ree·*tsa*·ta
Murano	*vetri* m pl *di*	*ve*·tree dee
glassware	*Murano*	moo·*ra*·no
paper goods	*articoli* m pl	ar·*tee*·ko·lee
	di carta	dee *kar*·ta
pottery	*ceramiche* f pl	che·*ra*·mee·ke
woodcarvings	*legno* m	*le*·nyo
	intagliato	een·ta·*lya*·to

key language

vocabolario essenziale

breakfast	*prima colazione* f	pree·ma ko·la·*tsyo*·ne
lunch	*pranzo* m	*pran*·dzo
dinner	*cena* f	*che*·na
afternoon snack	*merenda* f	me·*ren*·da
daily special	*piatto* m *del giorno*	*pya*·to del *jor*·no
set menu	*menu* m *turistico*	me·*noo* too·ree·*stee*·ko
snack	*spuntino* m	spoon·*tee*·no
eat	*mangiare*	man·*ja*·re
drink	*bere*	*be*·re
Enjoy the meal!	*Buon appetito!*	bwon a·pe·*tee*·to

cheap & cheerful

bar/caffè m   bar/ka·*fe*
serve drinks but also offer light meals such as bread
rolls and snacks

osteria/trattoria f   os·te·*re*·a/tra·to·*ree*·a
provide simple food and some local specialities

paninoteca f   pa·nee·no·*te*·ka
serves delicious sandwiches made with cheese and cold
meats

tavola calda f   *ta*·vo·la *kal*·da
a buffet offering local specialities, pizza, roasted meats
and salads

pizzeria f   pee·tse·*ree*·a
specialises in *pizza* and *calzoni* (a folded pizza dish),
usually prepared in a woodfired oven

ristorante m   ree·sto·*ran*·te
a more sophisticated eatery; expect a higher standard of
service, a more expensive menu and a decent wine list

finding a place to eat

Can you recommend a ...?	Potrebbe consigliare un ...?	po·tre·be kon·see·lya·re oon ...
cafe	bar	bar
restaurant	ristorante	rees·to·ran·te

Where would you go for (a) ...?	Dove andrebbe per ...?	do·ve an·dre·be per ...
business lunch	un pranzo d'affari	oon pran·dzo da·fa·ree
cheap meal	un pasto economico	oon pas·to e·ko·no·mee·ko
celebration	una celebrazione	oo·na che·le·bra·tsyo·ne
local specialities	le specialità locali	le spe·cha·lee·ta lo·ka·lee

listen for ...

do·ve vwo·le se·der·see
Dove vuole sedersi? — Where would you like to sit?

e al kom·ple·to
È al completo. — We're fully booked.

e·ko
Ecco! — Here you go!

ko·me la vwo·le ko·ta
Come la vuole cotta? — How would you like that cooked?

ko·za le por·to
Cosa Le porto? — What can I get for you?

non a·bya·mo ta·vo·lee
Non abbiamo tavoli. — We have no tables.

sya·mo kyoo·zee
Siamo chiusi. — We're closed.

Caldo	*kal·*do	**Hot**
Donne	*do·*ne	**Women**
Freddo	*fre·*do	**Cold**
Gabinetti	ga·bee·*ne·*tee	**Toilets**
Prenotato	pre·no·*ta·*to	**Reserved**
Riservato	ree·ser·*va·*to	**Reserved**
Uomini	*wo·*mee·nee	**Men**

I'd like to reserve	*Vorrei prenotare*	vo·ray pre·no·*ta·*re
a table for ...	*un tavolo per ...*	oon *ta·*vo·lo per ...
(two) people	*(due) persone*	*(doo·*e) per·*so·*ne
(eight) o'clock	*le (otto)*	le *(o·*to)
I'd like ..., please.	*Vorrei ...,*	vo·ray ...
	per favore.	per fa·*vo·*re
a table for (four)	*un tavolo per*	oon *ta·*vo·lo per
	(quattro)	*(kwa·*tro)
the menu	*il menù*	eel me·*noo*
the drink list	*la lista delle*	la *lee·*sta *de·*le
	bevande	be·*van·*de
the (non-)smoking	*(non) fumatori*	(non) foo·ma·*to·*ree
section		
Do you have ...?	*Avete ...?*	a·*ve·*te ...
children's meals	*pasti per*	*pas·*tee per
	bambini	bam·*bee·*nee
a menu in English	*un menù*	oon me·*noo*
	in inglese	een een·*gle·*ze

Are you still serving food?
Servite ancora da mangiare? ser·*vee·*te an·*ko·*ra da man·*ja·*re

How long is the wait?
Quanto si deve aspettare? *kwan·*to see *de·*ve as·pe·*ta·*re

eating out

145

at the restaurant

I'd like the menu, please.
Vorrei il menù, per favore. vo·ray eel me·noo per fa·vo·re

Is it self-serve?
È self-service? e self·ser·vees

We're just having drinks.
Prendiamo solo da bere. pren·dya·mo so·lo da be·re

What would you recommend?
Cosa mi consiglia? ko·za mee kon·see·lya

I'll have what they're having.
Vorrei quello che stanno vo·ray kwe·lo ke sta·no
mangiando loro. man·jan·do lo·ro

I'd like a local speciality.
Vorrei una specialità vo·ray oo·na spe·cha·lee·ta
di questa regione. dee kwe·sta re·jo·ne

What's in that dish?
Quali ingredienti ci kwa·li een·gre·dyen·tee chee
sono in questo piatto? so·no een kwe·sto pya·to

Does it take long to prepare?
Ci vuole molto per chee vwo·le mol·to per
prepararlo? pre·pa·rar·lo

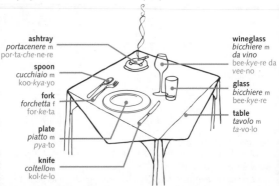

ashtray
portacenere m
por·ta·che·ne·re

spoon
cucchiaio m
koo·kya·yo

fork
forchetta f
for·ke·ta

plate
piatto m
pya·to

knife
coltello m
kol·te·lo

wineglass
bicchiere m
da vino
bee·kye·re da
vee·no

glass
bicchiere m
bee·kye·re

table
tavolo m
ta·vo·lo

look for ...

Antipasti	an·tee·*pas*·tee	Appetisers
Zuppe	*tsoo*·pe	Soups
Primi (Piatti)	*pree*·mee (*pya*·tee)	Entrees
Insalate	een·sa·*la*·te	Salads
Contorni	kon·*tor*·nee	Side Dishes
Pasti Leggeri	*pas*·tee le·*je*·ree	Light Meals
Secondi (Piatti)	se·*kon*·dee (*pya*·tee)	Main Courses
Dolci	*dol*·chee	Desserts
Bevande	be·*van*·de	Drinks
Aperitivi	a·pe·ree·*tee*·vee	Aperitifs
Bibite	*bee*·bee·te	Soft Drinks
Liquori	lee·*kwo*·ree	Spirits
Birre	*bee*·re	Beers
Vini della Casa	*vee*·nee *de*·la *ka*·za	House Wines
Vini Locali	*vee*·nee lo·*ka*·lee	Local Wines
Vini Frizzanti	*vee*·nee free·*tsan*·tee	Sparkling Wines
Vini Bianchi	*vee*·nee *byan*·kee	White Wines
Vini Rossi	*vee*·nee *ro*·see	Red Wines
Vini Rosati	*vee*·nee ro·*za*·tee	Roses
Vini da Dessert	*vee*·nee da de·*sert*	Dessert Wines
Digestivi	dee·jes·*tee*·vee	Digestifs

For more words you might see on a menu, see the **culinary reader**, page 161, and the dictionary.

Is ... included in the bill?	*Il ... è compreso nel conto?*	eel ... e kom·*pre*·zo nel *kon*·to
the cover charge	*coperto*	ko·*per*·to
service	*servizio*	ser·*vee*·tsyo
Please bring ...	*Mi porta ..., per favore?*	mee *por*·ta ... per fa·*vo*·re
the bill	*il conto*	eel *kon*·to
a cloth	*uno strofinaccio*	*oo*·no stro·fee·*na*·cho
a glass	*un bicchiere*	oon bee·*kye*·re

Is there (any Parmesan cheese)?
C'è (del parmigiano)?   che (del par·mee·*ja*·no)

I didn't order this.
Questo non l'ho ordinato.   *kwe*·sto non lo or·dee·*na*·to

hot 'n' saucy

Pasta comes in all shapes and sizes from the standard *spaghetti* spa·ge·tee to potato *gnocchi* nyo·kee and bow-shaped *farfalle* far·fa·le. There are even more varieties of pasta sauce and each region boasts its own speciality. Here are just a few you might come across. Note that *alla* a·la and *all'* al mean 'in the style of'.

aglio e olio   a·lyo e o·lyo
oil, garlic and sometimes chilli

al ragù   al ra·goo
meat (minced veal or pork), vegetables, lemon peel and nutmeg

all'amatriciana   a·la·ma·tree·cha·na
pig's cheek, lard, white wine, tomato, chilli and sheep's cheese

alla carbonara   a·la kar·bo·na·ra
bacon, butter, eggs and sheep's cheese

alla partenopea   a·la par·te·no·pe·a
mozzarella, tomato, bread crust, capers, olives, anchovies, basil, oil, chilli and salt

alla pescatora   a·la pes·ka·to·ra
fish, tomato and sweet herbs

alla pommarola   a·la po·ma·ro·la
tomato

alla puttanesca   a·la poo·ta·nes·ka
garlic, anchovies, black olives, capers, tomato, oil and chilli

cacio e pepe   ka·cho e pe·pe
black pepper and sheep's cheese

con il tonno   kon eel to·no
with tuna

con le vongole   kon le von·go·le
with clams

con tartufo di Norcia   kon tar·too·fo dee nor·cha
with Norcia truffles

talking food

That was delicious!
Era squisito!   e·ra skwee·zee·to

My compliments to the chef.
Complimenti al cuoco!   kom·plee·men·tee al kwo·ko

I'm full.
Sono sazio/a. m/f   so·no sa·tsyo/a

I love ...	*Vado matto/a*	va·do ma·to/a
	per ... m/f	per ...
this dish	*questo piatto*	kwe·sto pya·to
the local	*la cucina*	la koo·chee·na
cuisine	*locale*	lo·ka·le

This is ...	*Questo/a è ...* m/f	kwe·sto/a e ...
(too) cold	*(troppo) freddo/a* m/f	(tro·po) fre·do/a
(too) hot	*(troppo) caldo/a* m/f	(tro·po) kal·do/a
spicy	*piccante* m&f	pee·kan·te
superb	*delizioso/a* m/f	de·lee·tsyo·zo/a

breakfast

What's a typical breakfast?
Qual'è la prima   kwa·le la pree·ma
colazione tipica?   ko·la·tsyo·ne tee·pee·ka

bacon	*pancetta* f	pan·che·ta
bread	*pane* m	pa·ne
butter	*burro* m	boo·ro
cereal	*cereali* m pl	che·re·a·lee
croissant	*cornetto* m	kor·ne·to
eggs	*uova* f pl	wo·va
omelette	*frittata* f	free·ta·ta
milk	*latte* m	la·te
muesli	*muesli* m	moos·lee
pastry	*pasta* f	pas·ta
toast	*pane* m *tostato*	pa·ne tos·ta·to

methods of preparation

I'd like it ...	*Lo/La vorrei ...* m/f	lo/la vo·*ray* ...
I don't want it ...	*Non lo/la voglio ...* m/f	non lo/la *vo*·lyo ...
boiled	*bollito/a* m/f	bo·*lee*·to/a
broiled	*cotto/a* m/f	*ko*·to/a
	a fuoco vivo	a *fwo*·ko *vee*·vo
deep-fried	*fritto/a* m/f *in*	*free*·to/a een
	abbondante olio	a·bon·*dan*·te o·lyo
fried	*fritto/a* m/f	*free*·to/a
grilled	*(cotto/a)* m/f *ai ferri*	(*ko*·to/a) ai *fe*·ree
medium	*non troppo*	non *tro*·po
	cotto/a m/f	*ko*·to/a
rare	*al sangue*	al *san*·gwe
re-heated	*riscaldato/a* m/f	rees·kal·*da*·to/a
steamed	*cotto/a* m/f *a vapore*	*ko*·to/a a va·*po*·re
well-done	*ben cotto/a* m/f	ben *ko*·to/a
with the	*con il*	kon eel
dressing	*condimento*	kon·dee·*men*·to
on the side	*a parte*	a *par*·te
without ...	*senza ...*	*sen*·tsa ...

For other specific meal requests, see **vegetarian & special meals**, page 159.

in the bar

Excuse me!
Scusi!   skoo·zee

I'll have (a glass of red wine).
Prendo (un bicchiere di   *pren*·do (oon bee·*kye*·re dee
vino rosso).   *vee*·no *ro*·so)

Same again, please.
Un altro, per favore.   oon *al*·tro per fa·*vo*·re

No ice, thanks.
Senza ghiaccio, grazie.   *sen*·tsa *gya*·cho *gra*·tsye

Straight, please.
Liscio, per favore.   *lee*·sho per fa·*vo*·re

I'll buy you a drink.
Ti offro da bere.   tee *of*·ro da *be*·re

What would you like?
Cosa prendi?   *ko*·za *pren*·dee

It's my round.
Offro io.   *of*·ro *ee*·o

You can get the next one.
La prossima la paghi tu.   la *pro*·see·ma la *pa*·gee too

How much alcohol does this contain?
Quanto alcool contiene?   *kwan*·to *al*·kol kon·*tye*·ne

Do you serve meals here?
Servite da mangiare qui?   ser·*vee*·te da man·*ja*·re kwee

nonalcoholic drinks

le bevande analcoliche

almond milk	*orzata* f	or·*dza*·ta
bitter cola	*chinotto* m	kee·*no*·to
fruit juice (bottled)	*succo* m *di frutta*	*soo*·ko dee *froo*·ta
fruit juice (fresh)	*spremuta* f	spre·*moo*·ta
grapefruit juice	*succo* m *di pompelmo*	*soo*·ko dee pom·*pel*·mo
lemonade	*limonata* f	lee·mo·*na*·ta
orange juice (bottled)	*succo* m *d'arancia*	*soo*·ko da·*ran*·cha
orange juice (fresh)	*spremuta* f *d'arancia*	spre·*moo*·ta da·*ran*·cha
orangeade	*aranciata* f	a·ran·*cha*·ta
soft drink	*bibita* f	*bee*·bee·ta
(cup of) tea ...	*(un) tè ...*	(oon) te ...
(cup of) coffee ...	*(un) caffè ...*	(oon) ka·*fe* ...
with milk	*con latte*	kon *la*·te
without/with	*senza/con*	*sen*·tsa/kon
(sugar)	*(zucchero)*	*(tsoo*·ke·ro)

... water	*acqua ...*	a·kwa ...
boiled	*bollita*	bo·*lee*·ta
mineral	*minerale*	mee·ne·ra·le
sparkling	*frizzante*	free·*tsan*·te
still	*naturale*	na·too·ra·le

coffee lovers

Italians often drink their coffee standing up at the bar, as many establishments charge extra for table service. Simply ask for a *caffè* ka·fe and you'll receive an *espresso* es·*pre*·so, but don't order a *latte* la·te unless you want a glass of milk. If you want to blend in, make sure you don't ask for coffee with milk in the afternoon.

caffè m **alla valdostana**   ka·fe a·la val·dos·ta·na
    with *grappa*, lemon peel and spices

caffè m **americano**   ka·fe a·me·ree·ka·no
    long and black

caffè m **corretto**   ka·fe ko·re·to
    with a dash of liqueur

caffè m **doppio**   ka·fe *do*·pyo
    long, strong and black

caffè m **macchiato**   ka·fe ma·kya·to
    strong coffee with a drop of milk

caffè m **ristretto**   ka·fe ree·*stre*·to
    super strong black coffee

caffellatte m   ka·fe·*la*·te
    coffee with milk – usually only consumed at breakfast

cappuccino m   ka·poo·*chee*·no
    coffee prepared with milk, served with a lot of froth and sprinkled with cocoa – considered a morning drink

espresso m   es·*pre*·so
    short black coffee

ristretto m   ree·*stre*·to
    very short black coffee

latte m   *la*·te
    milk

FOOD

alcoholic drinks

You shouldn't have too many problems getting what you want at the bar. Some Italian spirits have made their way into English (eg, *sambuca* and *grappa*) and similarly Italian has adopted the English names for classics like *gin*, *rum* and *whiskey*.

amaro (bitter liqueur)	*amaro* m	a·*ma*·ro
brandy	*cognac* m	ko·nyak
champagne	*champagne* m	sham·*pa*·nye
cocktail	*cocktail* m	kok·tayl
draught beer	*birra* f *a la spina*	*bee*·ra a la *spee*·na
grappa (grape spirits)	*grappa* f	*gra*·pa
wine	*vino* m	*vee*·no

a shot of ...	*un sorso di ...*	oon *sor*·so dee ...
a bottle of	*una bottiglia*	*oo*·na bo·*tee*·lya
... wine	*di vino ...*	dee *vee*·no ...
a glass of	*un bicchiere*	oon bee·*kye*·re
... wine	*di vino ...*	dee *vee*·no ...
dessert	*da dessert*	da de·*sert*
red	*rosso*	*ro*·so
rose	*rosato*	ro·*za*·to
sparkling	*spumante*	spoo·*man*·te
white	*bianco*	*byan*·ko
a ... of beer	*... di birra*	... dee *bee*·ra
bottle	*una bottiglia*	*oo*·na bo·*tee*·lya
glass	*un bicchiere*	oon bee·*kye*·re
jug	*una caraffa*	*oo*·na ka·*ra*·fa
pint	*una pinta*	*oo*·na *peen*·ta

one too many?

Cheers!
Salute! — sa·*loo*·te

Thanks, but I don't feel like it.
Grazie, ma non mi va. — *gra*·tsye ma non mee va

No thanks, I'm driving.
No, grazie, devo guidare. — no *gra*·tsye *de*·vo gwee·*da*·re

I don't drink alcohol.
Non bevo. — non *be*·vo

I'm tired, I'd better go home.
Sono stanco/a, è meglio che vada a casa. m/f — *so*·no *stan*·ko/a e *me*·lyo ke *va*·da a *ka*·za

Where's the toilet?
Dov'è il gabinetto? — do·ve eel ga·bee·*ne*·to

This is hitting the spot.
Ci voleva proprio! — chee vo·*le*·va *pro*·pryo

I'm feeling drunk.
Mi sento un po' ubriaco/a. m/f — mee *sen*·to oon po oo·bree·*a*·ko/a

I really, really love you.
Ti amo molto molto. — tee *a*·mo *mol*·to *mol*·to

I think I've had one too many.
Penso d'aver bevuto troppo. — *pen*·so da·ver be·*voo*·to *tro*·po

Can you call a taxi for me?
Mi puoi chiamare un tassì? — mee pwoy kya·*ma*·re oon ta·*see*

I don't think you should drive.
È meglio che non guidi. — e *me*·lyo ke non gwee·dee

I'm pissed.
Ho la ciucca. — o la *choo*·ka

I feel ill.
Mi sento male. — mee *sen*·to *ma*·le

key language

il vocabolario essenziale

cooked	*cotto/a* m/f	*ko·ta/a*
dried	*secco/a* m/f	*se·ko/a*
fresh	*fresco/a* m/f	*fres·ko/a*
frozen	*congelato/a* m/f	*kon·je·la·to/a*
raw	*crudo/a* m/f	*kroo·do/a*
smoked	*affumicato/a* m/f	*a·foo·mee·ka·to/a*

shop till you drop

alimentari m	*a·lee·men·ta·ree*	grocery store
caseificio m	*ka·ze·ee·fee·cho*	creamery
enoteca f	*e·no·te·ka*	wine shop
formaggeria f	*for·ma·je·ree·a*	cheese shop (also sells other dairy products)
macelleria f	*ma·che·le·ree·a*	butcher
mercato m	*mer·ka·to*	market
pasticceria f	*pas·tee·che·ree·a*	cake shop
pastificio m	*pas·tee·fee·cho*	specialist pasta shop
pescheria f	*pes·ke·ree·a*	fish shop
polleria f	*po·le·ree·a*	poultry shop
salumeria f	*sa·loo·me·ree·a*	delicatessen
tabacchi m	*ta·ba·kee*	tobacconist
torrefazione f	*to·re·fa·tsyo·ne*	coffee roasting house

buying food

How much?
Quanto/a? m/f — kwan·to/a

How much is (a kilo of cheese)?
Quanto costa (un chilo di formaggio)? — kwan·to kos·ta (oon kee·lo dee for·ma·jo)

What's the local speciality?
Qual'è la specialità di questa regione? — kwa·le la spe·cha·lee·ta dee kwe·sta re·jo·ne

What's that?
Cos'è? — ko·ze

Can I taste it?
Lo/La posso assaggiare? m/f — lo/la po·so a·sa·ja·re

Can I have a bag, please?
Posso avere un sacchetto, per favore? — po·so a·ve·re oon sa·ke·to per fa·vo·re

I'd like ...	*Vorrei ...*	vo·ray ...
100 grams	*un etto*	oo·ne·to
200 grams	*due etti*	doo·e e·tee
a kilo	*un chilo*	oon kee·lo
(two) kilos	*(due) chili*	(doo·e) kee·lee
a bottle	*una bottiglia*	oo·na bo·tee·lya
a dozen	*una dozzina*	oo·na do·dzee·na
a jar	*un barattolo*	oon ba·ra·to·lo
a packet	*un sacchetto*	oon sa·ke·to
a piece	*un pezzo*	oon pe·tso
(three) pieces	*(tre) pezzi*	(tre) pe·tsee
a slice	*una fetta*	oo·na fe·ta
(six) slices	*(sei) fette*	(say) fe·te
a tin	*una scatola*	oo·na ska·to·la
some ...	*alcuni/e ...* m/f	al·koo·nee/al·koo·ne ...
that one	*quello/a* m/f	kwe·lo/a
this one	*questo/a* m/f	kwe·sto/a

Enough.	*Basta, grazie.*	*bas*·ta *gra*·tsye
A bit more.	*Un po' di più.*	oon po dee pyoo
Less.	*(Di) Meno.*	(dee) *me*·no

Do you have ...?	*Avete ...?*	a·*ve*·te ...
anything	*qualcosa di*	kwal·*ko*·za dee
cheaper	*meno costoso*	*me*·no kos·*to*·zo
other kinds	*altri tipi*	*al*·tree *tee*·pee

For food items, see the **culinary reader**, page 161, and the **dictionary**.

listen for ...

de·*see*·de·ra *al*·tro	
Desidera altro?	Would you like anything else?
e (*oo*·na gor·gon·*dzo*·la)	
È (una gorgonzola).	That's (a gorgonzola).
e e·zow·*ree*·to/a	
È esaurito/a. m/f	There's none left.
e poy	
E poi?	Anything else?
ko·za de·*see*·de·ra	
Cosa desidera?	What would you like?
non ne o	
Non ne ho.	I don't have any.
po·so a·yoo·*tar*·la	
Posso aiutarLa?	Can I help you?
so·no (*cheen*·kwe e·*oo*·ro)	
Sono (cinque euro).	That's (five euros).

Where can I find	*Dove posso trovare*	do·ve po·so tro·va·re
the ... section?	*il reparto ...?*	eel re·par·to ...
dairy	*dei latticini*	day la·tee·chee·nee
frozen goods	*dei surgelati*	day soor·je·la·tee
fruit and	*della frutta e*	de·la froo·ta e
vegetable	*verdura*	ver·doo·ra
meat	*della carne*	de·la kar·ne
poultry	*del pollame*	del po·la·me

Where's the health-food section/store?

Dov'è il reparto cibi	do·ve eel re·par·to chee·bee
macrobiotici?	ma·kro·bee·o·tee·chee

cooking utensils

utensili da cucina

Could I please borrow (a corkscrew)?

Posso prendere in prestito	po·so pren·de·re een pres·tee·to
(un cavatappi), per favore?	(oon ka·va·ta·pee) per fa·vo·re

Where's (a saucepan)?

Dov'è (un tegame)?	do·ve (oon te·ga·me)

For more cooking implements, see the **dictionary**.

vegetarian & special meals
piatti vegetariani & diete speciali

ordering food

ordinare da mangiare

Is there a ...	C'è un	che oon
restaurant near	ristorante ...	rees·to·ran·te ...
here?	qui vicino?	kwee vee·chee·no
halal	halal	a·lal
kosher	kasher	ka·sher
vegetarian	vegetariano	ve·je·ta·rya·no

Do you have (vegetarian) food?
Avete piatti (vegetariani)?   a·ve·te pya·tee (ve·je·ta·rya·nee)

I'm vegan.
Sono vegetaliano/a. m/f   so·no ve·je·ta·lya·no/a

I don't eat (fish).
Non mangio (pesce).   non man·jo (pe·she)

Is it cooked with (oil)?
È cotto con (olio)?   e ko·to kon (o·lyo)

Is this ...?	È ...?	e ...
cholesterol-free	senza	sen·tsa
	colesterolo	ko·le·ste·ro·lo
decaffeinated	decaffeinato/a m/f	de·ka·fey·na·to/a
free of animal	senza prodotti	sen·tsa pro·do·tee
produce	animali	a·nee·ma·lee
free-range	ruspante	roos·pan·te
genetically	geneticamente	je·ne·tee·ka·men·te
modified	modificato/a m/f	mo·dee·fee·ka·to/a
gluten-free	senza glutine	sen·tsa gloo·tee·ne
low fat/	a basso	a ba·so
sugar	contenuto	kon·te·noo·to
	lipidico/	lee·pee·dee·ko/
	glucosio	gloo·ko·zyo
organic	biologico/a m/f	bee·o·lo·jee·ko/a
salt-free	senza sale	sen·tsa sa·le

Could you	Potreste preparare	po·tres·te pre·pa·ra·re
prepare a meal	un pasto senza ...?	oon pas·to sen·tsa ...
without ...?		
butter	burro	boo·ro
eggs	uova	wo·va
meat/fish	brodo di carne/	bro·do dee kar·ne/
stock	pesce	pe·she
pork	carne di maiale	kar·ne dee ma·ya·le
poultry	pollame	po·la·me
red meat	carne rossa	kar·ne ro·sa

listen for ...

kon·tro·lo kon eel kwo·ko
Controllo con il cuoco. **I'll check with the cook.**

pwo man·ja·re ...
Può mangiare ...? **Can you eat ...?**

too·to kon·tye·ne (la kar·ne)
Tutto contiene (la carne). **It all has (meat) in it.**

special diets & allergies

diete speciali & allergie

I'm on a special diet.
Seguo una dieta speciale. se·gwo oo·na dye·ta spe·cha·le

I'm allergic	Sono	so·no
to ...	allergico/a ... m/f	a·ler·jee·ko/a ...
dairy produce	ai latticini	ai la·tee·chee·nee
eggs	alle uova	a·le wo·va
fish	al pesce	al pe·she
gelatin	alla gelatina	a·la je·la·tee·na
gluten	al glutine	al gloo·tee·ne
honey	al miele	al mye·le
MSG	al glutammato	al gloo·ta·ma·to
	monosodico	mo·no·so·dee·ko
nuts	alle noci	a·le no·chee
peanuts	alle arachidi	a·le a·ra·kee·dee
seafood	ai frutti di mare	ai froo·tee dee ma·re
shellfish	ai crostacei	ai kros·ta·che·ee

This miniguide to Italian cuisine is designed to help you navigate menus. Italian nouns, and adjectives affected by gender, have their gender indicated by ⓜ and/or ⓕ. If it's a plural noun, you'll also see pl.

A

abbacchio ⓜ a·ba·kyo *young lamb*
— **alla cacciatora** a·la ka·cha·to·ra
lamb casserole with spices, white wine & anchovies
— **a scottadito** a·sko·ta·dee·to
lamb cutlets fried in oil

acciughe ⓕ pl a·choo·ge
anchovies (often preserved in salt)

aceto ⓜ a·che·to *vinegar*

acquacotta ⓕ a·kwa·ko·ta
soup prepared with tomato, peppers, celery, eggs, artichokes or mushrooms

acquapazza ⓕ a·kwa·pa·tsa
'crazy water' – a type of fish soup

aglio ⓜ a·lyo *garlic*
— **e olio** ⓜ e o·lyo
garlic & olive oil pasta sauce

agnello ⓜ a·nye·lo *lamb*
— **ai funghi** ai foon·gee
with mushrooms
— **al forno** al for·no
with garlic & sometimes potatoes
— **da latte** da la·te
very young milk-fed lamb

agnolini ⓜ pl a·nyo·lee·nee *round pasta stuffed with stewed beef, eggs, cheese & other ingredients*

agnolotti ⓜ pl **ripieni** a·nyo·lo·tee
ree·pye·nee *pasta stuffed with meat, herbs, eggs & parmesan*

agro, all' ag·ro, al
with oil & lemon dressing

albicocca ⓕ al·bee·ko·ka *apricot*

alborella ⓕ al·bo·re·la
common freshwater fish

alici ⓕ pl a·lee·chee *anchovies*
— **a crudo** a kroo·do
raw, marinated in oil & spices

al dente al den·te *'to the tooth' – describes cooked pasta & rice that are still slightly hard*

all'/alla ... al/a·la ... *in the style of ...*

alloro ⓜ a·lo·ro *bay leaf*

al sangue al san·gwe *rare (cooked)*

amaretti ⓜ pl a·ma·re·tee
almond biscuits (macaroons)

amatriciana a·ma·tree·cha·na, al
spicy sauce with salami, tomato, capsicums & cheese

ananas ⓜ a·na·nas *pineapple*

anatra ⓕ a·na·tra *duck*
— **al sale** al sa·le
roast duck cooked in a crust of salt

angiulottus ⓜ an·joo·lo·toos
stuffed square pasta served with meat sauce or tomato sauce

anguilla ⓕ an·gwee·la *eel*

anice ⓜ a·nee·che *aniseed*

annoglia ⓕ a·no·lya
dry-cured pork sausage with chilli

anolini ⓜ pl a·no·lee·nee *stuffed round pasta with braised beef, cheese, parmesan, egg & breadcrumbs*

aragosta ⓕ a·ra·go·sta *lobster • crayfish*

arancia ⓕ a·ran·cha *orange*

arancia, all' a·ran·cha, al
sprinkled or baked with orange juice

arancini ⓜ pl a·ran·chee·nee *rice-balls stuffed with a meat mixture*

aranzada ⓕ a·ran·tsa·da *almond nougat*

arborio ⓜ ar·bo·ryo
short-grain rice used for risotto

aringa ⓕ a·reen·ga *herring*

arista ⓕ a·ree·sta *loin – generally pork*
— **alla fiorentina** a·la fyo·ren·tee·na
baked with spices

aromi ⓜ pl a·ro·mee *herbs*

arrabbiata, all' a·ra·bya·ta, al
'angry-style' – with spicy sauce

arrosticini ⓜ a·ros·tee·chee·nee
  *skewered & roasted meat – often
  lamb*
arrosto/a ⓜ/ⓕ a·ro·sto/a *roasted*
  — **alla griglia** a·la gree·lya *barbecued*
artigianale ar·tee·ja·na·le *home-made*
asiago ⓜ a·zya·go *hard white cheese*
asparagi ⓜ pl as·pa·ra·jee *asparagus*
aspro/a ⓜ/ⓕ as·pro/a *sour*

B

babà ⓜ ba·ba
  dessert containing sultanas
baccalà ⓜ ba·ka·la *dried salted cod*
  — **alla pizzaiola** a·la pee·tsa·yo·la
  with a tomato sauce
  — **mantecato** man·te·ka·to
  mixed to a puree
baci ⓜ pl ba·chee *'kisses' – type of
  chocolate • type of pastry or biscuit*
bagnetto ba·nye·to ver·de
  parsley & garlic sauce
barbabietola ⓕ bar·ba·bye·to·la
  beetroot
basilico ⓜ ba·zee·lee·ko *basil*
batsoà ⓜ bat·so·a
  boned, boiled & fried pig's trotters
battuto ⓜ ba·too·to
  *soup or meat seasoning prepared
  with lard & vegetables*
bavetta ⓕ ba·ve·ta *long, thick pasta*
bel paese ⓜ bel pa·e·ze
  soft, creamy cheese
besciamella ⓕ be·sha·me·la
  bechamel sauce
bescó'cc ⓜ bes·koch
  almond biscuits soaked in grappa
bianchetti ⓜ pl byan·ke·tee
  whitebait fried in oil
bianco d'uovo byan·ko dwo·vo
  egg white
bigné ⓜ bee·nye *cream puff*
bigoli ⓜ pl bee·go·lee
  thick, wholemeal flour spaghetti
bisció'la ⓕ bee·sho·la
  cake with nuts, dried figs & raisins
biscotti ⓜ pl bees·ko·tee *biscuits*
biscó'cc ⓜ bees·koch *see* bescó'cc
bisi ⓜ pl bee·zee *peas*

bistecca ⓕ bees·te·ka *steak*
  — **alla fiorentina** a·la fyo·ren·tee·na
  tasty, thick loin steak with its bone
bitto ⓜ bee·to *cow's milk cheese*
blanc manger ⓜ blank man·je *sweet
  white dessert with milk, sugar & vanilla*
bocconcini ⓜ pl bo·kon·chee·nee
  *tiny portions of mozzarella • can
  refer to anything bite-sized*
boghe ⓕ bo·ge een
  ska·be·sho *marinated, floured fish,
  browned in oil*
bollito bo·lee·to *boiled*
bollito (Bú'i) ⓜ bo·lee·to (boo·ee)
  mixed boiled meat with various sauces
bomba ⓕ **di riso** bom·ba dee ree·zo
  *baked rice with stewed pigeon, eggs,
  mushrooms, truffles & sausage*
bombas ⓕ bom·bas
  stewed veal meatballs
bonèt ⓜ bo·net
  *baked pudding of macaroons, cocoa,
  coffee, marsala & rum*
bostrengo ⓜ bos·tren·go
  *cake prepared with boiled rice,
  chocolate, sugar, spices & pine nuts*
boudin ⓜ boo·deen *blood sausage*
bra ⓕ bra *mild cheese*
braciola ⓕ bra·cho·la *chop • cutlet*
braciolone napoletano ⓜ bra·cho·lo·ne
  na·po·le·ta·no *steak rolled & filled with
  bacon, provolone & other ingredients*
branzi ⓜ pl bran·dzee *soft table cheese*
branzino ⓕ bran·dzee·no *sea bass*
brasato ⓜ bra·za·to *beef marinated in red
  wine & spices, then stewed*
brasare bra·za·re *to cook slowly*
brioche ⓕ bree·osh *breakfast pastry*
brochat ⓜ bro·shat
  *sweet, thick cream made with milk,
  wine & sugar & eaten with rye bread*
brodetto di pesce bro·de·to dee pe·she
  fish soup
brodo ⓜ bro·do *broth*
brôs ⓜ broos
  *creamy paste made from older
  cheese with herbs, spices & grappa*
bruschetta ⓕ broos·ke·ta *stale bread
  sliced, toasted, rubbed with garlic &
  flavoured with salt, pepper & olive oil*

bruscitt ⓜ broo·*sheet*
beef pieces cooked with red wine &
served with polenta or mashed potatoes

brutti ma buoni ⓜ pl
broo·tee ma bwo·nee
'ugly but good' – hazelnut macaroons

bucatini ⓜ pl boo·ka·*tee*·nee
long hollow tubes of pasta

buccellato ⓜ **di Lucca** boo·che·*la*·to dee
loo·ka traditional ring-shaped cake

budino ⓜ boo·*dee*·no
milk-based pudding

bugie ⓕ pl boo·*jee*·e 'lies' – small ribbons
of sweet pastry covered with icing sugar

burro ⓜ *boo*·ro butter

burtléina ⓕ boort·*lay*·na
little omelette prepared with water,
flour, lard & onion, served with salami

busecca ⓕ boo·ze·ka tripe

bussolà ⓜ **vicentino**
boo·so·*la* vee·chen·*tee*·no
sponge cake based dessert

C

caciotta ⓕ ka·*cho*·ta
semi-soft mild cheese

cacciucco ⓜ **(alla livornese)**
ka·*choo*·ko (a·la lee·vor·*ne*·ze) fish
soup with at least five kinds of fish

cacio ⓜ *ka*·cho
cheese in general • a creamy cheese

caciocavallo ⓜ ka·cho·ka·va·lo hard
cow's milk cheese from southern Italy

cacioricotta ⓕ ka·cho·ree·*ko*·ta
small round cheese made from cow/
sheep/goat's milk curd

caciuni ⓜ pl ka·*choo*·nee
big ravioli or puff pastry filled with egg
yolks, cheeses, sugar & lemon peel

caffè ⓜ ka·*fe* coffee (also see page 152)

calamari ⓜ pl ka·la·*ma*·ree
calamari • squid

calhiettes ⓜ **tradizionali** ka·*lyet*
tra·dee·tsyo·na·lee mixture of raw,
grated potatoes, left-over meat,
minced lard, onion, flour & eggs
mixed & boiled, normally used to
prepare dumplings & omelettes

calzone ⓜ kal·*tso*·ne
fried or baked flat bread made with
two thin sheets of pasta stuffed with
any number of ingredients

canederli ⓜ pl ka·ne·der·le·
big dumplings made with stale bread,
speck & other ingredients such as
liver, cheese, spinach or dried prunes

cannaroni ⓜ pl ka·na·ro·nee
large pasta tubes

cannella ⓕ ka·ne·la cinnamon

cannelloni ⓜ pl ka·ne·*lo*·nee
tubes of pasta stuffed with spinach,
minced roast veal, ham, eggs,
parmesan & spices

cannoli ⓜ pl **(ripieni)** ka·no·lee
(ree·pye·nee) sweet pastry tubes filled
with a mixture of sugar, candied fruit,
sweet ricotta & other ingredients

cantarelli ⓜ pl kan·ta·re·lee
chanterelle mushrooms

cantucci ⓜ pl kan·too·chee
crunchy, hard biscuits made with
aniseed & almonds

capasante ⓕ pl ka·pa·san·te scallops

capocollo ⓜ ka·po·ko·lo dry-cured pork
sausage washed with red wine

capelli ⓜ pl **d'angelo** ka·pe·lee
dan·je·lo 'angel's hair' – long, thin
strands of pasta

cappellacci ⓜ pl **di zucca** ka·pe·*la*·chee
dee *tsoo*·ka small pasta, filled with
pumpkin & parmesan

cappelletti ⓜ pl ka·pe·*le*·tee
similar to **tortellini**, only larger

cappello ⓜ **da prete** ka·pe·lo da pre·te
boiled lower part of the pig's trotter,
served with salsa verde or mustard

capperi ⓜ pl *ka*·pe·ree capers

cappon ⓜ **magro** ka·pon ma·gro
salad with vegetables, fish & shellfish,
dressed with a rich green sauce

capra ⓕ *ka*·pra goat • goat's cheese

caprese ⓕ ka·pre·ze salad with
tomato, basil & **mozzarella**

capretto ⓜ ka·pre·to *kid (goat)*

caprino ⓜ ka·pree·no *tart goat cheese often mixed at the table into a paste*

carbonada ⓕ kar·bo·na·da *diced, salted beef cooked in red wine*

carbonara kar·bo·na·ra, a·la *pasta sauce with egg, cheese & pancetta*

carciofi ⓜ pl kar·cho·fee *artichokes*

cardoncelli ⓜ pl kar·don·che·lee *type of mushroom, similar to oyster mushrooms*

carnaroli ⓜ pl kar·na·ro·lee *short grain rice used for risotto*

carne ⓕ kar·ne *meat*
   — **equina** e·kwee·na *horse meat*
   — **suina** swee·na *pork*
   — **trita/tritata** tree·ta/tree·ta·ta *mince meat*

carota ⓕ ka·ro·ta *carrot*

carpa ⓕ kar·pa *carp*

carpaccio ⓜ kar·pa·cho *very thin slices of raw meat*

carpione ⓜ kar·pyo·ne *fried fish preserved in a marinade of oil & spices*

carta ⓕ **da musica** kar·ta da moo·zee·ka *thin & very crunchy bread*

cartoccio ⓜ kar·to·cho *cooking method where fish, chicken or game are tightly wrapped in tinfoil & baked*

cascà ⓕ **di carloforte** kas·ka dee kar·lo·for·te *couscous with vegetables, minced meat & spices*

câsonséi ⓜ pl ka·zon·say *rectangles of pasta usually stuffed with parmesan, vegetables & sausage*

cassata ⓕ ka·sa·ta *ice cream or sponge cake stuffed with sweet ricotta, vanilla, chocolate, pistachios, candied fruit & liqueur*

cassola ⓕ ka·so·la *fish-soup with tomato sauce & herbs*

casoncelli ⓜ pl ka·zon·che·lee *pasta stuffed with meat and, depending on the region, spinach, eggs, raisins, almond biscuits, cheese or breadcrumbs*

castagnaccio ⓜ ka·sta·nya·cho *cake made with chestnut flour & sprinkled with pine nuts & rosemary*

castagne ⓕ pl ka·sta·nye *chestnuts*

castelmagno ⓜ ka·stel·ma·nyo *nutty blue cheese*

casunzei ⓜ pl ka·zoon·say *kind of ravioli stuffed with pumpkin or spinach, ham & cinnamon – served with smoked ricotta*

caulada ⓕ kow·la·da *cabbage-based soup with meat, mint & garlic*

cavallucci ⓜ pl ka·va·loo·chee *white sweets made with candied orange, nuts & spices*

cavatelli ⓜ pl ka·va·te·lee *small, round home-made pasta – often served with tomato sauce, oil & rocket*

cavolo ⓜ ka·vo·lo *cabbage*

cavolfiore ⓜ ka·vol·fyo·re *cauliflower*

cazzimperio ⓜ ka·tseem·pe·ree·o *fresh & crunchy vegetables dunked into a tasty sauce*

cazzmar ⓜ kats·mar *sliced sausage containing lamb's entrails, liver & giblets*

cecenielli ⓜ pl che·che·nye·lee *very small fish that can be fried or put on pizzas*

ceci ⓜ pl che·chee *chickpeas*

cefalo ⓜ che·fa·lo *mullet*

cervello ⓜ cher·ve·lo *brain*

cervo ⓜ cher·vo *venison*

cevapcici ⓜ pl che·vap·chee·chee *spicy fresh pork, beef or lamb sausages*

chenella ⓕ ke·ne·la *meatballs (sometimes fishballs)*

chinulille ⓕ pl kee·noo·lee·le *ravioli stuffed with sugar, ricotta, egg yolks, fried lemon & orange peel*

chiodino ⓜ kyo·dee·no *honey coloured fungus – mushroom that must be cooked*

ciabatta ⓕ cha·ba·ta *crisp, flat & long bread*

cialzons ⓜ pl chal·tsons *ravioli stuffed with ricotta, spinach, sultanas, chocolate & sometimes chicken & herbs*

ciambelle ⓕ pl **al mosto** cham·be·le al mos·to *ring-shaped cakes made with grape must*

ciammotta ① cha·mo·ta
mixed vegetable-fry

cianfotta ① chan·fo·ta
stew with vegetables, garlic & basil

ciaudedda ① chow·de·da
vegetable stew with artichokes,
onions & potatoes

ciavarro ⓜ cha·va·ro spring soup made
with cereals & legumes

cibuddau ⓜ chee·boo·da·oo
onion-based dish

cicala ① chee·ka·la crustacean

ciccioli ⓜ pl chee·cho·lee
tasty pieces of crispy fat

ciceri ⓜ pl **e tria** ① chee·che·ree e
tree·a dish of boiled chickpeas &
pasta, served with onions

cicirata ① chee·chee·ra·ta small, sweet
balls fried & covered with honey

ciliegia ① chee·lee·e·ja cherry

cima ① chee·ma breast, normally veal

cime ① **di rapa** chee·me dee ra·pa
turnip tops

cioccolato ⓜ cho·ko·la·to chocolate
— **fondente** fon·den·te
cooking chocolate

cipollata ① chee·po·la·ta
dish with pork, spare ribs, stale bread
& a lot of white onion

cipolle ① pl chee·po·le onions
— **ripiene** ree·pye·ne
stuffed half onions
— **selvatiche** sel·va·tee·ke
wild onions

coccois ⓜ ko·ko·ees flat bread made
with salty cheese & crackling

cocomero ⓜ ko·ko·me·ro watermelon

coda ① ko·da tail • angler fish

cognà ⓜ ko·nya
apple, pear, fig & grape sauce

coietas ① pl ko·ye·tas roulades made
with savoy cabbage & meat sauce

colombo/a ⓜ/① ko·lom·bo/a
dove • pigeon • type of cake

conchiglie ① pl kon·kee·lye
pasta shells

condimento ⓜ kon·dee·men·to dressing

confetti ⓜ pl kon·fe·tee
sugar-coated almonds

coniglio ⓜ ko·nee·lyo rabbit

conserva ① kon·ser·va preserve
— **di pomodoro** dee po·mo·do·ro
traditional tomato sauce

cornetto ⓜ kor·ne·to breakfast pastry

coscia ① ko·sha leg • haunch

costata ① kos·ta·ta beef steak (rib)
— **alla napoletana** a·la na·po·le·ta·na
with oil, tomato sauce, oregano,
garlic & white wine
— **di manzo alla pizzaiola**
dee man·dzo a·la pee·tsa·yo·la
with garlic, oil, tomatoes & oregano

costine ① pl kos·tee·ne ribs
— **di maiale** dee ma·ya·le
pork spare ribs grilled on stone

costoletta ① kos·to·le·ta veal cutlet

cotechinata ① ko·te·kee·na·ta roulade
of pig rind stuffed with garlic, parsley
& lard cooked with tomato sauce

cotechino ⓜ ko·te·kee·no
boiled pork sausage
— **in galera** een ga·le·ra
'in prison' – meatloaf stuffed with
a boiled **cotechino**

cotoletta ① ko·to·le·ta
(veal) cutlet usually breaded & fried
— **alla bolognese** a·la bo·lo·nye·ze
breaded veal cutlet sauteed with
butter & baked with cured ham &
fresh parmesan
— **alla milanese** a·la mee·la·ne·ze
veal loin steak breaded & fried in
butter

cotto/a ⓜ/① ko·to/ta cooked
ben — ben well done
non troppo — non tro·po medium rare
poco — po·ko rare

cozze ① pl ko·tse mussels

crema ① **inglese** kre·ma een·gle·ze
custard

cren ⓜ kren horseradish

crescenza ① kre·shen·tsa
fresh, soft cheese, see **stracchino**

crespella ① kres·pe·la thin fritter

crespelle ① pl **bagnate** kres·pe·le
ba·nya·te pasta with savoury filling
served in chicken stock

crocchette ⓕ pl kro·*ke*·te *croquettes of mashed potatoes & various ingredients*

crostacei ⓜ pl kro·*sta*·chay *crustaceans*

crostata ⓕ kro·*sta*·ta *fruit tart • crust*

crostini ⓜ pl kro·*stee*·nee *slices of bread toasted with savoury toppings*

crostoi ⓜ kro·*stoy* *little fritters with sweet or savoury fillings*

crostoli ⓜ pl kro·*sto*·lee *fried sweet pastry with icing sugar • small flat bread*

crucetta ⓕ kroo·*che*·ta *sweet made with figs stuffed with nuts & arranged as a cross*

crudo/a ⓜ/ⓕ *kroo*·do/a *raw*

crumiri ⓜ pl kroo·*mee*·ree *type of dry biscuits*

crusca ⓕ *kroos*·ka *bran*

culatello ⓜ **(di Busseto)** koo·la·*te*·lo (dee boo·*se*·to) *ham made of salted & spiced pig's rump*

culingiones ⓜ pl koo·leen·*jo*·nes *kind of ravioli stuffed with potatoes or chard, sheep's cheese, garlic & mint*

cupeta ⓕ koo·*pe*·ta *nougat stuffed between two wafers*

cuscus ⓜ koos·koos *couscous*

cutturiddi ⓜ pl koo·too·*ree*·dee *lamb stew with chilli, tomatoes, small onions & celery*

D

di/d' ... dee/d ... *from ...*

datteri ⓜ pl *da*·te·ree *dates (fruit)*
— **di mare** dee *ma*·re *type of mussel*

della casa *de*·la *ka*·za *'of the house' – house speciality*

diavola, alla *dya*·vo·la, *a*·la *spicy dish*

diavolicchio ⓜ dya·vo·*lee*·kyo *dynamite chilli*

ditali(ni) ⓜ pl dee·*ta*·lee/dee·ta·*lee*·nee *small bits of pasta often used in soups*

dolce *dol*·che *dessert • sweet • soft*

dolcelatte ⓜ dol·che·*la*·te *soft mild blue cheese*

dolcetti ⓜ pl **di pasta di mandorle** dol·*che*·tee dee *pas*·ta dee man·*dor*·le *traditional sweets made with marzipan, sugar & egg whites*

E

erbazzone ⓜ er·ba·*tso*·ne *baked pasta stuffed with spinach, lard, spices, parmesan, eggs & parsley*
— **dolce** *dol*·che *sweet baked shortcrust pastry filled with boiled & chopped chards mixed with* **ricotta**, *sugar & almonds*

erbe ⓕ pl *er*·be *herbs*

F

fagiano ⓜ fa·*ja*·no *pheasant*

fagioli ⓜ pl fa·*jo*·lee *beans – usually dried*

fagiolini ⓜ pl fa·jo·*lee*·nee *green beans*

false salsicce ⓕ *fal*·se sal·*see*·che *'false sausages' – sausages made with lard & potatoes & coloured with beet*

farcito ⓜ far·*chee*·to *stuffed food*

farfalle ⓕ pl far·*fa*·le *butterfly-shaped pasta*

farina ⓕ fa·*ree*·na *flour*

farinata ⓕ fa·ree·*na*·ta *thin, flat bread made from chickpea flour*

farro ⓜ *fa*·ro *spelt – an ancient grain*

fasoi ⓜ pl **col muset** fa·*zoy* kol myoo·*zet* *dish with dried beans, sausage, pork rind & spices*

fatto/a ⓜ/ⓕ *fa*·to/a *made*
— **a mano** a *ma*·no *made by hand*
— **in casa** een *ka*·za *home-made • made on the premises*

favata ⓕ fa·*va*·ta *rustic dish of broad beans, lard, pork, sausages, tomatoes & herbs*

fave ⓕ pl *fa*·ve *broad beans*

fegato ⓜ *fe*·ga·to *liver*

felino ⓜ fe·*lee*·no *type of salami*

ferri, ai *fe*·ree, ai *grilled on an open fire*

fesa ⓕ *fe*·za *northern Italian word for veal*

fetta ⓕ *fe*·ta *a slice of meat, cheese, etc*

fettuccine ⓕ pl fe·too·*chee*·ne *long ribbon-shaped pasta*
— **alla romana** *a*·la ro·*ma*·na *'Roman-style' – served with meat sauce, mushrooms & sheep's cheese*

fiadoni ⓜ pl **alla trentina** fya·do·nee a·la tren·tee·na *little sweets stuffed with almonds, honey, cinnamon & rum*

fiandolein ⓜ fyan·do·layn *'egg flip' made with yolks, milk, sugar & lemon peel*

fico ⓜ fee·ko *fig*

filoncino ⓜ fee·lon·chee·no *breadstick*

finanziera ⓕ fee·nan·tsye·ra *sweetbreads, mushrooms & chicken livers in a creamy sauce*

finocchio ⓜ fee·no·kyo *fennel*

fior di latte ⓕ fyor dee *la*·te *fresh & very soft cheese • a gelato flavour*

fiori ⓜ pl fyo·ree *flowers – some, especially zucchini flowers, are commonly eaten* — **di zucca farciti** dee tsoo·ka far·chee·tee *stuffed, fried zucchini or squash flowers*

focaccia ⓕ fo·ka·cha *flat bread often filled/topped with cheese, ham, vegetables & other ingredients*

foglia ⓕ **d'alloro** fo·lya da·lo·ro *bay leaf*

fondo ⓜ fon·do *stock*

fondua ⓕ fon·doo·a *fontina cheese melted with butter & eggs & topped with thin slices of truffle*

fontina ⓕ fon·tee·na *sweet & creamy cheese, similar to Gruyère*

formaggio ⓜ for·ma·jo *cheese*

forno, al for·no, al *cooked in an oven*

fragole ⓕ pl fra·go·le *strawberries*

freddo/a ⓜ/ⓕ fre·do/a *cold (temperature)*

fresco/a ⓜ/ⓕ fres·ko/a *fresh*

fregola ⓕ fre·go·la *type of couscous*

fregnacce ⓕ pl fre·nya·che *thin rolled pancakes stuffed with meat*

frisceu ⓜ free·she·oo *fritters with lettuce, whitebait, zucchini, liver, brain, dried cod, pumpkin, etc*

frisedde ⓕ free·ze·de *big ring-shaped cakes, boiled, baked then served with tomatoes, oil, salt & oregano*

fritole ⓕ pl free·to·le *fritters containing sultanas, pine nuts, candied lemon & liqueur*

frittata ⓕ free·ta·ta *thick omelette slice, served hot or cold*

frittatensuppe ⓕ pl free·ta·ten·soo·pe *thin omelettes cut into strips & served with meat stock*

frittatine ⓕ pl **di farina al miele di fichi** free·ta·tee·ne dee fa·ree·na al mye·le dee fee·kee *pancakes folded & stuffed with fig honey*

frittelle ⓕ pl free·te·le *fritters*

frittelloni ⓜ pl free·te·lo·nee *boiled spinach tortellini sautéed with butter, sultanas & cheese, then fried in lard*

fritto/a ⓜ/ⓕ free·to/a *fried*

frito ⓜ **misto** free·to mees·to *a mixture of various ingredients, depending on the region & time of year, fried in olive oil (some versions contain offal)* — **abruzzese** a·broo·tse·ze *diced artichokes & boiled fennel, breaded & fried*

frumento ⓜ froo·men·to *wheat*

frutta ⓕ froo·ta *fruit* — **secca** se·ka *dried fruit*

frutti ⓜ pl **di mare** froo·tee dee ma·re *sea food*

fugazza ⓕ foo·ga·tsa *very rich, tasty sweet pastry*

funghi ⓜ pl foon·gee *mushrooms*

fusilli ⓜ pl foo·zee·lee *corkscrew shaped pasta*

G

galani ⓜ pl ga·la·nee *layered strips of fried pastry sprinkled with icing sugar*

gallina ⓕ ga·lee·na *chicken • hen*

gambero ⓜ gam·be·ro *prawn • shrimp*

gamberoni ⓜ pl gam·be·ro·nee *prawns*

gambon ⓜ gam·bon *pig's leg, boned, pressed & matured*

garagoli ⓜ pl ga·ra·go·lee *shellfish similar to periwinkles*

garganelli ⓜ pl gar·ga·ne·lee *short pasta served with various sauces*

gattò ⓜ **di patate e salsiccia** ga·to dee pa·ta·te e sal·see·cha *baked meatloaf made with mashed potato, eggs, ham & cheeses*

gelato ⓜ je·la·to *ice cream*

genovese, alla je·no·ve·ze, a·la *sauce including olive oil, garlic & herbs*

gerstensuppe ⓕ ger·sten·soo·pe *barley-soup with onions, parsley, spices & speck*

gianduiotto ⓜ jyan·doo·yo·to *hazelnut chocolate*

giardiniera ⓕ jar·dee·nye·ra *pickled vegetables*

girello ⓜ jee·re·lo *round cut of meat*

gnocchi ⓜ pl nyo·kee *small dumplings – most commonly potato dumplings*

gnocchetti ⓜ pl nyo·ke·tee *small shell-shaped pasta*

gnocco di pane (al prosciutto) nyo·ko dee pa·ne (al pro·shoo·to) *pieces of bread fried in a mixture of butter, eggs, milk (& ham)*

goregone ⓜ go·re·go·ne *freshwater lake fish*

gorgonzola ⓕ gor·gon·dzo·la *spicy, sweet, creamy blue vein cow's milk cheese*

grana (padano) gra·na (pa·da·no) *hard cheese, also refers to cheeses such as* **parmigiano**

granchio ⓜ gran·kyo *crab*

granita ⓕ gra·nee·ta *finely crushed flavoured ice*

granseola ⓕ gran·se·o·la *spider crab*

grano ⓜ gra·no *wheat*

gran(o)turco ⓜ gra·n(o)·toor·ko *maize*

grappa ⓕ gra·pa *distilled grape must*

grissini ⓜ pl gree·see·nee *breadsticks*

guanciale ⓜ gwan·cha·le *cheek, usually pig's*

gubana ⓕ goo·ba·na *sweet pastry*

I

impanada ⓕ eem·pa·na·da *savoury tart stuffed with vegetables & many kinds of meat & fish*

impepata di cozze eem·pe·pa·ta dee ko·tse *fish-based dish prepared with mussels & lemon*

infarinata ⓕ een·fa·ree·na·ta *polenta as a soup, or fried in strips, with various meat & vegetable combinations*

insalata ⓕ een·sa·la·ta *salad*
— **caprese** ka·pre·ze *with* **mozzarella**, *tomato & basil*
— **di carne cruda** dee kar·ne kroo·da *with raw minced meat*

involtini ⓜ pl een·vol·tee·nee *stuffed rolls of meat or fish*
— **di carne** dee kar·ne *small veal slices, rolled up, stuffed, pierced on kebabs & baked or grilled*
— **siciliani** see·chee·lya·nee *meat rolled in breadcrumbs, stuffed with egg, ham & cheese*

J

jota ⓕ yo·ta *soup with beans, milk, & polenta • soup with beans, potatoes, sauerkraut & smoked pork rinds*

L

laganelle e fagioli la·ga·ne·le e fa·jo·le·dee *sheets of pasta served in a bean soup*

lamponi ⓜ pl lam·po·nee *raspberries*

lasagne ⓕ pl la·za·nye *flat sheets of egg pasta*
— **alla bolognese** a·la bo·lo·nye·ze *baked lasagne with meat sauce, bechamel & parmesan*

lattuga ⓕ la·too·ga *lettuce*

lavarelli ⓜ pl la·va·re·lee *fresh water whitefish*

lecca-lecca ⓕ le·ka le·ka *lollipop*

lenticchie ⓕ pl len·tee·kye *lentils*

lepre ⓜ lep·re *hare*

lesso/a ⓜ/ⓕ le·so *boiled*

liscio/a ⓜ/ⓕ lee·sho/a *smooth – describes pasta with a smooth surface*

lianeddè ⓕ pl lya·ne·de *noodles with chickpeas or rabbit sauce*

lievito ⓜ lye·vee·to *yeast*

limone ⓜ lee·mo·ne *lemon*

lingua ⓕ leen·gwa *tongue*

linguine ⓕ pl leen·gwee·ne *long thin ribbons of pasta*

luccio ⓜ loo·cho *pike*

luganega ① loo·ga·ne·ga *pork sausage*

luganiga di verze ① loo·ga·nee·ga dee ver·dze *cabbage sausage stuffed with mince, cheese, eggs & breadcrumbs*

lumache ① pl loo·ma·ke *snails*

luppoli ⓜ pl loo·po·lee *hops*

M

maccaruni ⓜ pl **di casa con ragù** ma·ka·roo·nee dee ka·za kon ra·goo *small pasta tubes served with tomato & meat sauce*

maccheroni ⓜ ma·ke·ro·nee *can refer to any tube pasta*
— **alla chitarra** a·la kee·ta·ra *square spaghetti, generally served with a meat sauce*
— **con la ricotta** kon la ree·ko·ta *pasta served with ricotta, sheep's cheese & sometimes also parmesan*

magro/a ⓜ/① mag·ro/a *thin • lean • meatless*

maturo/a ⓜ/① ma·too·ro/a *ripe*

maiale ⓜ ma·ya·le *pork*

mais ⓜ ma·eez *maize*

malfatti ⓜ pl mal·fa·tee *dumplings with spinach, eggs & cheese*

malloreddus ⓜ pl ma·lo·re·doos *dumplings with saffron in a meat sauce*

maltagliati ⓜ pl mal·ta·lya·tee *odd shapes of pasta*

mandorle ① pl man·dor·le *almonds*

manteca ① man·te·ka *fresh cheese rolled in a ball and stuffed with butter*

mantecato ⓜ man·te·ka·to *any ingredients pounded to a paste*

manzo ⓜ man·dzo *beef*

maraschino ⓜ ma·ras·kee·no *cherry liqueur*

marcetto ⓜ mar·che·to *very spicy cheese paste*

marille ① ma·ree·le *crazily-shaped pasta designed to retain the maximum amount of sauce*

marinara, alla ma·ree·na·ra, a·la *dish containing seafood*

maritozzi ⓜ pl ma·ree·to·tsee *small, soft sweet cakes stuffed with pine nuts, sultanas, orange peel & fruit*

marrone ⓜ ma·ro·ne *large chestnut*

marsala ① mar·sa·la *fortified wine*

marubini ⓜ pl ma·roo·bee·nee *pasta stuffed with toasted bread, parmesan, marrow & eggs*

mascarpone ⓜ mas·kar·po·ne *very soft & creamy cheese*

maturo/a ⓜ/① ma·too·ro/a *ripe*

mazzafegato ① pl ma·tsa·fe·ga·to *matured dry-cured pork sausage, made with minced liver, kidney, tripe & lung*

mela ① me·la *apple*

melagrana ① me·la·gra·na *pomegranate*

melanzanata ① **(di Lecce)** me·lan·dza·na·ta (dee le·che) *eggplant pasta sauce • baked eggplant, tomato, onion, basil & sheep's cheese*

melanzane ① pl me·lan·dza·ne *eggplants • aubergines*
— **ripiene** ree·pye·ne *baked eggplants stuffed with their pulp, eggs, cheese, herbs, spices & bread*
— **violette** vee·o·le·te *purple eggplant*

meringa ① me·reen·ga *meringue*

merlano ① mer·la·no *whiting*

merluzzo ⓜ mer·loo·tso *cod*

mesta ⓜ **e fasoi** ⓜ pl mes·ta e fa·zoy *polenta cooked with beans*

miele ⓜ mye·le *honey*

migliaccio ⓜ **'e cigule** ① pl mee·lya·cho e chee·goo·le *baked polenta with pork, sausages, sheep's cheese & pepper*

milanese, alla mee·la·ne·ze, a·la *any sauce associated with Milan – normally includes butter*

millecosedde ⓜ mee·le·ko·ze·de *hearty soup with vegetables, legumes & short pasta*

minestra ① mee·ne·stra *general word for soup*
— **alla pignata** a·la pee·nya·ta *with beans, pork & vegetables*
— **cò i cece** ko ee che·che *with chickpeas & pasta*

minestrone ⓜ mee·ne·*stro*·ne
traditional soup usually including many vegetables & sometimes pasta or rice, bacon cubes & pork rinds

misticanza ⓕ mees·tee·*kan*·tsa
salad with mixed greens

misto/a ⓜ/ⓕ *mees*·to/a *mixed*

mollusco ⓜ mo·*loo*·sko *mollusc*

montasio ⓜ mon·*ta*·zyo *hard cheese*

montato/a ⓜ/ⓕ mon·*ta*·to/a *whipped*

morbido/a ⓜ/ⓕ *mor*·bee·do *soft*

mortadella ⓕ **(di Bologna)**
mor·ta·*de*·la (dee bo·*lo*·nya)
salami made with minced pork, lard & black pepper

mostaccioli ⓜ pl mos·ta·*cho*·lee *small, sweet, chocolate-coated biscuits*

mozzetta ⓕ mot·*tse*·ta *salami made with haunch of mountain-goat or chamois, salted & dried*

mozzarella ⓕ mo·tsa·*re*·la *soft, fresh white cheese made from cow's milk*
— di bufala dee boo·fa·la
made from buffalo's milk
— in carrozza een ka·*ro*·tsa
on slices of bread, battered & fried

'mpanada ⓕ m·pa·*na*·da see **impanada**

'mpepata ⓕ **di cozze** m·pe·*pa*·ta dee *ko*·tse see **impepata di cozze**

muggine ⓜ *moo*·jee·ne *mullet*

N

napoletana, alla na·po·le·*ta*·na, *a*·la
from or in the style of Naples – usually includes tomatoes & garlic

nasello ⓜ na·*ze*·lo *hake*

'ndugghia ⓕ n·*doo*·gya *dry-cured pork & fennel-seed sausage*

nero ⓜ **di seppia/calamaro** *ne*·ro dee se·pya/ka·la·*ma*·ro *squid/calamari ink*

nocciola ⓕ no·*cho*·la *hazelnut*

noce ⓕ *no*·che *nut • walnut*
— di cocco dee *ko*·ko *coconut*
— moscata mos·*ka*·ta *nutmeg*

norma, alla *nor*·ma, *a*·la
pasta sauce with eggplant & tomato

nostrano ⓜ nos·*tra*·no
hard cheese • local, home-made or domestic produce

O

oca ⓕ *o*·ka *goose*

offelle ⓕ pl o·*fe*·le
sweet biscuits with mixed dried fruit

olio ⓜ *o*·lyo
oil – almost always olive oil

ombrichelli ⓜ pl om·bree·*ke*·lee
coarse home-made spaghetti

opinus ⓜ o·pee·noos
pine-cone-shaped biscuits sprinkled with melted sugar & egg whites

orata ⓕ o·*ra*·ta *bream • gilthead*

orecchiette ⓕ pl o·re·kye·te
shell-shaped, hand-made pasta, served with vegetables & olive oil or a rich meat sauce

orzo ⓜ *or*·dzo *barley*
— e fagioli e fa·*jo*·lee
thick barley & bean broth

ossi di morti ⓜ pl o·see dee *mor*·tee
'bones of the dead' – very hard crunchy biscuits

ossobuco ⓜ o·so·*boo*·ko *veal shanks*
— milanese mee·la·*ne*·ze *cut into small pieces & cooked with spices*

ostriche ⓕ pl os·tree·ke *oysters*

P

pagnottella ⓕ pa·nyo·*te*·la *bread roll*

palle ⓕ pl *pa*·le *balls*
— del nonno del *no*·no
'grandpa's balls' – sweet fried ricotta balls • crinkly pork sausages
— di riso dee *ree*·zo
stuffed rice croquettes

palombo ⓜ pa·*lom*·bo *dove • pigeon*
— alla todina a·la to·*dee*·na
roasted pigeon

pan ⓜ **biscotto condito** pan bees·*ko*·to kon·*dee*·to *toasted bread with oil, tomatoes, herbs*

panadas ⓕ pl pa·*na*·das see **pancotto**

pancetta ⓕ pan·*che*·ta *salt-cured bacon*

pancotto ⓜ pan·*ko*·to
soup made with boiled bread, cheese & eggs or fresh tomatoes

pane ⓜ *pa*·ne bread
 — **all'olio** a·*lo*·lyo bread with oil
 — **aromatico** a·ro·ma·*tee*·ko herb or vegetable bread
 — **carasau** ka·ra·zow long-lasting bread eaten by shepherds
 — **casereccio** ka·ze·re·cho firm, floury loaf
 — **col mosto** kol *mos*·to bread with nuts, anise, almonds, raisins, sugar & must
 — **di segale** dee se·ga·le rye bread
 — **frattau** fra·tow slices of bread with sheep's cheese, tomato or meat sauce, boiling broth & eggs
 — **fresa** fre·za flat, crispy bread
 — **integrale** een·te·gra·le wholemeal bread
 — **pugliese** poo·*lye*·ze large, crusty loaf
 — **salato** sa·la·to salty bread
 — **toscano** tos·ka·no crumbly, unsalted bread
 — **unto** oon·to slices of bread toasted with garlic, olive oil, salt & pepper
panelle ⓘ pl pa·ne·le fried chickpea fritters
panforte ⓜ **(senese)** pan·for·te (se·ne·ze) hard cake made with almonds, fruit & spices
panino ⓜ pa·nee·no bread roll
paniscia ⓘ **novarese** pa·nee·sha no·va·re·ze rice-based dish with onion, sausage & soup
panna ⓘ *pa*·na cream
 — **cotta** ko·ta thick creamy dessert
panpepato ⓜ pan·pe·pa·to sweet, ring-shaped cake
pan ⓜ **speziale** pan spe·cha·le bread with honey, nuts, raisins & fruit
panzanella ⓘ pan·tsa·ne·la Tuscan bread served with tomato sauce, onion, lettuce, anchovies, basil, olive oil, vinegar & salt
panzerotti ⓜ pl pan·tse·ro·tee filled pasta or pastries in a half-moon shape

paparot ⓜ pa·pa·rot spinach & corn soup
papassinas ⓘ pl pa·pa·see·nas small, sweet cone-shaped cakes
pappa ⓘ *pa*·pa baby food
 — **col pomodoro** kol po·mo·*do*·ro soup made with thin slices of stale bread, tomatoes & spices
pappardelle ⓘ pl pa·par·de·le wide, flat pasta ribbons
 — **alla lepre** a·la le·pre with stewed hare, red wine & tomato sauce
parmigiana, alla par·mee·ja·na, a·la any type of cheesy sauce
parmigiana ⓘ **di melanzane** par·mee·ja·na dee me·lan·dza·ne fried eggplant layered with eggs, basil, tomato sauce, onion & **mozzarella**
parmigiano ⓜ **(reggiano)** par·mee·ja·no (re·ja·no) parmesan cheese and often simply called **grana**
parrozzo ⓜ pa·ro·tso sweet bread, sometimes chocolate coated
passatelli ⓜ pl pa·sa·te·lee small dumplings made with eggs, parmesan, ox marrow & nutmeg
pasta ⓘ *pas*·ta general name for the numerous types of pasta shapes • dough • pastry
 — **col bianchetto** kol byan·ke·to spaghetti with a whitebait, tomato, garlic & chilli sauce
 — **cresciuta** kre·shoo·ta anchovy or courgette flower fritters
 — **e fagioli** e fa·jo·lee bean soup with pasta
 — **fresca** fres·ka general term for freshly made pasta
pastasciutta ⓘ pas·ta·shoo·ta dry pasta
pastissada/pastizzada ⓘ pas·tee·sa·da/pas·tee·tsa·da stew prepared with beef, ox or horse meat & vegetables
patate ⓘ pl pa·ta·te potatoes
pecorino ⓜ **(romano)** pe·ko·ree·no (ro·ma·no) hard & spicy cheese made from ewe's milk
penne ⓘ pl pe·ne short & tubular pasta

pepe ⓜ *pe·pe* pepper

peperonata ⓕ *pe·pe·ro·na·ta*
capsicum, onion & tomato stew

peperoncini ⓜ pl *pe·pe·ron·chee·nee*
hot chilli

peperoni ⓜ pl *pe·pe·ro·nee*
peppers • capsicum

— **ripieni** *ree·pye·nee*
stuffed with various fillings

pere ⓕ pl *pe·ra* pears

— **imbottite** *eem·bo·tee·te*
baked stuffed pears

persico ⓜ *per·see·ko* perch

pesca ⓕ *pe·ska* peach

pesce ⓜ *pe·she* fish

pesto ⓜ *pes·to*
sauce prepared with fresh basil, pine
nuts, olive oil, garlic, cheese & salt

petto ⓜ *pe·to* breast

pettole ⓕ pl *pe·to·le* home-made, long
thin, ribbons of pasta

piadina ⓕ *pya·dee·na* flat round bread

piccagge ⓕ pl *pee·ka·je*
long ribbon pasta served with pesto
or an artichoke & mushroom sauce

piccata ⓕ *pee·ka·ta*
veal with a lemon & **Marsala** sauce

picchi pacchiu ⓜ *pee·kee pa·kyoo*
pasta sauce with tomato & chilli

pici ⓜ pl *pee·chee*
fresh pasta, like thick spaghetti

piccione ⓜ *pee·cho·ne* squab • pigeon

picula ⓕ **ad caval** *pee·koo·la ad ka·val*
horse meat stew

pinoli ⓜ pl *pee·no·lee* pine nuts

pinza ⓕ **padovana** *peen·tsa
pa·do·va·na* sweet pastry

pinzimonio ⓜ *peen·tsee·mo·nyo*
seasoned virgin olive oil for dipping
(see also **cazzimperio**)

pioparello ⓜ *pyo·pa·re·lo*
common flat mushroom

pisarei ⓜ pl **e fasó** ⓜ pl
pee·za·ray e fa·zo
small dumplings flavoured with
tomato sauce, bacon & boiled beans

piselli ⓜ pl *pee·ze·lee* green peas

pistum ⓜ *pees·toom* sweet & sour
dumplings served with pork stock

pitta ⓕ *pee·ta* soft & flat loaf of bread

pitte ⓕ *pee·te* fring-shaped cake

pizza ⓕ *pee·tsa*
there are more than 50 kinds of
pizza, with varying bases and toppings

— **a(l) taglio** *a(l) ta·lyo* slice of pizza

— **dolce di Pasqua**
dol·che dee pas·kwa
sweet pizza dough with dried fruits

— **Margherita** *mar·ge·ree·ta* topped
with simple ingredients such as oil,
tomato, **mozzarella**, basil & oregano

— **rustica** *roos·tee·ka*
topped with various combinations of
ham, salami, sausage, egg or cheese

pizzaiola, alla *pee·tsa·yo·la, a·la*
a tomato & oil sauce

pizzoccheri ⓜ pl *pee·tso·ke·ree*
short, buckwheat pasta with cabbage
& potatoes

polenta ⓕ *po·len·ta* corn meal porridge

— **al ragù** *al ra·goo*
served with a meat sauce

— **concia** *kon·cha*
flavoured with a variety of cheeses

— **e osei** *e o·zay*
served with sparrows, thrushes or
larks • sponge cake with jam

— **pasticciata** *pas·tee·cha·ta*
baked with meat sauce,
mushrooms & cheese

— **sulla spianatoria** *soo·la
spya·na·to·rya* with sausages, tomato
& sheep's cheese served from a
spianatoria (pastry board) placed in
the middle of the table

— **taragna** *ta·ra·nya*
originally buckwheat **polenta**

polipo ⓜ *po·lee·po* octopus (see **polpi**)

pollo ⓜ *po·lo* chicken

— **alla diavola** *a·la dya·vo·la*
grilled with red pepper or chilli

— **con peperoni e patate al coccio**
kon pe·pe·ro·nee e pa·ta·te al ko·cho
slowly cooked in a terracotta pot
with sage, potatoes & capsicum

polpette ⓜ pol·pe·te *meatballs*
polpettine ⓕ pl pol·pe·tee·ne
small meatballs
　— di carne con salsa di pomodoro
　dee kar·ne kon sal·sa dee
　po·mo·do·ro *in tomato sauce*
polpettone ⓜ pol·pe·to·ne *meatloaf*
polpi ⓜ pl pol·pee
octopus (also called **polipi***)*
　— alla luciana a·la loo·cha·na
　sliced octopus with tomatoes, oil,
　garlic, parsley & lemon
　— in purgatorio een poor·ga·to·ryo
　stewed with tomato, parsley,
　chilli & garlic
pomodori ⓜ pl po·mo·do·ree
tomatoes
　— secchi se·kee *sun-dried tomatoes*
pomodorini ⓜ pl po·mo·do·ree·nee
tiny tomatoes • *sun-dried tomatoes*
pompelmo ⓜ pom·pel·mo *grapefruit*
porchetta ⓕ por·ke·ta
stuffed suckling pig
porcini ⓜ pl por·chee·nee
ceps (type of mushrooms)
porco ⓜ por·ko *pig*
potizza ⓕ po·tee·tsa *soft cake prepared*
with leavened pastry
prataiolo ⓜ pra·ta·yo·lo
popular button mushroom
preboggion ⓜ pre·bo·jon
mixture of wild herbs
prosciutto ⓜ pro·shoo·to *basic name*
for many types of thinly-sliced ham
　— affumicato a·foo·mee·ka·to
　smoked salami
　— San Daniele san da·nye·le
　sweet & delicate ham
provola ⓕ pro·vo·la *semi-hard cheese*
made from buffalo & cow's milk
provolone ⓜ pro·vo·lo·ne *rich medium*
hard cheese made from cow's milk
prugna ⓕ proo·nya *plum*
puttanesca, alla poo·ta·ne·ska, a·la
'whore's style' – *tomato, chilli,*
anchovies & black olive pasta sauce

Q

quaglie ⓕ pl kwa·lye *quails*
quartirolo ⓜ kwar·tee·ro·lo
sweet & delicate soft cheese
quattro formaggi kwa·tro for·ma·jee
pasta sauce with four different
cheeses
quattro stagioni kwa·tro sta·jo·nee
pizza with different toppings on
each quarter

R

rabarbaro ⓜ ra·bar·ba·ro *rhubarb*
radicchio ⓜ ra·dee·kyo *chicory*
　— rosso ro·so *slightly bitter*
　vegetable with long leaves
rafano ⓜ **tedesco** ra·fa·no te·des·ko
horseradish
ragù ⓜ ra·goo *generally a meat sauce*
but sometimes vegetarian
　— alla bolognese a·la bo·lo·nye·ze
　sauce of minced veal & pork
　— alla napoletana a·la na·po·le·ta·na
　sauce made with chunks of meat,
　vegetables & red wine
rambasicci ⓜ pl ram·ba·zee·chee
stuffed cabbage leaves
rapa ⓕ ra·pa *turnip*
ravioli ⓜ pl ra·vee·o·lee *pasta squares*
usually stuffed with meat, parmesan
cheese & breadcrumbs
　— liguri lee·goo·ree
　sometimes filled with ricotta *& herbs*
raviolini ⓜ pl ra·vee·o·lee·nee
small ravioli
ravioloni ⓜ pl ra·vee·o·lo·nee
large ravioli
razza ⓕ ra·tsa *skate*
ri(so) ⓜ **in cagnon** ree(·zo) een ka·nyon
rice sauteed in garlic, butter, sage &
sprinkled with parmesan
ribes ⓜ **nero** ree·bes ne·ro *blackcurrant*
ribes ⓜ **rosso** ree·bes ro·so *redcurrant*
ribollita ⓕ ree·bo·lee·ta
reheated & thickened vegetable soup
ricciarelli ⓜ pl ree·cha·re·lee
almond biscuits

ricotta ① ree·ko·ta
fresh, moist, white cheese
— **affumicata** a·foo·mee·ka·ta
smoked
— **infornata** een·for·na·ta
oven baked

rigaglie ① pl ree·ga·lye giblets

rigatoni ⓜ pl ree·ga·to·nee
short, fat tubes of pasta
— **con la pagliata** kon la pa·lya·ta
served with small intestines of calves

ripieno ⓜ ree·pye·no stuffing

risi ⓜ pl **e bisi** ⓜ pl ree·zee e bee·zee
thick rice-based soup with peas

risi ⓜ pl **e bruscandoli** ⓜ pl ree·zee e
broos·kan·do·lee bitter hop sprouts
cooked in a broth with rice

riso ⓜ ree·zo rice
— **al salto** al sal·to
boiled rice sauteed with saffron
— **comune** ko·moo·ne
lowest quality, usually used in soups
— **fino** fee·no
good quality with large grains
— **semifino** se·mee·fee·no
slightly better quality than comune,
with larger grains
— **superfino** soo·per·fee·no
best quality rice, used in risotto

risotto ⓜ ree·zo·to
rice dish slowly cooked in broth to a
creamy consistency
— **alla milanese** a·la mee·la·ne·ze
with ox marrow, meat stock &
saffron
— **alla monzese** a·la mon·dze·ze
with sausage & saffron or red wine
— **alla piemontese** a·la pye·mon·te·ze
with white wine & truffles (& sometimes tomato sauce)
— **alla sbirraglia** a·la sbee·ra·lya
with chicken breasts
— **alla trevisana** a·la tre·vee·za·na
with sausage or chicken livers
— **allo zafferano** a·lo dza·fe·ra·no
see risotto alla milanese
— **con filetti di pesce persico**
kon fee·le·tee dee pe·she per·see·ko
with perch fillets
— **con le rane** kon le ra·ne
with frog legs, frog broth & herbs
— **nero** ne·ro black risotto with
chard, onion, cuttlefish & their ink
— **polesano** po·le·za·no
with eel, grey mullet, bass, white
wine & fish broth

robiola ① ro·byo·la soft cheese made
mainly from cow's milk

romana, alla ro·ma·na, a·la
sauce, usually tomato based

rombo ⓜ rom·bo turbot

rosolata ① ro·zo·la·ta saute

rosbif ⓜ roz·beef roast beef

rospo ⓜ ros·po angler fish

rosumada ① ro·zoo·ma·da
egg-nog with red wine

rotolo ⓜ ro·to·lo folded sheet of pasta
filled with spinach, ricotta or meat

ruchetta ① roo·ke·ta rocket

rucola ① roo·ko·la rocket

rum-babà ⓜ room ba·ba
babà sprinkled with rum & sugar

ruta ① roo·ta rue (bitter herb)

S

sa fregula ① sa fre·goo·la a soup with
small balls of flour & saffron

sagne chine ① sa·nye kee·ne baked
pasta with meatballs, eggs & cheese

salama ① **da sugo ferrarese** sa·la·ma
da soo·go fe·ra·re·ze pork sausage

salame ① **di Felino** sa·la·me dee
fe·lee·no dry-cured pork sausage

salami ⓜ pl sa·la·mee
generally any type of (pork) sausage

salamino ⓜ sa·la·mee·no small salami

salato/a ⓜ/① sa·la·to/a salty

sale ⓜ sa·le salt

salmì ⓜ sal·mee marinade with
spices & sometimes wine

salmone ⓜ sal·mo·ne salmon

salsa ① sal·sa sauce
— **alfredo** al·fre·do with butter,
cream, parmesan & parsley
— **alla checca** a·la ke·ka
cold sauce with tomatoes, olives,
basil, capers & oregano

— alla pizzaiola a·la pee·tsa·yo·la
pizza-style sauce

— di cren dee kren
with grated radish & apples, onion, broth & white wine

— di pomodoro al tonno e funghi dee po·mo·do·ro al to·no e foon·gee
with tuna, mushroom & tomato

— di pomodoro alla siciliana dee po·mo·do·ro a·la see·chee·lya·na
with eggplant, anchovies, olives, capers, tomato & garlic

— verde ver·de *green sauce with herbs, capers, olives, nuts, anchovies, breadcrumbs, garlic & vinegar*

saltimbocca ① sal·teem·bo·ka
'jump into the mouth' – bite-sized

salume ⓜ sa·loo·me *salami*

sanguinaccio ⓜ san·gwee·na·cho
black pudding made with pig's blood, olives & cocoa

saor, in sowr, een *sweet & sour, vinegar-based marinade for fish*

sarago ⓜ sa·ra·go *white bream*

sarde ① pl sar·de *sardines*

— a scapece a ska·pe·che
fried sardines

— alla marchigiana a·la mar·kee·ja·na
baked, marinated sardines

sardele in saor ① pl sar·de·le een sowr
dish with fried, marinated pilchards

sartù ⓜ 'e riso ⓜ sar·too e ree·zo
savoury rice dish

sas melicheddas ⓜ pl sas me·lee·ke·das
marzipan cakes sprinkled with sugar

sausa ① d'avie sow·sa da·vee·e
honey, nut & mustard sauce

savoiardi ⓜ pl sa·vo·yar·dee
ladyfinger biscuits

sbrofadej ⓜ z·bro·fa·day *thin pasta*

— in brodo een bro·do *served in broth*

scagliuozzoli ⓜ pl ska·lyoo·o·tso·lee
fried polenta & provolone

scaloppine ① pl ska·lo·pee·ne *thin cutlets, usually veal, pork or turkey*

— al marsala al mar·sa·la
lean veal cutlet with marsala

scamorza ① ska·mor·tsa
soft, white cheese, similar to mozzarella & often smoked

scampi ⓜ pl skam·pee
a small type of lobster

scapece ⓜ ska·pe·che *vinegar-based marinade usually used for fish*

— di Vasto dee va·sto
dish prepared with sliced & fried fish, preserved in a marinade

scarole ⓜ ska·ro·le
bitter leafy vegetable

schiaffettuni ⓜ pl chini skya·fe·too·nee kee·nee *maccheroni with pork & eggs*

schmorbraten ⓜ shmor·bra·ten
veal marinated & cooked in wine & tomato sauce

sciatt ⓜ schat
soft, round fritters containing grappa

scimú'd ⓜ shee·mood
salted & spicy skim milk cheese

sciroppo ⓜ shee·ro·po *syrup*

scivateddi ⓜ shee·va·te·dee
thick spaghetti served with meat sauce & ricotta

scottiglia ① sko·tee·lya
rich stew with tomatoes & meat

sebadas ⓜ se·ba·das *large, round & sweet ravioli with cheese & honey*

seccia ① 'mbuttunata se·cha m·boo·too·na·ta *stuffed cuttlefish stewed with tomato sauce*

selvaggina ① sel·va·jee·na *game*

semifreddo ⓜ se·mee·fre·do *can refer to many soft, creamy desserts*

— al torrone al to·ro·ne *dessert with milk, vanilla, eggs & nougat*

semola ① se·mo·la *bran • semolina*

semolino ⓜ se·mo·lee·no *semolina*

senape ① se·na·pe *mustard*

seno ⓜ se·no *breast*

seppia ① se·pya *cuttlefish*

serpe ⓜ ser·pe *cake with marzipan, almonds, icing sugar or chocolate*

sfogliatelle ① pl sfo·lya·te·le
cake or pastry stuffed with ricotta, cinnamon, candied fruit & vanilla

sformato ⓜ sfor·*ma*·to *flan*
— **di spinaci con cibreo al vinsanto**
dee spee·*na*·chee kon chee·*bre*·o
al veen·*san*·to *flan with spinach &
served with liver*

sgombro ⓜ *sgom*·bro *mackerel*

sogliola ⓕ so·*lyo*·la *sole*

sopa ⓕ **còada** *so*·pa ko·a·da *soup of
meat stock, pigeon, cheese & bread*

soppressa ⓕ so·*pre*·sa *pork sausage*

soppressata ⓕ so·pre·*sa*·ta *matured
raw salami made with minced pig's
tongue, lean pork & spices* • *soft
salami made with pork & lard*
— **molisana** mo·lee·*za*·na
large pork sausage

sorbetto ⓜ sor·*be*·to *sorbet*

sott'aceti ⓜ pl so·ta·*che*·tee *pickles*

sott'olio ⓜ so·to·*lyo preserved in oil*

spaghetti ⓜ pl spa·*ge*·tee
ubiquitous long thin strands of pasta

spä'tzle ⓕ *spa*·tsle *little dumplings
that can be served in broth*

speck ⓜ spek *type of smoked ham*

spiedino/spiedo ⓜ spye·*dee*·no/
spye·do *skewer*

spezie ⓕ pl *spe*·tsye *spices*

spigola ⓕ *spee*·go·la *sea bass*

spinaci ⓜ pl spee·*na*·chee *spinach*

sponga(r)da ⓕ spon·*ga(r)*·da
*sweet pastry with vanilla, egg &
sometimes mixed dried fruits*

spugnola ⓕ spoo·*nyo*·la
morel (sponge-like mushroom)

stecchi ⓜ pl *ste*·kee *sticks* • *kebabs*
— **alla ligure** a·la lee·*goo*·re
*with veal, chicken, sweetbread,
eggs, mushrooms, artichokes & spices*

stiacciata ⓕ stya·*cha*·ta *sweet bun*

stinco ⓜ *steen*·ko *shank*

stoccafisso ⓜ sto·ka·*fee*·so
stockfish (small air-dried cod)
— **a brandacujun** a bran·da·*koo*·yoon
creamy dish of potatoes & stockfish
— **accomodato** a·ko·mo·*da*·to
*stockfish cooked in a casserole with
anchovies or mushrooms*

stracchino ⓜ stra·*kee*·no
soft & delicate cheese

stracciatella ⓕ stra·cha·*te*·la
broth with whipped egg & parmesan

stracotto ⓜ stra·*ko*·to *beef stew*

stracotto/a ⓜ/ⓕ stra·*ko*·to/a
cooked for a long time • *overcooked*

stravecchio ⓜ stra·*ve*·kyo
'very old' – aged for a long time

stringozzi ⓜ pl streen·*go*·tsee *short pasta
served with tomato or meat sauce*

strinù ⓕ stree·*noo*
tasty sausage, usually grilled

stroscia ⓕ **(di Pietrabruna)** *stro*·sha
(dee pye·tra·*broo*·na) *sweet cake*

strozzapreti ⓜ pl stro·tsa·*pre*·tee
long strips of pasta • *dumplings
made with spinach, chard & ricotta*

strudel ⓜ *stroo*·del *pastry with a
stuffing including apples*

stufatino ⓜ stoo·fa·*tee*·no *lean veal
stewed with tomatoes & spices*

supa ⓕ **barbetta** soo·pa bar·*be*·ta
rich meat & vegetable stock

suppa ⓕ *soo*·pa *soup*

suppli ⓜ soo·*plee fried rice balls
(similar to crocchettes)*

suricitti ⓜ pl soo·ree·*chee*·tee
flavoured polenta dumplings

susamelli ⓜ pl soo·za·*me*·lee
's'-shaped biscuits

T

tacchino ⓜ ta·*kee*·no *turkey*
— **alla gosutta** a·la go·*zoo*·ta
turkey casserole with fennel & broth
— **con sugo di melagrana**
kon soo·go dee me·la·*gra*·na
with pomegranate sauce

tagliatelle ⓕ ta·lya·*te*·le
long, ribbon-shaped pasta
— **alla salsa di noci** a·la *sal*·sa dee
no·chee *with nuts, oil, butter, ricotta
& parmesan*

— con finocchio selvatico kon
fee·no·kyo sel·va·tee·ko *served with a
fennel, bacon & parsley sauce*

taglierini ⓜ pl ta·lye·ree·nee
thin strips of pasta

— al ragù al ra·goo
served with meat sauce

tagliolini (blò blò) ⓜ pl ta·lyo·lee·nee
(blo blo) *thin strips of pasta in broth,
with grated cheese*

tajarin ⓜ pl ta·ya·reen *thin pasta
usually served with meat sauce*

taleggio ⓜ ta·le·jo *sweet, soft & fatty
cheese with a soft rind*

taralli ⓜ pl ta·ra·lee
boiled & baked pretzel-like biscuits

tartufo ⓜ tar·too·fo *truffle (very
expensive kind of fungus)*

tè ⓜ te *tea*

tegamata ⓕ **di maiale**
te·ga·ma·ta dee ma·ya·le
casserole of pork & fennel seed

tegame, in te·ga·me, een *fried • braised*

tegole ⓜ pl **d'Aosta** te·go·le da·os·ta
almond biscuits

testaiò ⓜ tes·ta·yo *squares of pasta
served with pesto & parmesan*

testaroli ⓜ pl tes·ta·ro·lee
discs of pasta, like pancakes

tiramisù ⓜ tee·ra·mee·soo *sponge
cake or savoiardi soaked in coffee &
arranged in layers with mascarpone,
then sprinkled with cocoa*

tòcco ⓜ **di carne** to·ko dee kar·ne
veal sauce

toma ⓕ to·ma
firm cow or sheep's cheese

— piemontese pye·mon·te·ze
a softer variety of toma

tomaxelle ⓕ pl to·ma·kse·le
veal roulade in wine & broth

tomino ⓜ to·mee·no
small fresh cheese

tonno ⓜ to·no *tuna*

torciarelli ⓜ pl **al tartufo** tor·cha·re·lee
al tar·too·fo *pasta served with a
sauce containing minced lean pork,
spices, mushrooms, truffles & cheese*

torcinelli ⓜ pl tor·chee·ne·lee
stewed lamb or kid entrails

torcolo ⓜ **di San Costanzo** tor·ko·lo
dee san kos·tan·dzo *ring-shaped cake*

torresani ⓜ pl to·re·za·nee
pigeon kebabs

torrone ⓜ to·ro·ne *nougat*

— al cioccolato al cho·ko·la·to
very soft chocolate nougat

torroni ⓜ pl **di semi di sesamo**
to·ro·nee dee se·mee dee se·za·mo
crunchy sweets with sesame seeds

torta ⓕ tor·ta *cake • tart • pie*

tortelli ⓜ pl tor·te·lee *fat, stuffed pasta*

— di San Leo dee san le·o
with spinach & cheeses

— di zucca dee tsoo·ka
with pumpkin

tortellini ⓜ pl tor·te·lee·nee *pasta filled
with meat, parmesan & egg*

tortelloni ⓜ pl tor·te·lo·nee
large tortellini

tosella ⓕ to·ze·la *fresh fried cheese*

totano ⓜ to·ta·no *type of squid*

tramezzino ⓜ tra·me·dzee·no
sandwich

Trebbiano ⓜ tre·bya·no
white grape found throughout Italy

trenette ⓕ pl **al pesto** tre·ne·te al
pes·to *long, flat pasta with pesto*

trifola ⓕ tree·fo·la *white truffle*

triglia ⓕ tree·lya *red mullet*

trota ⓕ tro·ta *trout*

tubetti ⓜ pl too·be·tee *short pasta tubes*

turcinelli ⓜ pl **arrostiti** toor·chee·ne·lee
a·ro·stee·tee *lamb-offal stew*

U

uardi ⓜ pl **e fasoi** ⓜ pl war·dee e
fa·zoy *soup with beans, barley, ham
bone & spices*

umbrici ⓜ pl oom·bree·chee
hand-made, thick spaghetti

uova ⓜ pl wo·va *eggs*

uva ⓕ pl oo·va *grapes*

— bianca byan·ka *green grapes*

— nera ne·ra *red grapes*

— passa pa·sa *raisins*

V

vapore, cotto/a a ⓜ/ⓕ va·po·re, ko·to/a a *steamed*
vecchio/a ⓜ/ⓕ ve·kyo/a *old • aged*
ventresca ⓕ **di tonno** ven·tres·ka dee to·no *tuna belly*
verdura/verdure ⓕ ver·doo·ra/ ver·doo·re *vegetable/vegetables*
verza ⓕ ver·dza *savoy cabbage*
vialone nano ⓜ vya·lo·ne na·no *short grain rice used for risotto*
vincisgrassi ⓜ pl veen·cheez·gra·see *rich, baked dish made of offal, cheese & sometimes, truffle*
viscidu ⓜ vee·shee·doo *dry, salty & sour cheese, sliced & pickled*
vitello ⓜ vee·te·lo *veal*
— **tonnato** to·na·to *thin slices of veal covered with a tuna, capers & anchovy sauce*
vongole ⓕ pl von·go·le *clams*

Z

zabaglione ⓜ dza·ba·lyo·ne *mousse-like dessert made of beaten egg, marsala & sugar*
zampetto ⓜ dzam·pe·to *calf, lamb or pig trotter*
zenzero ⓜ dzen·dze·ro *ginger*

zeppule ⓕ pl **'e cicenielli** ⓜ pl dze·poo·le e chee·che·nye·lee *fritters with cheese & anchovies*
zeppule ⓕ pl **'e San Giuseppe** dze·poo·le e san joo·ze·pe *small, fried ring-shaped cakes*
zimin ⓜ pl dzee·meen *soup with beans, pork & chards • dish with calamari & chard*
ziti ⓜ pl dzee·tee *long fat hollow pasta*
zucca ⓕ tsoo·ka *pumpkin*
— **gialla in agrodolce** ja·la een a·gro·dol·che *fried & served with spices & capers*
zucchero ⓜ tsoo·ke·ro *sugar*
zuccotto ⓜ **fiorentino** tsoo·ko·to fyo·ren·tee·no *sponge cake with liqueur, custard, chocolate & whipped cream*
zuppa ⓕ tsoo·pa *soup, usually thick*
— **alla canavesana** a·la ka·na·ve·za·na *soup base of bread, cabbage, butter, lard, onions & garlic*
— **di ceci** dee che·chee *rich chickpea soup*
— **di pesce alla marinara** dee pe·she a·la ma·ree·na·ra *fish soup*
— **'e zuffritto** e tsoo·free·to *sauce prepared with pig's offal, red wine & tomato sauce.*

emergencies

le emergenze

Help!	*Aiuto!*	a·*yoo*·to
Stop!	*Fermi!*	*fer*·mee
Go away!	*Vai via!*	vai *vee*·a
Thief!	*Ladro!*	*la*·dro
Fire!	*Al fuoco!*	al *fwo*·ko
Watch out!	*Attenzione!*	a·ten·*tsyo*·ne

Call the police!
Chiami la polizia!   kya·mee la po·lee·*tsee*·a

Call a doctor!
Chiami un medico!   kya·mee oon *me*·dee·ko

Call an ambulance!
Chiami un'ambulanza!   kya·mee o·nam·boo·*lan*·tsa

It's an emergency!
È un'emergenza!   e oo·ne·mer·*jen*·tsa

There's been an accident.
C'è stato un incidente.   che *sta*·to oon een·chee·*den*·te

Can you help me, please?
Mi può aiutare,   mee pwo a·yoo·*ta*·re
per favore?   per fa·*vo*·re

I have to use the telephone.
Devo fare una telefonata.   *de*·vo fa·re oo·na te·le·fo·*na*·ta

I'm lost.
Mi sono perso/a. m/f   mee *so*·no *per*·so/a

signs

Carabinieri	ka·ra·bee·*nye*·ree	**Police (military)**
Polizia	po·lee·*tsee*·a	**Police (civilian)**
Pronto Soccorso	*pron*·to so·*kor*·so	**Casualty**
Questura	kwes·*too*·ra	**Police Headquarters (civilian)**

Do you have a first-aid kit?
Avete una cassetta   a·ve·te *oo*·na ka·*se*·ta
di pronto soccorso?   dee *pron*·to so·*kor*·so

Where are the toilets?
Dove sono i gabinetti?   *do*·ve *so*·no ee ga·bee·*ne*·tee

police

la polizia

Where's the police station?
Dov'è il posto di   do·ve eel *pos*·to dee
polizia?   po·lee·*tsee*·a

I want to report an offence.
Voglio fare una denuncia.   *vo*·lyo fa·re *oo*·na de·*noon*·cha

I have insurance.
Ho l'assicurazione.   o la·see·koo·ra·*tsyo*·ne

(My bag) was stolen.
Mi hanno rubato   mee *a*·no roo·*ba*·to
(la mia borsa).   (la *mee*·a *bor*·sa)

I've lost (my wallet).
Ho perso (il mio   o *per*·so (eel *mee*·o
portafoglio).   por·ta·*fo*·lyo)

I've been robbed.
Sono stato/a derubato/a. m/f   *so*·no *sta*·to/a de·roo·*ba*·to/a

I've been raped.
Sono stato/a violentato/a. m/f   *so*·no *sta*·to/a vyo·len·*ta*·to/a

---

cop shops

In Italy, both the *polizia* po·lee·*tsee*·a (civilian police) and the *carabinieri* ka·ra·bee·*nye*·ree (police force administered by the Ministry of Defence) handle police tasks. Both forces investigate crimes, but the *posto di polizia* *pos*·to dee po·lee·*tsee*·a (regular civilian police station) or the *questura* kwes·*too*·ra (the police headquarters) is where to go to report a theft. Nevertheless, if you happen to be closer to the *carabinieri*, they'll redirect you from their *caserma* ka·*ser*·ma (barracks) if necessary.

| It was him. | E' stato lui. | e sta·to loo·ee |
| It was her. | E' stata lei. | e sta·ta lay |

He/She tried to ... me.	Ha cercato di ...	a cher·ka·to dee ...
assault	aggredirmi	a·gre·deer·mee
rape	violentarmi	vyo·len·tar·mee
rob	derubarmi	de·roo·bar·mee

I want to contact my ...	Vorrei contattare ...	vo·ray kon·ta·ta·re ...
embassy	la mia ambasciata	la mee·a am·ba·sha·ta
consulate	il mio consolato	eel mee·o kon·so·la·to

Can I call someone?
Posso chiamare qualcuno? po·so kya·ma·re kwal·koo·no

Can I call a lawyer?
Posso chiamare un avvocato? po·so kya·ma·re oo·na·vo·ka·to

Can I have a lawyer (who speaks English)?
Posso avere un avvocato (che parli inglese)? po·so a·ve·re oo·na·vo·ka·to (ke par·lee een·gle·ze)

Is there a fine we can pay to clear this?
C'è una multa che possiamo pagare per chiarire tutto questo? che oo·na mool·ta ke po·sya·mo pa·ga·re per kya·ree·re too·to kwe·sto

Can I have a copy, please?
Potrei avere una copia, per favore? po·tray a·ve·re oo·na ko·pya per fa·vo·re

This drug is for personal use.
Questo medicinale è per uso personale. kwe·sto me·dee·chee·na·le e per oo·zo per·so·na·le

I have a prescription for this drug.
Ho una ricetta per questa medicina. o oo·na re·che·ta per kwe·sta me·dee·chee·na

I (don't) understand.
(Non) Capisco. (non) ka·pees·ko

What am I accused of?
Di che cosa sono stato/a accusato/a? m/f — dee ke ko·za so·no sta·to/a a·koo·za·to/a

I'm sorry.
Mi scusi. — mee skoo·zee

I apologise.
Mi dispiace. — mee dees·pya·che

I didn't realise I was doing anything wrong.
Non sapevo che facessi qualcosa di male. — non sa·pe·vo ke fa·che·see kwal·ko·za dee ma·le

I didn't do it.
Non sono stato/a io. m/f — non so·no sta·to/a ee·o

I'm innocent.
Sono innocente. — so·no ee·no·chen·te

the police may say ...

You'll be charged with ...	*Sarai accusato/a di ...* m/f	sa·rai a·koo·za·to/a dee ...
He'll/She'll be charged with ...	*Lui/Lei sarà accusato/a di ...* m/f	loo·ee/lay sa·ra a·koo·za·to/a dee ...
assault	*aggressione*	a·gre·syo·ne
disturbing the peace	*disturbo della quiete pubblica*	dees·toor·bo de·la kwye·te poo·blee·ka
murder	*omicidio*	o·mee·chee·dyo
not having a visa	*non avere un visto*	no·na·ve·re oon vee·sto
possession (of illegal substances)	*possesso (di sostanze illecite)*	po·se·so (dee sos·tan·tse ee·le·chee·te)
rape	*stupro*	stoo·pro
shoplifting	*taccheggio*	ta·ke·jo
speeding	*eccesso di velocità*	e·che·so dee ve·lo·chee·ta
theft	*furto*	foor·to

doctor

il medico

Where's the nearest ...?	Dov'è ... più vicino/a? m/f	do·ve ... pyoo vee·chee·no/a
(night) chemist	la farmacia f (di turno)	la far·ma·chee·a (dee toor·no)
dentist	il/la dentista m/f	eel/la den·tee·sta
doctor	il medico m	eel me·dee·ko
hospital	l'ospedale m	los·pe·da·le
medical centre	l'ambulatorio m	lam·boo·la·to·ryo
optometrist	l'ottico m	lo·tee·ko

I need a doctor (who speaks English).
Ho bisogno di un medico (che parli inglese).
o bee·zo·nyo dee oon me·dee·ko (ke par·lee een·gle·ze)

Could I see a female doctor?
Posso vedere una dottoressa?
po·so ve·de·re oo·na do·to·re·sa

Can the doctor come here?
Può venire qui il medico?
pwo ve·nee·re kwee eel me·dee·ko

I've been vaccinated for ...	Sono stato/a vaccinato/a per ... m/f	so·no sta·to/a va·chee·na·to/a per ...
He's/She's been vaccinated for ...	Lui/Lei è stato/a vaccinato/a per ... m/f	loo·ee/lay e sta·to/a va·chee·na·to/a per ...
hepatitis A/B/C	l'epatite A/B/C	le·pa·tee·te a/bee/chee
tetanus	il tetano	eel te·ta·no
typhoid	il tifo	eel tee·fo

I need ...	*Ho bisogno di ...*	o bee·zo·nyo dee ...
new contact	*nuove lenti a*	nwo·ve len·tee a
lenses	*contatto*	kon·ta·to
new glasses	*nuovi occhiali*	nwo·vee o·kya·lee

I've run out of my medication.
Ho finito la mia   o fee·nee·to la mee·a
medicina.   me·dee·chee·na

Can I have a receipt for my insurance?
Potrebbe darmi una   po·tre·be dar·mee oo·na
ricevuta per   ree·che·voo·ta per
l'assicurazione?   la·see·koo·ra·tsyo·ne

the doctor may say ...

What's the problem?
Qual'è il problema?   kwa·le eel pro·ble·ma

Where does it hurt?
Dove Le fa male?   do·ve le fa ma·le

Do you have a temperature?
Ha la febbre?   a la fe·bre

How long have you been like this?
Da quanto (tempo) è che   da kwan·to (tem·po) e ke
si sente così?   see sen·te ko·zee

Have you had this before?
Si è mai sentito/a   see e mai sen·tee·to/a
così prima? m/f   ko·zee pree·ma

Are you sexually active?
È sessualmente   e se·swal·men·te
attivo/a? m/f   a·tee·vo/a

Have you had unprotected sex?
Ha avuto rapporti   a a·voo·to ra·por·tee
non protetti?   non pro·te·tee

the doctor may say ...

Are you allergic to anything?
È allergico/a
a qualcosa? m/f

e a·*ler*·jee·ko/a
a kwal·*ko*·za

Are you on medication?
Sta prendendo
medicine?

sta pren·*den*·do
me·dee·*chee*·ne

Are you pregnant?
È incinta?

e een·*cheen*·ta

How long are you travelling for?
Per quanto tempo
viaggia?

per *kwan*·to *tem*·po
vee·a·ja

Do you ...?
drink	*Beve?*	*be*·ve
smoke	*Fuma?*	*foo*·ma
take drugs	*Si droga?*	see *dro*·ga

You need to be admitted to hospital.
Deve essere ricoverato/a
in ospedale. m/f

de·ve e·se·re ree·ko·ve·*ra*·to/a
ee·nos·pe·*da*·le

You should have it checked when you go home.
Dovrebbe farlo
controllare dal
medico quando
ritorna a casa.

dov·*re*·be *far*·lo
kon·tro·*la*·re dal
me·dee·ko *kwan*·do
re·*tor*·na a *ka*·za

You should return home for treatment.
Dovrebbe tornare
a casa per
farsi curare.

do·vre·be tor·*na*·re
a *ka*·za per
far·see koo·*ra*·re

You're a hypochondriac.
È un ipocondriaco/a. m/f

e oo·nee·po·kon·*drya*·ko/a

Go and enjoy your holiday!
Vada a godersi
le vacanze!

va·da a go·*der*·see
le va·*kan*·tse

symptoms & conditions

I'm sick.
Mi sento male.   mee sen·to ma·le

My friend is sick.
Il mio amico è malato. m   eel mee·o a·mee·ko e ma·la·to
La mia amica è malata. f   la mee·a a·mee·ka e ma·la·ta

It hurts here.
Mi fa male qui.   mee fa ma·le kwee

I've been injured.
Sono stato/a ferito/a. m/f   so·no sta·to/a fe·ree·to/a

I've been vomiting.
Ho vomitato alcune volte.   o vo·mee·ta·to al·koo·ne vol·te

I can't sleep.
Non riesco a dormire.   non ryes·ko a dor·mee·re

I have an infection.
Ho un'infezione.   o oon een·fe·tsyo·ne

I have a rash.
Ho uno sfogo.   o oo·no sfo·go

Please use a new syringe.
Usi una siringa   oo·see oo·na see·reen·ga
nuova, per favore.   nwo·va per fa·vo·re

I have my own syringe.
Ho con me la mia siringa.   o kon me la mee·a see·reen·ga

I don't want a blood transfusion.
Non voglio una   non vo·lyo oo·na
trasfusione di sangue.   tras·foo·syo·ne dee san·gwe

I feel ...	Ho ...	o ...
dizzy	il capogiro	eel ka·po·gee·ro
hot and cold	vampate di	vam·pa·te dee
	calore	ka·lo·re
nauseous	la nausea	la now·ze·a
shivery	i brividi	ee bree·vee·dee

I feel ...	Mi sento ...	mee *sen*·to ...
better	meglio	*me*·lyo
strange	strano/a m/f	*stra*·no/a
weak	debole	*de*·bo·le
worse	peggio	*pe*·jo

I feel ...	Sono ...	*so*·no ...
anxious	ansioso/a m/f	an·*syo*·zo/a
depressed	depresso/a m/f	de·*pre*·so/a

I have a ...	Ho ...	o ...
cold	un raffreddore	oon ra·fre·*do*·re
cough	la tosse	la *to*·se
fever	la febbre	la *fe*·bre
headache	mal di testa	mal deé *tes*·ta
heart	un problema	oon pro·*ble*·ma
condition	cardiaco	kar·*dee*·a·ko
migraine	un'emicrania	oo·ne·mee·*kra*·nya

I'm ...	Sono ...	*so*·no ...
asthmatic	asmatico/a m/f	az·*ma*·tee·ko/a
diabetic	diabetico/a m/f	dee·a·*be*·tee·ko/a
epileptic	epilettico/a m/f	e·pee·*le*·tee·ko/a

I've (recently) had ...
Ho avuto ... (di recente).   o a·*voo*·to ... (dee re·*chen*·te)

He's/She's (recently) had ...
Ha avuto ... (di recente).   a a·*voo*·to ... (dee re·*chen*·te)

I'm on medication for ...
Prendo la medicina   *pren*·do la me·dee·*chee*·na
per ...   per ...

He/She is on medication for ...
Prende la medicina   *pren*·de la me·dee·*chee*·na
per ...   per ...

For more symptoms and conditions, see the **dictionary**.

women's health

I think I'm pregnant.
Penso di essere incinta. pen·so dee e·se·re een·cheen·ta

I'm pregnant.
Sono incinta. so·no een·cheen·ta

I'm on the Pill.
Prendo la pillola. pren·do la pee·lo·la

I haven't had my period for (two) weeks.
Sono (due) settimane so·no (doo·e) se·tee·ma·ne
che non mi vengono le ke non mee ven·go·no le
mestruazioni. mes·troo·a·tsyo·nee

I've noticed a lump/swelling here.
Ho notato un nodulo/ o no·ta·to oon no·doo·lo/
gonfiore qui. gon·fyo·re kwee

I have period pain.
Ho dolori mestruali. o do·lo·ree mes·trwa·lee

I have a rash.
Ho uno sfogo. o oo·no sfo·go

the doctor may say ...

Are you using contraception?
Prende contraccettivi? pren·de kon·tra·che·tee·vee

Are you menstruating?
Ha le mestruazioni? a le mes·troo·a·tsyo·nee

Are you pregnant?
È incinta? e een·cheen·ta

When did you last have your period?
Quand'è l'ultima volta kwan·de lool·tee·ma vol·ta
che Le sono venute le ke le so·no ve·noo·te le
mestruazioni? mes·troo·a·tsyo·nee

You're pregnant.
È incinta. e een·cheen·ta

I need ...	Ho bisogno ...	o bee·zo·nyo ...
contraception	di	dee
	contraccettivi	kon·tra·che·tee·vee
the morning-	della pillola del	de·la pee·lo·la del
after pill	mattino dopo	ma·tee·no do·po
a pregnancy	di un test di	dee oon test dee
test	gravidanza	gra·vee·dan·tsa

allergies

I'm allergic	Sono	so·no
to ...	allergico/a ... m/f	a·ler·jee·ko/a ...
He/She is	È allergico/a ... m/f	e a·ler·jee·ko/a ...
allergic to ...		
antibiotics	agli	a·lyee
	antibiotici	an·tee·bee·o·tee·chee
anti-	agli	a·lyee
inflammatories	antinfiammatori	an·teen·fya·ma·to·ree
aspirin	all'aspirina	a·las·pee·ree·na
bees	alle api	a·le a·pee
codeine	alla codeina	a·la ko·de·ee·na
penicillin	alla	a·la
	penicillina	pe·nee·chee·lee·na
pollen	al polline	al po·lee·ne
sulphur-based	agli	a·lyee
drugs	medicinali	me·dee·chee·na·lee
	a base di zolfo	a ba·ze dee dzol·fo

I have a skin allergy.

Ho un'allergia alla pelle.   o oo·na·ler·jee·a a·la pe·le

For food-related allergies, see **vegetarian & special meals**, page 160.

parts of the body

My (stomach) hurts.
Mi fa male (lo stomaco).   mee fa *ma*·le (lo *sto*·ma·ko)

I can't move (my ankle).
Non riesco a muovere   non *ryes*·ko a *mwo*·ve·re
(la caviglia).   (la ka·*vee*·lya)

I have a cramp (in my foot).
Ho crampi (al piede).   o *kram*·pee (al *pye*·de)

(My throat) is swollen.
(La gola) è gonfia.   (la *go*·la) e *gon*·fya

For more parts of the body, see the **dictionary**.

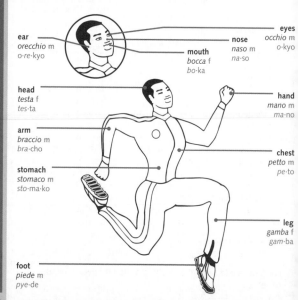

ear
orecchio m
o·re·kyo

nose
occhio m   eyes
naso m   *occhio* m
na·so   o·kyo

mouth
bocca f
bo·ka

head
testa f
tes·ta

hand
mano m
ma·no

arm
braccio m
bra·cho

chest
petto m
pe·to

stomach
stomaco m
sto·ma·ko

leg
gamba f
gam·ba

foot
piede m
pye·de

chemist

I need something for (diarrhoea).
Ho bisogno di   o bee·zo·nyo dee
qualcosa per (la diarrea).   kwal·ko·za per (la dee·a·re·a)

Do I need a prescription for (antihistamines)?
C'è bisogno di una   che bee·zo·nyo dee oo·na
ricetta per (gli   re·che·ta per (lyee
antistaminici)?   an·tee·sta·mee·nee·chee)

How many times a day?
Quante volte al giorno?   kwan·te vol·te al jor·no

Will it make me drowsy?
Mi farà dormire?   mee fa·ra dor·mee·re

For pharmaceutical items, see the **dictionary**.

listen for ...

de·ve kom·ple·ta·re eel cheek·lo
  Deve completare il   **You must complete the**
  ciclo.   **course.**

doo·e vol·te al jor·no (kon ee pas·tee)
  Due volte al giorno   **Twice a day**
  (con i pasti).   **(with food).**

kwe·sto la mai pre·so
  Questo l'ha mai preso?   **Have you taken this before?**

sa·ra pron·to fra (ven·tee mee·noo·tee)
  Sarà pronto fra   **It'll be ready to pick up in**
  (venti minuti).   **(20 minutes).**

dentist

I have a ...	*Ho ...*	o ...
broken tooth	*un dente rotto*	oon den·te ro·to
cavity	*una cavità*	oo·na ka·vee·ta
toothache	*mal di denti*	mal dee den·tee

I need a/an ...	Ho bisogno di ...	o bee·zo·nyo dee ...
anaesthetic	un anestetico	oo·na·nes·te·tee·ko
filling	un'otturazione	oo·no·too·ra·tsyo·ne
crown	una corona	oo·na ko·ro·na

I've lost a filling.
Ho perso un'otturazione.   o per·so oo·no·too·ra·tsyo·ne

My dentures are broken.
La mia dentiera è rotta.   la mee·a den·tye·ra e ro·ta

My gums hurt.
Mi fanno male le gengive.   mee fa·no ma·le le jen·jee·ve

My orthodontic braces broke.
Mi si è rotto l'apparecchio.   mee see e ro·to la·pa·re·kyo

My orthodontic braces fell off.
Mi è caduto l'apparecchio.   mee e ka·doo·to la·pa·re·kyo

I don't want it extracted.
Non voglio che mi venga   non vo·lyo ke mee ven·ga
tolto.   tol·to

Ouch!
Ahi!   a·ee

listen for ...

a·pra be·ne la bo·ka
  Apra bene la bocca.   **Open wide.**

non le fa·ra ma·le per nyen·te
  Non Le farà male per niente.   **This won't hurt a bit.**

for·se le fa·ra oon po ma·le
  Forse Le farà un po' male.   **This might hurt a little.**

mor·da kwe·sto
  Morda questo.   **Bite down on this.**

sha·kwee
  Sciacqui!   **Rinse!**

tor·nee kwee ke non o fee·nee·to
  *Torni qui che non
  ho finito.*   **Come back, I haven't
finished.**

SUSTAINABLE TRAVEL

As the climate change debate heats up, the matter of sustainability becomes an important part of the travel vernacular. In practical terms, this means assessing our impact on the environment and local cultures and economies – and acting to make that impact as positive as possible. Here are some basic phrases to get you on your way …

communication & cultural differences

I'd like to learn some of your local dialects.

Vorrei imparare qualche
dialetto regionale.

vo·*ray* eem·pa·*ra*·re *kwal*·ke
dee·a·*le*·to re·jo·*na*·le

Would you like me to teach you some English?

Vuole che le insegni
un po' d'inglese?

vwo·le ke le een·*se*·nyee
oon po deen·*gle*·ze

Is this a local or national custom?

Questa è un'usanza
locale o nazionale?

kwe·sta e oon oo·*san*·tsa
lo·*ka*·le o na·tsyo·*na*·le

I respect your customs.

Rispetto le vostre usanze.

rees·*pe*·to le *vos*·tre oo·*san*·tse

community benefit & involvement

What sorts of issues is this community facing?

Quali problemi ci sono
da queste parti?

kwa·lee prob·*le*·mee chee *so*·no
da *kwe*·ste *par*·tee

climate change	*cambiamento* m *del clima*	kam·bya·*men*·to del *klee*·ma
organised crime	*criminalità* f *organizzata*	kree·mee·na·lee·*ta* or·ga·nee·*dza*·ta

racism	*razzismo* m	ra·*tsees*·mo
relations between church and state	*rapporti* m pl *fra Chiesa e Stato*	ra·*por*·tee fra *kye*·za e *sta*·to
unemployment	*disoccupazione* f	dees·o·ku·pa·*tsyo*·ne

I'd like to volunteer my skills.

Vorrei offrirvi la mia competenza.

vo·*ray* o·*freer*·vee la *mee*·a kom·pe·*ten*·tsa

Are there any volunteer programs available in the area?

Ci sono programmi di volontariato da queste parti?

chee *so*·no pro·*gra*·mee dee vo·lon·ta·*rya*·to da *kwe*·ste *par*·tee

environment

Where can I recycle this?

Dove lo posso riciclare?   *do*·ve lo *po*·so ree·chee·*kla*·re

transport

Can we get there by public transport?

Possiamo arrivarci con i mezzi pubblici?

po·*sya*·mo a·ree·*var*·chee kon ee *me*·dzee poo·blee·chee

Can we get there by bike?

Possiamo arrivarci in bicicletta?

po·*sya*·mo a·ree·*var*·chee een bee·chee·*kle*·ta

I'd prefer to walk there.

Preferisco andarci a piedi.

pre·fe·*rees*·ko an·*dar*·chee a *pye*·dee

accommodation

I'd like to stay at a locally run hotel.

Vorrei stare in un albergo a gestione locale.

vo·*ray sta*·re een oon al·*ber*·go a jes·*tyo*·ne lo·*ka*·le

Can I turn the air conditioning off and open the window?

Posso spegnere l'aria	po·so spe·nye·re la·ree·a
condizionata e aprire	kon·dee·tsyo·na·ta e a·pree·re
la finestra?	la fee·nes·tra

There's no need to change my sheets.

Non c'è bisogno di	non che bee·zo·nyo dee
cambiare le lenzuola.	kam·bya·re le len·tswo·la

shopping

Where can I buy locally produced goods/souvenirs?

Dove posso comprare	do·ve po·so kom·pra·re
oggetti/souvenirs di	o·je·tee/soov·neer dee
produzione locale?	pro·doo·tsyo·ne lo·ka·le

Do you sell Fair Trade products?

Vendete prodotti del	ven·de·te pro·do·tee del
Commercio Equo e Solidale?	ko·mer·cho e·kwo e so·lee·da·le

food

Do you sell ...?	*Vendete ...?*	ven·de·te ...
locally produced	*prodotti*	pro·do·tee
food	*alimentari*	a·lee·men·ta·ree
	locali	lo·ka·lee
organic	*prodotti*	pro·do·tee
produce	*biologici*	bee·o·lo·jee·chee

Can you tell me which traditional foods I should try?

Mi può dire quali piatti	mee pwo dee·re kwa·lee pya·tee
tradizionali dovrei	tra·dee·tsyo·na·lee do·vray
provare?	pro·va·re

sightseeing

Are cultural tours available?

Si possono fare	see po·so·no fa·re
gite culturali?	jee·te kool·too·ra·lee

Does your company ...?	La vostra agenzia ...?	la vos·tra a·jen·tsee·a ...
donate money to charity	fa offerte a organizzazioni umanitarie	fa o·fer·te a or·ga·nee·tsa·tsyo·nee oo·ma·nee·ta·rye
hire local guides	assume guide del posto	as·soo·me gwee·de del pos·to
visit local businesses	visita imprese locali	vee·see·ta eem·pre·se lo·ka·lee
Does the guide speak ...?	La guida parla ...?	la gwee·da par·la ...
Abruzzese	Abruzzese	a·broo·tse·ze
Apulian	Pugliese	poo·lee·e·ze
Calabrian	Calabrese	ka·la·bre·ze
Emiliano-Romagnolo	Emiliano-Romagnolo	e·mee·lee·a·no ro·ma·nyo·lo
Friulian	Friulano	free·oo·la·no
Laziale	Laziale	la·tsee·a·le
Ligurian	Ligure	lee·goo·re
Lombard	Lombardo	lom·bar·do
Marchigiano	Marchigiano	mar·kee·ja·no
Neapolitan	Napoletano	na·po·le·ta·no
Piemontese	Piemontese	pee·e·mon·te·ze
Romanesque	Romanesco	ro·ma·nes·ko
Sardinian	Sardo	sar·do
Sicilian	Siciliano	see·chee·lee·a·no
Tuscan	Toscano	tos·ka·no
Umbrian	Umbro	oom·bro
Venetian	Veneto	ve·ne·to

Nouns in this dictionary, and adjectives affected by gender, have their gender indicated by ⓜ and/or ①. If it's a plural noun, you'll also see pl. Where a word that could be either a noun or a verb has no gender indicated ①, it's a verb.

A

aboard *a bordo* a bor·do
abortion *aborto* ⓜ a·bor·to
above *sopra* so·pra
abroad *all'estero* a·les·te·ro
accident *incidente* ⓜ een·chee·den·te
accommodation *alloggio* ⓜ a·lo·jo
acupuncture *agopuntura* ①
   a·go·poon·too·ra
adaptor *spina* ① *multipla*
   spee·na mool·tee·pla
addicted *dipendente* ⓜ/①
   dee·pen·den·te
address *indirizzo* ⓜ een·dee·ree·tso
administration *amministrazione* ①
   a·mee·nee·stra·tsyo·ne
admission price *prezzo* ⓜ *d'ingresso*
   pre·tso deen·gre·so
admit (let in) *far entrare* far en·tra·re
adult *adulto/a* ⓜ/① a·dool·to/a
adventure *avventura* ① a·ven·too·ra
advertisement *annuncio* ⓜ a·noon·cho
aerobics *aerobica* ① a·e·ro·bee·ka
Africa *Africa* ① a·free·ka
after *dopo* do·po
afternoon *pomeriggio* ⓜ po·me·ree·jo
aftershave *dopobarba* ⓜ do·po·bar·ba
again *di nuovo* dee nwo·vo
age *età* ① e·ta
aggressive *aggressivo/a* ⓜ/①
   a·gre·see·vo/a
agree *essere d'accordo* e·se·re da·kor·do
agriculture *agricoltura* ①
   a·gree·kol·too·ra
AIDS *AIDS* ⓜ a·eedz
air *aria* ① a·rya

airmail *via* ① *aerea* vee·a a·e·re·a
air-conditioned *ad aria condizionata*
   ad a·rya kon·dee·tsyo·na·ta
airline *linea* ① *aerea* lee·ne·a a·e·re·a
airport *aeroporto* ⓜ a·e·ro·por·to
airport tax *tassa* ① *aeroportuale*
   ta·sa a·e·ro·por·twa·le
aisle (plane, train) *corridoio* ⓜ
   ko·ree·do·yo
alarm clock *sveglia* ① sve·lya
alcohol *alcol* ⓜ al·kol
all (singular) *tutto/a* ⓜ/① too·to/a
all (plural) *tutti/e* ⓜ/① too·tee/too·te
allergy *allergia* ① a·ler·jee·a
almond *mandorla* ① man·dor·la
alone *da solo/a* ⓜ/① da so·lo/a
already *già* ja
also *anche* an·ke
altar *altare* ⓜ al·ta·re
altitude *quota* ① kwo·ta
always *sempre* sem·pre
ambassador
   ambasciatore/ambasciatrice ⓜ/①
   am·ba·sha·to·re/am·ba·sha·tree·che
ambulance *ambulanza* ①
   am·boo·lan·tsa
America *America* ① a·me·ree·ka
amount *quantità* ① kwan·tee·ta
ancient *antico/a* ⓜ/① an·tee·ko/a
and *e* e
angry *arrabbiato/a* ⓜ/① a·ra·bya·to/a
animal *animale* ⓜ a·nee·ma·le
ankle *caviglia* ① ka·vee·lya
annual *annuale* a·noo·a·le
answer *risposta* ① rees·pos·ta
ant *formica* ① for·mee·ka
antibiotics *antibiotici* ⓜ pl
   an·tee·bee·o·tee·che

antihistamines *antistaminici* ⓜ pl
an-tee-sta-*mee*-nee-chee

antinuclear *antinucleare*
an-tee-noo-kle-*a*-re

antique *pezzo* ⓜ *di antiquariato*
pe-tso dee an-tee-kwa-*rya*-to

antiseptic *antisettico* ⓜ an-tee-se-*tee*-ko

appendix *appendice* ⓕ a-pen-*dee*-che

apple *mela* ⓕ *me*-la

appointment *appuntamento* ⓜ
a-poon-ta-*men*-to

apricot *albicocca* ⓕ al-bee-*ko*-ka

archaeological *archeologico/a* ⓜ/ⓕ
ar-ke-o-lo-jee-ko/a

architect *architetto* ⓜ ar-kee-*te*-to

architecture *architettura* ⓕ
ar-kee-te-*too*-ra

argue *litigare* lee-*tee*-ga-re

arm *braccio* ⓜ *bra*-cho

aromatherapy *aromaterapia* ⓕ
a-ro-ma-te-ra-*pee*-a

arrest *arrestare* a-res-*ta*-re

arrivals *arrivi* ⓜ pl a-*ree*-vee

arrive *arrivare* a-ree-*va*-re

art *arte* ⓕ *ar*-te

art gallery *galleria* ⓕ *d'arte*
ga-le-*ree*-a *dar*-te

artist *artista* ⓜ&ⓕ ar-*tee*-sta

ashtray *portacenere* ⓜ por-ta-*che*-ne-re

Asia *Asia* ⓕ *a*-zya

ask (a question) *domandare*
do-man-*da*-re

ask (for something) *richiedere*
ree-*kye*-de-re

aspirin *aspirina* ⓕ as-pee-*ree*-na

asthma *asma* ⓕ *az*-ma

athletics *atletica* ⓕ at-*le*-tee-ka

aubergine *melanzana* ⓕ me-lan-*dza*-na

aunt *zia* ⓕ *tsee*-a

Australia *Australia* ⓕ ow-*stra*-lya

Austria *Austria* ⓕ ow-*stree*-a

automatic *automatico/a* ⓜ/ⓕ
ow-to-*ma*-tee-ko/a

automatic teller machine (ATM)
Bancomat ⓜ *ban*-ko-mat

autumn *autunno* ⓜ ow-*too*-no

avenue *viale* ⓜ vee-*a*-le

awful *orrendo/a* ⓜ/ⓕ o-*ren*-do/a

B

B&W (film) *in bianco e nero*
een *byan*-ko e *ne*-ro

baby *bimbo/a* ⓜ/ⓕ *beem*-bo/a

baby food *cibo* ⓜ *da bebè*
chee-bo da be-*be*

baby powder *borotalco* ⓜ bo-ro-*tal*-ko

babysitter *baby-sitter* ⓜ&ⓕ
be-bee-*see*-ter

back (body) *schiena* ⓕ *skye*-na

backpack *zaino* ⓜ *dzai*-no

bacon *pancetta* ⓕ pan-*che*-ta

bad *cattivo/a* ⓜ/ⓕ ka-*tee*-vo/a

bag (general) *borsa* ⓕ *bor*-sa

bag (shopping) *sacchetto* ⓜ sa-*ke*-to

baggage *bagaglio* ⓜ ba-*ga*-lyo

baggage allowance *bagaglio*
consentito ba-*ga*-lyo kon-sen-*tee*-to

baggage claim *ritiro* ⓜ *bagagli*
ree-*tee*-ro ba-*ga*-lyee

bakery *panetteria* ⓕ pa-ne-te-*ree*-a

balance (account) *saldo* ⓜ *sal*-do

balcony *balcone* ⓜ bal-*ko*-ne

ball (dancing) *ballo* ⓜ *ba*-lo

ball (inflated) *pallone* ⓜ pa-*lo*-ne

ball (sports) *palla* ⓕ *pa*-la

ballet *balletto* ⓜ ba-*le*-to

band (music) *gruppo* ⓜ *groo*-po

bandage *fascia* ⓕ *fa*-sha

Band-aids *cerotti* ⓜ pl che-*ro*-tee

bank (money) *banca* ⓕ *ban*-ka

bank account *conto* ⓜ *in banca*
kon-to een *ban*-ka

banknote *banconota* ⓕ ban-ko-*no*-ta

baptism *battesimo* ⓜ ba-*te*-zee-mo

bar *locale* ⓜ lo-*ka*-le

bar fridge *frigobar* ⓜ *free*-go-bar

barber *barbiere* ⓜ bar-*bye*-re

baseball *baseball* ⓜ *bays*-bol

basket *cestino* ⓜ ches-*tee*-no

basketball *pallacanestro* ⓕ
pa-la-ka-*ne*-stro

bath *bagno* ⓜ *ba*-nyo

bathing suit *costume* ⓜ *da bagno*
kos-*too*-me da *ba*-nyo

bathroom *bagno* ⓜ *ba*-nyo

battery (for car) *batteria* ① ba·te·*ree*·a
battery (general) *pila* ① *pee*·la
be *essere* e·se·re
beach *spiaggia* ① *spya*·ja
beans *fagioli* ⓜ pl fa·*jo*·lee
beansprouts *germogli* ⓜ pl *(di soia)*
  jer·*mo*·lyee (dee *so*·ya)
beautician *estetista* ⓜ&① es·te·*tee*·sta
beautiful *bello/a* ⓜ/① *be*·lo/a
beauty salon *parrucchiere* ⓜ
  pa·roo·*kye*·re
because *perché* per·*ke*
bed *letto* ⓜ *le*·to
bedding *coperte* ① pl e *lenzuola* ① pl
  ko·*per*·te e len·*zwo*·la
bedroom *camera* ① *da letto*
  ka·me·ra da *le*·to
bee *ape* ① *a*·pe
beef *manzo* ⓜ *man*·dzo
beer *birra* ① *bee*·ra
beetroot *barbabietola* ① bar·ba·*bye*·to·la
before *prima* *pree*·ma
beggar *mendicante* ⓜ&①
  men·dee·*kan*·te
begin *cominciare* ko·meen·*cha*·re
behind *dietro* *dye*·tro
Belgium *Belgio* ⓜ *bel*·jo
below *sotto* *so*·to
best *migliore* mee·*lyo*·re
bet *scommessa* ① sko·*me*·sa
better *migliore* mee·*lyo*·re
between *fra* fra
bible *bibbia* ① *bee*·bya
bicycle *bicicletta* ① bee·chee·*kle*·ta
big *grande* *gran*·de
bike chain *catena* ① *di bicicletta*
  ka·*te*·na dee bee·chee·*kle*·ta
bike lock *lucchetto* ⓜ loo·*ke*·to
bike path *ciclopista* ① chee·klo·*pee*·sta
bill (account) *conto* ⓜ *kon*·to
binoculars *binocolo* ⓜ bee·*no*·ko·lo
bird *uccello* ⓜ oo·*che*·lo
birthday *compleanno* ⓜ kom·ple·*a*·no
biscuit *biscotto* ⓜ bees·*ko*·to
bite (dog) *morso* ⓜ *mor*·so
bite (insect) *puntura* ① poon·*too*·ra
black *nero/a* ⓜ/① *ne*·ro/a
blanket *coperta* ① ko·*per*·ta

blind *cieco/a* ⓜ/① *chye*·ko/a
blister *vescica* ① ve·*shee*·ka
blocked *bloccato/a* ⓜ/① blo·*ka*·to/a
blonde *biondo/a* ⓜ/① *byon*·do/a
blood *sangue* ⓜ *san*·gwe
blood group *gruppo* ⓜ *sanguigno*
  groo·po san·*gwee*·nyo
blood pressure *pressione* ① *del sangue*
  pre·*syo*·ne del *san*·gwe
blood test *analisi* ① *del sangue*
  a·*na*·lee·zee del *san*·gwe
blue (dark) *blu* bloo
blue (light) *azzurro/a* ⓜ/① a·*dzoo*·ro/a
board (plane/ship) *salire su* sa·*lee*·re su
boarding house *pensione* ① pen·*syo*·ne
boarding pass *carta* ① *d'imbarco*
  kar·ta deem·*bar*·ko
boat *barca* ① *bar*·ka
body *corpo* ⓜ *kor*·po
bone *osso* ⓜ *o*·so
book *libro* ⓜ *lee*·bro
book (make a booking) *prenotare*
  pre·no·*ta*·re
booked out *completo/a* ⓜ/①
  kom·*ple*·to/a
bookshop *libreria* ① lee·bre·*ree*·a
boots *stivali* ⓜ pl stee·*va*·lee
boots (ski) *scarponi* ⓜ pl *(da sci)*
  skar·*po*·nee (da shee)
boots (soccer) *scarpette* ① pl skar·*pe*·te
border *confine* ⓜ kon·*fee*·ne
bored *annoiato/a* ⓜ/① a·no·ya·to/a
boring *noioso/a* ⓜ/① no·yo·zo/a
borrow *prendere in prestito*
  pren·de·re een pres·*tee*·to
bottle *bottiglia* ① bo·*tee*·lya
bottle opener *apribottiglie* ⓜ
  a·pree·bo·*tee*·lye
(at the) bottom *(in) fondo* ⓜ
  (een) *fon*·do
bowl *piatto* ⓜ *fondo* pya·to *fon*·do
box *scatola* ① *ska*·to·la
boxing *pugilato* ⓜ poo·jee·*la*·to
boy *bambino* ⓜ bam·*bee*·no
boy(friend) *ragazzo* ⓜ ra·*ga*·tso
bra *reggiseno* ⓜ re·jee·*se*·no
Braille *braille* ⓜ bray
brake *freno* ⓜ *fre*·no

brave *coraggioso/a* ⓜ/ⓕ ko·ra·jo·zo/a
bread *pane* ⓜ pa·ne
  rye bread *pane* ⓜ *di segala*
  pa·ne dee se·ga·la
  sourdough bread *pane* ⓜ *a pasta
  acida* pa·ne a pas·ta a·chee·da
  wholemeal bread *pane* ⓜ *integrale*
  pa·ne een·te·gra·le
break *rompere* rom·pe·re
break down *guastarsi* gwas·tar·see
breakfast *(prima) colazione* ⓕ
  (pree·ma) ko·la·tsyo·ne
breast *seno* ⓜ se·no
breathe *respirare* res·pee·ra·re
brewery *fabbrica di birra* ⓕ
  fa·bree·ka dee bee·ra
bribe *corrompere* ko·rom·pe·re
bridge *ponte* ⓜ pon·te
briefcase *valigetta* ⓕ va·lee·je·ta
brilliant *brillante* ⓜ/ⓕ bree·lan·te
bring *portare* por·ta·re
broken *rotto/a* ⓜ/ⓕ ro·to/a
broken down *guastato/a* ⓜ/ⓕ
  gwas·ta·to/a
bronchitis *bronchite* ⓕ bron·kee·te
brother *fratello* ⓜ fra·te·lo
brown *marrone* ⓜ/ⓕ ma·ro·ne
bruise *livido* ⓜ lee·vee·do
bucket *secchio* ⓜ se·kyo
Buddhist *buddista* ⓜ&ⓕ boo·dee·sta
budget *bilancio* ⓜ bee·lan·cho
buffet (meal) *pasto* ⓜ *freddo*
  pas·to fre·do
bug *insetto* ⓜ een·se·to
build *costruire* kos·troo·ee·re
builder *costruttore/costruttrice* ⓜ/ⓕ
  kos·troo·to·re/kos·stroo·tree·che
building *edificio* ⓜ e·dee·fee·cho
burn *bruciare* broo·cha·re
bus (city) *autobus* ⓜ ow·to·boos
bus (coach) *pullman* ⓜ pool·man
bus station *stazione* ⓕ *d'autobus*
  sta·tsyo·ne dow·to·boos
bus stop *fermata* ⓕ *d'autobus*
  fer·ma·ta dow·to·boos
business *affari* ⓜ pl a·fa·ree
business class *classe* ⓕ *business*
  kla·se beez·nes

business person *uomo/donna d'affari*
  ⓜ/ⓕ wo·mo/do·na da·fa·ree
business studies *commercio* ⓜ
  ko·mer·cho
business trip *viaggio* ⓜ *d'affari*
  vee·a·jo da·fa·ree
busker *musicista* ⓜ&ⓕ *di strada*
  moo·zee·chee·sta dee stra·da
but *ma* ma
butcher's shop *macelleria* ⓕ
  ma·che·lee·ree·a
butter *burro* ⓜ boo·ro
butterfly *farfalla* ⓕ far·fa·la
button *bottone* ⓜ bo·to·ne
buy *comprare* kom·pra·re

C

cabbage *cavolo* ⓜ ka·vo·lo
cable car *funivia* ⓕ foo·nee·vee·a
cafe *bar* ⓜ bar
cake *torta* ⓕ tor·ta
cake shop *pasticceria* ⓕ
  pa·stee·che·ree·a
calculator *calcolatrice* ⓕ
  kal·ko·la·tree·che
calendar *calendario* ⓜ ka·len·da·ryo
camera *macchina* ⓕ *fotografica*
  ma·kee·na fo·to·gra·fee·ka
camera shop *fotografo* ⓜ fo·to·gra·fo
camp *campeggiare* kam·pe·ja·re
camp site *campeggio* ⓜ kam·pe·jo
camping store *negozio* ⓜ *da campeggio*
  ne·go·tsyo da kam·pe·jo
can (tin) *scatola* ⓕ ska·to·la
can *potere* po·te·re
can opener *apriscatole* ⓜ
  a·pree·ska·to·le
Canada *Canada* ⓜ ka·na·da
cancel *cancellare* kan·che·la·re
cancer *cancro* ⓜ kan·kro
candle *candela* ⓕ kan·de·la
candy *dolciumi* ⓜ pl dol·choo·mee
cantaloupe *melone* ⓜ me·lo·ne
capsicum *peperone* ⓜ pe·pe·ro·ne
car *macchina* ⓕ ma·kee·na
car hire *autonoleggio* ⓜ ow·to·no·le·jo

car owner's title
libretto Ⓜ *di circolazione*
lee·*bre*·to dee cheer·ko·la·*tsyo*·ne
car park *parcheggio* Ⓜ par·*ke*·jo
car racing *automobilismo* Ⓜ
ow·to·mo·bee·*leez*·mo
car registration *bollo* Ⓜ *di circolazione*
bo·lo dee cheer·ko·la·*tsyo*·ne
caravan *roulotte* Ⓕ roo·*lot*
cards *carte* Ⓕ pl *kar*·te
carpenter *carpentiere* Ⓜ kar·pen·*tye*·re
carrot *carota* Ⓕ ka·*ro*·ta
carry *portare* por·*ta*·re
carry-on luggage *bagaglio* Ⓜ *a mano*
ba·*ga*·lyo a *ma*·no
carton *scatola* Ⓕ *ska*·to·la
cash *soldi* Ⓜ pl *sol*·dee
cash a cheque *riscuotere un assegno*
ree·*skwo*·te·re oon a·*se*·nyo
cash register *cassa* Ⓕ *ka*·sa
cashew *noce* Ⓕ *(di acagiù)*
no·che (dee a·ka·joo)
cashier *cassiere/a* Ⓜ/Ⓕ ka·*sye*·re/a
casino *casinò* Ⓜ ka·zee·*no*
cassette *cassetta* Ⓕ ka·*se*·ta
castle *castello* Ⓜ kas·*te*·lo
cat *gatto* Ⓜ *ga*·to
cathedral *duomo* Ⓜ *dwo*·mo
Catholic *cattolico/a* Ⓜ/Ⓕ ka·*to*·lee·ko/a
cauliflower *cavolfiore* Ⓜ ka·vol·*fyo*·re
cave *grotta* Ⓕ *gro*·ta
caviar *caviale* Ⓜ ka·*vya*·le
CD *cidì* Ⓜ chee·*dee*
celebration *celebrazione* Ⓕ
che·le·bra·*tsyo*·ne
cell phone *(telefono) cellulare* Ⓜ
(te·*le*·fo·no) che·loo·*la*·re
cent *centesimo* Ⓜ chen·*te*·zee·mo
centimetre *centimetro* Ⓜ
chen·*tee*·me·tro
central heating *riscaldamento* Ⓜ
centrale rees·kal·da·*men*·to chen·*tra*·le
centre *centro* Ⓜ *chen*·tro
cereal *cereali* Ⓜ pl che·re·*a*·lee
certificate *certificato* Ⓜ
cher·tee·fee·*ka*·to
chain *catena* Ⓕ ka·*te*·na
chair *sedia* Ⓕ *se*·dya

chairlift (skiing) *seggiovia* Ⓕ se·jo·*vee*·a
championships *campionato* Ⓜ
kam·pyo·*na*·to
chance *fortuna* Ⓕ for·*too*·na
change (coins) *spiccioli* Ⓜ pl
spee·cho·lee
change (money) *resto* Ⓜ *res*·to
change *cambiare* kam·*bya*·re
change room (sport) *spogliatoio* Ⓜ
spo·lya·*to*·yo
charming *affascinante* a·fa·shee·*nan*·te
chat up *agganciare* a·gan·*cha*·re
cheap *economico/a* Ⓜ/Ⓕ
e·ko·no·mee·ko/a
cheat *imbrogliare* eem·bro·*lya*·re
check (bill) *conto* Ⓜ *kon*·to
check *controllare* kon·tro·*la*·re
check-in (airport) *accetazione* Ⓕ
a·che·ta·*tsyo*·ne
check-in (hotel) *registrazione* Ⓕ
re·jee·stra·*tsyo*·ne
cheese *formaggio* Ⓜ for·*ma*·jo
chef *cuoco/a* Ⓜ/Ⓕ *kwo*·ko/a
chemist *farmacista* Ⓜ&Ⓕ
far·ma·*chee*·sta
cheque *assegno* Ⓜ a·*se*·nyo
chess *scacchi* Ⓜ pl *ska*·kee
chest *petto* Ⓜ *pe*·to
chicken *pollo* Ⓜ *po*·lo
chickpeas *ceci* Ⓜ pl *che*·chee
child *bambino/a* Ⓜ/Ⓕ bam·*bee*·no/a
child seat *seggiolino* Ⓜ se·jo·*lee*·no
child minding (group) *asilo nido* Ⓜ
a·*zee*·lo *nee*·do
chilli *peperoncino* Ⓜ pe·pe·ron·*chee*·no
chilli sauce *salsa* Ⓕ *di peperoncino rosso*
sal·sa dee pe·pe·ron·*chee*·no *ro*·so
chiropractor *chiropratico* Ⓜ
kee·ro·*pra*·tee·ko
chocolate *cioccolato* Ⓜ cho·ko·*la*·to
Christian *cristiano/a* Ⓜ/Ⓕ krees·*tya*·no/a
Christmas *Natale* Ⓜ na·*ta*·le
church *chiesa* Ⓕ *kye*·za
cider *sidro* Ⓜ *see*·dro
cigar *sigaro* Ⓜ *see*·ga·ro
cigarette *sigaretta* Ⓕ see·ga·*re*·ta
cigarette lighter *accendino* Ⓜ
a·chen·*dee*·no

cinema *cinema* ⓜ chee·ne·ma

circus *circo* ⓜ cheer·ko

citizenship *cittadinanza* ⓕ
chee·ta·dee·nan·tsa

city *città* ⓕ chee·ta

class *classe* ⓕ kla·se

classical *classico/a* ⓜ/ⓕ kla·see·ko/a

clean *pulito/a* ⓜ/ⓕ poo·lee·to/a

cleaning *pulizia* ⓕ poo·lee·tsee·a

client *cliente* ⓜ&ⓕ klee·en·te

cliff *scogliera* ⓕ sko·lye·ra

climb *scalare* ska·la·re

cloakroom *guardaroba* ⓜ gwar·da·ro·ba

clock *orologio* ⓜ o·ro·lo·jo

close (nearby) *vicino/a* ⓜ/ⓕ
vee·chee·no/a

close (shut) *chiudere* kyoo·de·re

closed *chiuso/a* ⓜ/ⓕ kyoo·zo/a

clothes line *corda* ⓕ *del bucato*
kor·da del boo·ka·to

clothing *abbigliamento* ⓜ
a·bee·lya·men·to

clothing store
negozio ⓜ *di abbigliamento*
ne·go·tsyo dee a·bee·lya·men·to

cloud *nuvola* ⓕ noo·vo·la

cloudy *nuvoloso/a* ⓜ/ⓕ noo·vo·lo·zo/a

clutch *frizione* ⓕ free·tsyo·ne

coach (bus) *pullman* ⓜ pool·man

coast *costa* ⓕ kos·ta

coat *cappotto* ⓜ ka·po·to

cocaine *cocaina* ⓕ ko·ka·ee·na

cockroach *scarafaggio* ⓜ ska·ra·fa·jo

cocoa *cacao* ⓜ ka·ka·o

coffee *caffè* ⓜ ka·fe

coins *monete* ⓕ pl mo·ne·te

cold *freddo/a* ⓜ/ⓕ fre·do/a

have a cold *essere raffreddato/a* ⓜ/ⓕ
e·se·re ra·fre·da·to/a

colleague *collega* ⓜ&ⓕ ko·le·ga

collect call *chiamata* ⓕ *a carico del
destinatario* kya·ma·ta a ka·ree·ko del
des·tee·na·ta·ryo

college *collegio* ⓜ *universitario*
ko·le·jo oo·nee·ver·see·ta·ryo

colour *colore* ⓜ ko·lo·re

comb *pettine* ⓜ pe·tee·ne

come *venire* ve·nee·re

comedy *commedia* ⓕ *comica*
ko·me·dya ko·mee·ka

comfortable *comodo/a* ⓜ/ⓕ ko·mo·do/a

commission *commissione* ⓕ
ko·mee·syo·ne

communion *comunione* ⓕ
ko·moo·nyo·ne

communist *comunista* ⓜ&ⓕ
ko·moo·nee·sta

companion *compagno/a* ⓜ/ⓕ
kom·pa·nyo/a

company (firm) *ditta* ⓕ dee·ta

compass *bussola* ⓕ boo·so·la

complain *lamentarsi* la·men·tar·see

complimentary (free) *gratuito/a* ⓜ/ⓕ
gra·too·ee·to/a

computer *computer* ⓜ kom·pyoo·ter

computer game *gioco* ⓜ *elettronico*
jo·ko e·le·tro·nee·ko

concert *concerto* ⓜ kon·cher·to

conditioner *balsamo* ⓜ *per i capelli*
bal·sa·mo per e ka·pe·lee

condom *preservativo* ⓜ pre·zer·va·tee·vo

confession (religious) *confessione* ⓕ
kon·fe·syo·ne

confirm (a booking) *confermare*
kon·fer·ma·re

connection (transport) *coincidenza* ⓕ
ko·een·chee·den·tsa

conservative
conservatore/conservatrice ⓜ/ⓕ
kon·ser·va·to·re/kon·ser·va·tree·che

constipation *stitichezza* ⓕ stee·tee·ke·tsa

consulate *consolato* ⓜ kon·so·la·to

contact lenses *lenti* ⓕ pl *a contatto*
len·tee a kon·ta·to

contraceptive *contraccettivo* ⓜ
kon·tra·che·tee·vo

contract *contratto* ⓜ kon·tra·to

convenience store *alimentari* ⓜ
a·lee·men·ta·ree

convent *convento* ⓜ kon·ven·to

cook *cuoco/a* ⓜ/ⓕ kwo·ko/a

cook *cucinare* koo·chee·na·re

cookie *biscotto* ⓜ bees·ko·to

corn flakes *fiocchi* ⓜ pl *di mais*
fyo·kee dee ma·ees

corner *angolo* ⓜ an·go·lo
correct *giusto/a* ⓜ/ⓕ joo·sto/a
corrupt *corrotto/a* ⓜ/ⓕ ko·ro·to/a
cost *costare* kos·ta·re
cot *culla* ⓕ koo·la
cotton *cotone* ⓜ ko·to·ne
cotton balls *batuffoli* ⓜ pl di cotone
ba·too·fo·lee dee ko·to·ne
cough *tossire* to·see·re
cough medicine *sciroppo* ⓜ per la tosse
shee·ro·po per la to·se
count *contare* kon·ta·re
counter (at bar) *bancone* ⓜ ban·ko·ne
country (nation) *paese* ⓜ pa·e·ze
countryside *campagna* ⓕ kam·pa·nya
courgette *zucchini* ⓜ pl tsoo·kee·nee
court (legal) *corte* ⓕ kor·te
court (tennis) *campo* ⓜ da tennis
kam·po da te·nees
cover charge (restaurant) *coperto* ⓜ
ko·per·to
cover charge (venue) *ingresso* ⓜ
een·gre·so
cow *mucca* ⓕ moo·ka
craft (product) *pezzo* ⓜ d'artigianato
pe·tso dar·tee·ja·na·to
craft (trade) *mestiere* ⓜ mes·tye·re
crash (accident) *incidente* ⓜ
een·chee·den·te
crazy *pazzo/a* ⓜ/ⓕ pa·tso/a
cream (food) *panna* ⓕ pa·na
cream cheese *formaggio* ⓜ fresco
for·ma·jo fres·ko
creche *asilo* ⓜ nido a·zee·lo nee·do
credit card *carta* ⓕ di credito
kar·ta dee kre·dee·to
cricket *cricket* ⓜ kree·ket
crime (infringment) *delitto* ⓜ de·lee·to
crime (issue) *criminalità* ⓕ
kree·mee·na·lee·ta
Croatia *Croazia* ⓕ kro·a·tsya
cross (religious) *croce* ⓕ kro·che
crowded *affollato/a* ⓜ/ⓕ a·fo·la·to/a
cucumber *cetriolo* ⓜ che·tree·o·lo
cup *tazza* ⓕ ta·tsa
currency exchange *cambio* ⓜ valuta
kam·byo va·loo·ta

current (electricity) *corrente* ⓕ ko·ren·te
current affairs *attualità* ⓕ a·too·a·lee·ta
curry *curry* ⓜ koo·ree
curry powder *polvere* ⓕ da curry
pol·ve·re da koo·ree
customs *dogana* ⓕ do·ga·na
cut *tagliare* ta·lya·re
cutlery *posate* ⓕ pl po·za·te
CV *curriculum vitae* ⓜ
koo·ree·koo·loom vee·te
cycle *andare in bicicletta*
an·da·re een bee·chee·kle·ta
cycling *ciclismo* ⓜ chee·kleez·mo
cyclist *ciclista* ⓜ&ⓕ chee·klee·sta
cystitis *cistite* ⓕ chees·tee·te

D

dad *papà* ⓜ pa·pa
damage *danno* ⓜ da·no
dance *ballare* ba·la·re
dancing *ballo* ⓜ ba·lo
dangerous *pericoloso/a* ⓜ/ⓕ
pe·ree·ko·lo·zo/a
dark *scuro/a* ⓜ/ⓕ skoo·ro/a
date (appointment) *appuntamento* ⓜ
a·poon·ta·men·to
date (day) *data* ⓕ da·ta
date (go out with) *uscire con*
oo·shee·re kon
date of birth *data* ⓕ di nascita
da·ta dee na·shee·ta
daughter *figlia* ⓕ fee·lya
day *giorno* ⓜ jor·no
day after tomorrow *dopodomani*
do·po·do·ma·nee
day before yesterday *altro ieri* ⓜ
al·tro ye·ree
dead *morto/a* ⓜ/ⓕ mor·to/a
deaf *sordo/a* ⓜ/ⓕ sor·do/a
deep *profondo/a* ⓜ/ⓕ pro·fon·do/a
delay *ritardo* ⓜ ree·tar·do
delicatessen *salumeria* ⓕ
sa·loo·me·ree·a
democracy *democrazia* ⓕ
de·mo·kra·tsee·a
demonstration (protest) *manifestazione*
ⓕ ma·nee·fes·ta·tsyo·ne

Denmark *Danimarca* ① da·nee·*mar*·ka
dental floss *filo* ⓜ *dentario* fee·lo den·*ta*·ree·o
dentist *dentista* ⓜ&① den·*tee*·sta
deodorant *deodorante* ⓜ de·o·do·*ran*·te
depart *partire* par·*tee*·re
department store *grande magazzino* ⓜ *gran*·de ma·ga·*dzee*·no
departure *partenza* ① par·*ten*·tsa
deposit (bank) *deposito* ⓜ de·*po*·zee·to
deposit (refundable) *caparra* ① ka·*pa*·ra
derailleur *deragliatore* ⓜ de·ra·lya·*to*·re
dessert *dolce* ⓜ *dol*·che
destination *destinazione* ①
des·tee·na·*tsyo*·ne
diabetes *diabete* ⓜ dee·a·*be*·te
dial tone *segnale* ⓜ *(acustico)*
se·*nya*·le (a·koos·tee·ko)
diaper *pannolino* ⓜ pa·no·*lee*·no
diaphragm *diaframma* ① dee·a·*fra*·ma
diarrhoea *diarrea* ① dee·a·*re*·a
diary *agenda* ① a·*jen*·da
dictionary *vocabolario* ⓜ vo·ka·bo·*la*·ryo
die *morire* mo·*ree*·re
diet *dieta* ① *dye*·ta
different *diverso/a* dee·*ver*·so/a
different (from) *differente (da)*
dee·fe·*ren*·te (da)
difficult *difficile* dee·*fee*·chee·le
digital *digitale* dee·jee·*ta*·le
dining car *carrozza* ① *ristorante*
ka·*ro*·tsa rees·to·*ran*·te
dinner *cena* ① *che*·na
direct *diretto/a* ⓜ/① dee·*re*·to/a
direct-dial *telefono* ⓜ *diretto*
te·*le*·fo·no dee·*re*·to
direction *direzione* ① dee·re·*tsyo*·ne
director (films) *regista* ⓜ&① re·*jee*·sta
dirty *sporco/a* ⓜ/① *spor*·ko/a
disabled *disabile* dee·za·*bee*·le
discount *sconto* ⓜ *skon*·to
discrimination *discriminazione* ①
dees·kree·mee·na·*tsyo*·ne
disease *malattia* ① ma·la·*tee*·a
disinfectant *disinfettante* ⓜ
deez·een·fe·*tan*·te
disk (computer) *dischetto* ⓜ dees·*ke*·to

disposable *usa e getta* oo·za e *je*·ta
dive *tuffarsi* ⓜ pl too·*far*·see
diving (sea) *immersioni* ① pl
ee·mer·*syo*·nee
divorced *divorziato/a* ⓜ/①
dee·vor·*tsya*·to/a
dizzy *stordito/a* ⓜ/① stor·*dee*·to/a
do *fare* *fa*·re
doctor *medico* ⓜ *me*·dee·ko
dog *cane* ⓜ *ka*·ne
doll *bambola* ① *bam*·bo·la
dollar *dollaro* ⓜ *do*·la·ro
door *porta* ① *por*·ta
dope (drugs) *roba* ① *ro*·ba
double *doppio/a* ⓜ/① *do*·pyo/a
double bed *letto* ⓜ *matrimoniale*
le·to ma·tree·mo·*nya*·le
double room *camera* ① *doppia*
ka·mer·a *do*·pya
down *giù* joo
dozen *dozzina* ① do·*dzee*·na
drag queen *travestito* ⓜ tra·ves·*tee*·to
drama *dramma* ⓜ *dra*·ma
dream *sogno* ⓜ *so*·nyo
dream *sognare* so·*nya*·re
dress *abito* ⓜ *a*·bee·to
drink *bevanda* ① be·*van*·da
drink *bere* *be*·re
drinkable *potabile* po·ta·*bee*·le
drive *guidare* gwee·*da*·re
drivers licence *patente* ① *(di guida)*
pa·*ten*·te (dee gwee·da)
drug (medicinal) *medicina* ①
me·dee·*chee*·na
drug addiction *tossicodipendenza* ①
to·see·ko·dee·pen·*den*·tsa
drug dealer *spacciatore/spacciatrice*
ⓜ/① spa·cha·to·re/spa·cha·*tree*·che
drugs (illegal) *droga* ① sg *dro*·ga
drums *batteria* ① ba·te·*ree*·a
drunk *ubriaco/a* ⓜ/① oo·bree·*a*·ko/a
dry *secco/a* ⓜ/① *se*·ko/a
dry *asciugare* a·shoo·*ga*·re
dry cleaning *lavaggio* ⓜ *a secco*
la·*va*·jo a *se*·ko

duck *anatra* ① a·na·tra
dummy (pacifier) *ciucciotto* ⑩ choo·*cho*·to
during *durante* doo·*ran*·te

E

each *ciascuno/a* ⑩/① chas·*koo*·no/a
ear *orecchio* ⑩ o·*re*·kyo
early *presto* ⑩/① *pres*·to
earplugs *tappi* ⑩ pl *per le orecchie* *ta*·pee per le o·*re*·kye
earrings *orecchini* ⑩ pl o·re·*kee*·nee
Earth *Terra* ① *te*·ra
earthquake *terremoto* ⑩ te·re·*mo*·to
east *est* ⑩ est
Easter *Pasqua* ① *pas*·kwa
easy *facile* fa·*chee*·le
eat *mangiare* man·*ja*·re
economy class *classe* ① *turistica* *kla*·se too·*ree*·stee·ka
eczema *eczema* ⑩ ek·*dze*·ma
education *istruzione* ① ees·troo·*tsyo*·ne
egg *uovo* ⑩ *wo*·vo
eggplant *melanzana* ① me·lan·*dza*·na
elections *elezioni* ① pl e·le·*tsyo*·nee
electrician *elettricista* ⑩&① e·le·tree·*chee*·sta
electricity *elettricità* ① e·le·tree·chee·*ta*
elevator *ascensore* ⑩ a·shen·*so*·re
email *email* ⑩ e·*mayl*
embarrassed *imbarazzato/a* ⑩/① eem·ba·ra·*tsa*·to/a
embassy *ambasciata* ① am·ba·*sha*·ta
emergency *emergenza* ① e·mer·*jen*·tsa
emotional *emotivo/a* ⑩/① e·mo·*tee*·vo/a
employee *impiegato/a* ⑩/① eem·pye·*ga*·to/a
employer *datore/datrice* ⑩/① *di lavoro* da·*to*·re/da·*tree*·ce dee la·*vo*·ro
empty *vuoto/a* ⑩/① *vwo*·to/a
end *fine* ① *fee*·ne
end *finire* fee·*nee*·re
endangered species *specie* ① *in via di estinzione* *spe*·che en *vee*·a dee es·teen·*tsyo*·ne
engagement (couple) *fidanzamento* ⑩ fee·dan·tsa·*men*·to

engine *motore* ⑩ mo·*to*·re
engineer *ingegnere* ⑩&① een·je·*nye*·re
England *Inghilterra* ① een·geel·*te*·ra
English *inglese* een·*gle*·ze
enjoy (oneself) *divertirsi* dee·ver·*teer*·see
enough *abbastanza* a·bas·*tan*·tsa
enter *entrare* en·*tra*·re
entertainment guide *guida* ① *agli spettacoli* *gwee*·da a·lyee spe·ta·*ko*·lee
entry *entrata* ① en·*tra*·ta
(padded) envelope *busta* ① *(imbottita)* *boo*·sta eem·bo·*tee*·ta
environment *ambiente* ⑩ am·*byen*·te
epilepsy *epilessia* ① e·pee·le·*see*·a
equipment *attrezzatura* ① a·tre·tsa·*too*·ra
escalator *scala* ① *mobile* *ska*·la *mo*·bee·le
euro *euro* ⑩ e·oo·ro
Europe *Europa* ① e·oo·*ro*·pa
European *europeo/a* ⑩/① e·oo·ro·*pe*·o/a
euthanasia *eutanasia* ① e·oo·ta·na·*zee*·a
evening *sera* ① *se*·ra
everything *tutto* ⑩ *too*·to
example *esempio* ⑩ e·*zem*·pyo
excellent *ottimo/a* ⑩/① o·*tee*·mo/a
excess bagage *bagaglio* ⑩ *in eccedenza* ba·*ga*·lyo een e·che·*den*·tsa
exchange *cambio* ⑩ *kam*·byo
exchange *cambiare* kam·*bya*·re
exchange rate *tasso* ⑩ *di cambio* *ta*·so dee *kam*·byo
excluded *escluso/a* ⑩/① es·*kloo*·zo/a
exhaust (car) *tubo* ⑩ *di scappamento* *too*·bo dee ska·pa·*men*·to
exhibition *esposizione* ① es·po·zee·*tsyo*·ne
exit *uscita* ① oo·*shee*·ta
expensive *caro/a* ⑩/① *ka*·ro/a
experience *esperienza* ① es·pe·*ryen*·tsa
exploitation *sfruttamento* ⑩ sfroo·ta·*men*·to
express *espresso/a* ⑩/① es·*pre*·so/a
express mail *posta* ① *prioritaria* *pos*·ta pree·o·ree·*ta*·rya
extension (visa) *proroga* ① pro·*ro*·ga
eye *occhio* ⑩ *o*·kyo
eye drops *collirio* ⑩ ko·*lee*·ryo

F

fabric *stoffa* ⓕ sto·fa
face *faccia* ⓕ fa·cha
factory *fabbrica* ⓕ fa·bree·ka
factory worker *operaio/a* ⓜ/ⓕ
o·pe·ra·yo/a
fall (autumn) *autunno* ⓜ ow·too·no
family *famiglia* ⓕ fa·mee·lya
family name *cognome* ⓜ ko·nyo·me
famous *famoso/a* ⓜ/ⓕ fa·mo·zo/a
fan (person) *tifoso/a* ⓜ/ⓕ tee·fo·zo/a
fan (machine) *ventilatore* ⓜ
ven·tee·la·to·re
fan belt *cinghia* ⓕ *della ventola*
cheen·gya de·la ven·to·la
far *lontano/a* ⓜ/ⓕ lon·ta·no/a
farm *fattoria* ⓕ fa·to·ree·a
farmer *agricoltore/agricoltrice* ⓜ/ⓕ
a·gree·kol·to·re/a·gree·kol·tree·che
fashion *moda* ⓕ mo·da
fast *veloce* ve·lo·che
fat *grasso/a* ⓜ/ⓕ gra·so/a
father *padre* ⓜ pa·dre
father-in-law *suocero* ⓜ swo·che·ro
faucet *rubinetto* ⓜ roo·bee·ne·to
fault (someone's) *colpa* ⓕ kol·pa
faulty *difettoso/a* ⓜ/ⓕ dee·fe·to·zo/a
favourite *preferito/a* ⓜ/ⓕ pre·fe·ree·to/a
fax *fax* ⓜ faks
fee *compenso* ⓜ kom·pen·so
feel *sentire* sen·tee·re
feelings *sentimenti* ⓜ pl sen·tee·men·tee
fence *recinto* ⓜ re·cheen·to
fencing (sport) *scherma* ⓕ sker·ma
ferry *traghetto* ⓜ tra·ge·to
festival *festa* ⓕ fes·ta
fever *febbre* ⓕ fe·bre
few *pochi/e* ⓜ/ⓕ po·kee/po·ke
fiance(e) *fidanzato/a* ⓜ/ⓕ
fee·dan·tsa·to/a
fiction *narrativa* ⓕ na·ra·tee·va
fig *fico* ⓜ fee·ko
fight *lite* ⓕ lee·te
film (cinema) *film* ⓜ feelm
film (roll for camera) *rullino* ⓜ
roo·lee·no
film speed *ASA* a·za

find *trovare* tro·va·re
fine (payment) *multa* ⓕ mool·ta
finger *dito* ⓜ dee·to
finish *finire* fee·nee·re
fire *fuoco* ⓜ fwo·ko
firewood *legna* ⓕ *da ardere*
le·nya da ar·de·re
first *primo/a* ⓜ/ⓕ pree·mo/a
first class *prima classe* ⓕ pree·ma kla·se
first-aid kit
valigetta ⓕ *del pronto soccorso*
va·lee·je·ta del pron·to so·kor·so
fish *pesce* ⓜ pe·she
fish shop *pescheria* ⓕ pe·ske·ree·a
fishing *pesca* ⓕ pe·ska
flag *bandiera* ⓕ ban·dye·ra
flash (camera) *flash* ⓜ flesh
flashlight (torch) *torcia* ⓕ *elettrica*
tor·cha e·le·tree·ka
flat *appartamento* ⓜ a·par·ta·men·to
flat *piatto/a* ⓜ/ⓕ pya·to/a
flea *pulce* ⓕ pool·che
flight *volo* ⓜ vo·lo
flood *inondazione* ⓕ ee·non·da·tzyo·nee
floor (ground) *pavimento* ⓜ
pa·vee·men·to
floor (storey) *piano* ⓜ pya·no
florist *fioraio* ⓜ&ⓕ fyo·ra·yo
flour *farina* ⓕ fa·ree·na
flower *fiore* ⓜ fyo·re
flu *influenza* ⓕ een·floo·en·tsa
fly *mosca* ⓕ mos·ka
fly *volare* vo·la·re
foggy *nebbioso/a* ⓜ/ⓕ ne·byo·zo/a
follow *seguire* se·gwee·re
food *cibo* ⓜ chee·bo
food poisoning
intossicazione ⓕ *alimentare*
een·to·see·ka·tsyo·ne a·lee·men·ta·re
food supplies *provviste* ⓕ pl *alimentari*
pro·vee·ste a·lee·men·ta·ree
foot *piede* ⓜ pye·de
football (soccer) *calcio* ⓜ kal·cho
footpath *marciapiede* ⓜ mar·cha·pye·de
foreign *straniero/a* ⓜ/ⓕ stra·nye·ro/a
forest *foresta* ⓕ fo·res·ta
forever *per sempre* per sem·pre

forget *dimenticare* dee·men·tee·*ka*·re
forgive *perdonare* per·do·*na*·re
fork *forchetta* ① for·*ke*·ta
form (paper) *modulo* ⓜ *mo*·doo·lo
fortnight *quindici giorni* ⓜ pl
  kween·dee·chee *jor*·nee
foyer *atrio* ⓜ *a*·tryo
fragile *fragile* *fra*·jee·le
France *Francia* ① *fran*·cha
free (gratis) *gratuito/a* ⓜ/①
  gra·*too*·ee·to/a
free (not bound) *libero/a* ⓜ/①
  lee·be·ro/a
freeze *congelare* kon·je·*la*·re
fresh *fresco/a* ⓜ/① *fres*·ko/a
fridge *frigorifero* ⓜ free·go·*ree*·fe·ro
friend *amico/a* ⓜ/① a·*mee*·ko/a
frozen *congelato/a* ⓜ/① kon·je·*la*·to/a
frozen foods *surgelati* ⓜ pl soor·je·*la*·tee
fruit *frutta* ① *froo*·ta
fruit juice (bottled) *succo* ⓜ *di frutta*
  soo·ko dee *froo*·ta
fruit juice (fresh) *spremuta* ①
  spre·*moo*·ta
fry *friggere* *free*·je·re
frying pan *padella* ① pa·*de*·la
full *pieno/a* ⓜ/① *pye*·no/a
full-time *a tempo pieno* a *tem*·po *pye*·no
fun *divertimento* ⓜ dee·ver·tee·*men*·to
have fun *divertirsi* dee·ver·*teer*·see
funeral *funerale* ⓜ foo·ne·*ra*·le
funny *divertente* dee·ver·*ten*·te
furniture *mobili* ⓜ pl *mo*·bee·lee
future *futuro* ⓜ foo·*too*·ro

G

game (play) *gioco* ⓜ *jo*·ko
game (sport) *partita* ① par·*tee*·ta
garage *garage* ⓜ ga·*raj*
garbage *spazzatura* ① pl spa·tsa·*too*·ra
garden *giardino* ⓜ jar·*dee*·no
gardening *giardinaggio* ⓜ jar·dee·*na*·jo
garlic *aglio* ⓜ a·lyo
gas (for cooking) *gas* ⓜ gaz
gas (petrol) *benzina* ① ben·*dze*·na

gas cartridge
  cartuccia ① *di ricambio del gas*
  kar·*too*·cha dee ree·*kam*·byo del gaz
gastroenteritis *gastroenterite* ①
  gas·tro·en·te·*ree*·te
gate *cancello* ⓜ kan·*che*·lo
gay *gay* gei
gears (bicycle) *cambio* ⓜ *kam*·byo
general *generale* je·ne·*ra*·le
Germany *Germania* ① jer·*ma*·nya
gift *regalo* ⓜ re·*ga*·lo
ginger *zenzero* ⓜ *dzen*·dze·ro
girl(friend) *ragazza* ① ra·*ga*·tsa
give *dare* *da*·re
glandular fever *mononucleosi* ⓜ
  mo·no·noo·kle·o·zee
glass (material) *vetro* ⓜ *ve*·tro
glass (drinking) *bicchiere* ⓜ bee·*kye*·re
glasses (spectacles) *occhiali* ⓜ pl
  o·*kya*·lee
gloves *guanti* ⓜ pl *gwan*·tee
go *andare* an·*da*·re
go out with *uscire con* oo·*shee*·re kon
goat *capra* ① *ka*·pra
god (general) *dio/dea* ⓜ/① *dee*·o/*de*·a
goggles (skiing) *occhiali* ⓜ pl *(da sci)*
  o·*kya*·lee (da shee)
gold *oro* ⓜ *o*·ro
golf ball *palla* ① *da golf* *pa*·la da golf
golf course *campo* ⓜ *da golf*
  kam·po da golf
good *buono/a* ⓜ/① *bwo*·no/a
government *governo* ⓜ go·*ver*·no
grams *grammi* ⓜ pl *gra*·mee
grandchild *nipote* ⓜ&① nee·*po*·te
grandfather *nonno* ⓜ *no*·no
grandmother *nonna* ① *no*·na
grapefruit *pompelmo* ⓜ pom·*pel*·mo
grapes *uva* ① pl *oo*·va
grass *erba* ① *er*·ba
grave (tomb) *tomba* ① *tom*·ba
great *ottimo/a* ⓜ/① o·*tee*·mo/a
green *verde* *ver*·de
greengrocer *fruttivendolo/a* ⓜ/①
  froo·tee·ven·*do*·lo/a
grey *grigio/a* ⓜ/① *gree*·jo/a
grocery *drogheria* ① dro·ge·*ree*·a
groundnut *arachide* ① a·ra·*kee*·de

grow *crescere* kre·she·re
guesthouse *pensione* ① pen·syo·ne
guide (audio) *guida* ① *audio*
gwee·da ow·dyo
guide (person) *guida* ① gwee·da
guide dog *cane* ⓜ *guida* ka·ne gwee·da
guidebook *guida* ① *(turistica)*
gwee·da (too·ree·stee·ka)
guided tour *visita* ① *guidata*
vee·zee·ta gwee·da·ta
guilty *colpevole* kol·pe·vo·le
guitar *chitarra* ① kee·ta·ra
gum (mouth) *gengiva* ① jen·jee·va
gum (chewing) *gomma* ① *da masticare*
go·ma da ma·stee·ka·re
gym *palestra* ① pa·le·stra
gymnastics *ginnastica* ① jee·nas·tee·ka
gynaecologist *ginecologo/a* ⓜ/①
jee·ne·ko·lo·go/a

H

hail *grandine* ① gran·dee·ne
hailstorm *grandinata* ① gran·dee·na·ta
haircut *taglio* ⓜ *di capelli*
ta·lyo dee ka·pe·lee
hairdresser *parrucchiere/a* ⓜ/①
pa·roo·kye·re/a
halal *halal* a·lal
half *mezzo* ⓜ me·dzo
hallucinate *allucinare* a·loo·chee·na·re
ham (boiled) *prosciutto* ⓜ *(cotto)*
pro·shoo·to (ko·to)
hammer *martello* ⓜ mar·te·lo
hammock *amaca* ① a·ma·ka
hand *mano* ① ma·no
handbag *borsetta* ① bor·se·ta
handball *pallamuro* ① pa·la·moo·ro
handicrafts *oggetti* ⓜ pl *d'artigianato*
o·je·tee dar·tee·ja·na·to
handkerchief *fazzoletto* ⓜ fa·tso·le·to
handlebars *manubrio* ⓜ ma·noo·bryo
handmade *fatto/a* ⓜ/① *a mano*
fa·to/a a ma·no
handsome *bello/a* ⓜ/① be·lo/a
happy *felice* ⓜ/① fe·lee·che
harassment *molestia* ① mo·les·tya
harbour *porto* ⓜ por·to

hard (not easy) *difficile* dee·fee·chee·le
hard (not soft) *duro/a* ⓜ/① doo·ro/a
hardware store *ferramenta* ①
fe·ra·men·ta
hash *hashish* ⓜ a·sheesh
hat *cappello* ⓜ ka·pe·lo
have *avere* a·ve·re
hay fever *febbre* ① *da fieno*
fe·bre da fye·no
he *lui* loo·ee
head *testa* ① tes·ta
headache *mal* ⓜ *di testa* mal de tes·ta
headlights *fari* ⓜ pl fa·ree
health *salute* ① sa·loo·te
hear *sentire* sen·tee·re
hearing aid *apparecchio* ⓜ *acustico*
a·pa·re·kyo a·koos·tee·ko
heart *cuore* ⓜ kwo·re
heart condition *problema* ⓜ *cardiaco*
pro·ble·ma kar·dee·a·ko
heat *caldo* ⓜ kal·do
heater *stufa* ① stoo·fa
heating *riscaldamento* ⓜ
rees·kal·da·men·to
heavy *pesante* pe·zan·te
height *altezza* ① al·te·tsa
helmet *casco* ⓜ kas·ko
help *aiutare* a·yoo·ta·re
hepatitis *epatite* ① e·pa·tee·te
herbalist *erborista* ⓜ&① er·bo·ree·sta
herbs *erbe* ① pl er·be
here *qui* kwee
heroin *eroina* ① e·ro·ee·na
herring *aringa* ① a·reen·ga
high *alto/a* ⓜ/① al·to/a
high school *scuola* ① *superiore*
skwo·la soo·pe·ryo·re
hike *escursione* ① *a piedi*
es·koor·syo·ne a pye·de
hiking *escursionismo* ⓜ *a piedi*
es·koor·syo·neez·mo a pye·de
hiking boots *scarponi* ⓜ pl skar·po·nee
hiking route *itinerario* ⓜ *escursionistico*
e·tee·ne·ra·ryo es·koor·syo·nee·stee·ko
hill *collina* ① ko·lee·na
Hindu *indù* ⓜ&① een·doo
hire *noleggiare* no·le·ja·re
historical *storico/a* ⓜ/① sto·ree·ko/a

history *storia* ⓕ *sto·rya*

hitchhike *fare l'autostop*
fa·re low·to·stop

HIV positive *sieropositivo/a* ⓜ/ⓕ
sye·ro·po·zee·tee·vo/a

hobby *passatempo* ⓜ *pa·sa·tem·po*

hockey *hockey* ⓜ *o·kee*

holidays *vacanze* ⓕ pl *va·kan·tse*

Holy Week *settimana* ⓕ *santa*
se·tee·ma·na san·ta

home *casa* ⓕ *ka·za*

homeless *senzatetto* ⓜ&ⓕ *sen·tsa·te·to*

homemaker *casalingo/a* ⓕ
ka·za·leen·go/a

homeopathy *omeopatia* ⓕ
o·me·o·pa·tee·a ·

homosexual *omosessuale* ⓜ&ⓕ
o·mo·se·swa·le

honey *miele* ⓜ *mye·le*

honeymoon *luna* ⓕ *di miele*
loo·na dee mye·le

horse *cavallo* ⓜ *ka·va·lo*

horse riding *andare a cavallo*
an·da·re a ka·va·lo

horseradish *rafano* ⓜ *ra·fa·no*

hospital *ospedale* ⓜ *os·pe·da·le*

hospitality *ospitalità* ⓕ *os·pee·ta·lee·ta*

hot *caldo/a* ⓜ/ⓕ *kal·do/a*

hot water *acqua* ⓕ *calda* a·kwa *kal·da*

hotel *albergo* ⓜ *al·ber·go*

hour *ora* ⓕ *o·ra*

house *casa* ⓕ *ka·za*

how *come* *ko·me*

how much *quanto/a* ⓜ/ⓕ *kwan·to/a*

hug *abbracciare* a·bra·cha·re

huge *enorme* e·nor·me

human rights *diritti* ⓜ pl *umani*
dee·ree·tee oo·ma·nee

(to be) hungry *avere fame* ⓕ
a·ve·re fa·me

hunting *caccia* ⓕ *ka·cha*

(to be) in a hurry *avere fretta* ⓕ
a·ve·re fre·ta

hurt *fare male* fa·re ma·le

husband *marito* ⓜ *ma·ree·to*

hydrating fluid *fluido* ⓜ *idratante*
floo·ee·do ee·dra·tan·te

I

I *io* ee·o

ice *ghiaccio* ⓜ *gya·cho*

ice axe *piccozza* ⓕ *pee·ko·tsa*

ice cream *gelato* ⓜ *je·la·to*

ice-cream parlour *gelateria* ⓕ
je·la·te·ree·a

ice hockey *hockey* ⓜ *su ghiaccio*
o·kee soo gya·cho

identification *documento* ⓜ *d'identità*
do·koo·men·to dee·den·tee·ta

identification card (ID) *carta* ⓕ
d'identità kar·ta dee·den·tee·ta

idiot *idiota* ⓜ&ⓕ ee·dyo·ta

if *se* se

ill *malato/a* ⓜ/ⓕ ma·la·to/a

illegal *illegale* ee·le·ga·le

immigration *immigrazione* ⓕ
ee·mee·gra·tsyo·ne

important *importante* eem·por·tan·te

impossible *impossibile* eem·po·see·bee·le

included *compreso/a* ⓜ/ⓕ kom·pre·zo/a

indicator (car) *freccia* ⓕ *fre·cha*

indigestion *indigestione* ⓕ
een·dee·je·styo·ne

industry *industria* ⓕ een·doos·trya

infection *infezione* ⓕ een·fe·tsyo·ne

inflammation *infiammazione* ⓕ
een·fya·ma·tsyo·ne

influenza *influenza* ⓕ een·floo·en·tsa

information *informazioni* ⓕ pl
een·for·ma·tsyo·nee

ingredient *ingrediente* ⓜ
een·gre·dyen·te

inhaler *inalatore* ⓜ ee·na·la·to·re

injection *iniezione* ⓕ ee·nye·tsyo·ne

injured *ferito/a* ⓜ/ⓕ fe·ree·to/a

injury *ferita* ⓕ fe·ree·ta

innocent *innocente* ee·no·chen·te

insect *insetto* ⓜ een·se·to

inside *dentro* den·tro

instructor (general) *istruttore/istruttrice*
ⓜ/ⓕ ee·stroo·to·re/ee·stroo·tree·che

instructor (skiing) *maestro/a* ⓜ/ⓕ
ma·es·tro/a

insurance *assicurazione* ⓕ
a·see·koo·ra·tsyo·ne

interesting *interessante* een·te·re·*san*·te
intermission *intervallo* ⓜ een·ter·*va*·lo
international *internazionale*
een·ter·na·tsyo·*na*·le
Internet (cafe) *Internet (point)* ⓜ
een·ter·net (poynt)
interpreter *interprete* ⓜ/ⓕ een·ter·*pre*·te
intersection *incrocio* ⓜ een·*kro*·cho
interview *colloquio* ⓜ *(selettivo)*
ko·*lo*·kwyo (se·le·*tee*·vo)
invite *invitare* een·vee·*ta*·re
Ireland *Irlanda* ⓕ eer·*lan*·da
iron (for clothes) *ferro* ⓜ *da stiro*
fe·ro da *stee*·ro
island *isola* ⓕ *ee*·zo·la
IT *informatica* ⓕ een·for·ma·*tee*·ka
Italian *italiano/a* ⓜ/ⓕ ee·ta·*lya*·no/a
Italy *Italia* ⓕ ee·*ta*·lya
itch *prurito* ⓜ proo·*ree*·to
itinerary *itinerario* ⓜ ee·tee·ne·*ra*·ryo
IUD *spirale* ⓕ spee·*ra*·le

J

jacket *giacca* ⓕ *ja*·ka
jail *prigione* ⓕ pree·*jo*·ne
jam *marmellata* ⓕ mar·me·*la*·ta
Japan *Giappone* ⓜ ja·*po*·ne
jar *barattolo* ⓜ ba·*ra*·to·lo
jealous *geloso/a* ⓜ/ⓕ je·*lo*·zo/a
jeans *jeans* ⓜ pl jeens
jet lag *disturbo* ⓜ pl *da fuso orario*
dees·*toor*·bee da *foo*·zo o·*ra*·ryo
jewellery *gioielli* ⓜ pl jo·*ye*·lee
Jewish *ebreo/a* ⓜ/ⓕ e·*bre*·o/a
job *lavoro* ⓜ la·*vo*·ro
jockey *fantino* ⓜ fan·*tee*·no
jogging *footing* ⓜ *foo*·teeng
joke *scherzo* ⓜ *sker*·tso
journalist *giornalista* ⓜ&ⓕ jor·na·*lee*·sta
judge *giudice* ⓜ *joo*·dee·che
judo *giudò* ⓜ joo·*do*
juice *succo* ⓜ *soo*·ko
jump *saltare* sal·*ta*·re
jumper *maglione* ⓜ ma·*lyo*·ne
jumper leads *cavi* ⓜ pl *con morsetti*
ka·vee kon mor·*se*·tee

K

key *chiave* ⓕ *kya*·ve
keyboard *tastiera* ⓕ tas·*tye*·ra
kick *dare un calcio* *da*·re oon *kal*·cho
kill *ammazzare* a·ma·*tsa*·re
kilogram *chilo* ⓜ *kee*·lo
kilometre *chilometro* ⓜ kee·*lo*·me·tro
kind *gentile* jen·*tee*·le
kindergarten *asilo* ⓜ a·*zee*·lo
king *re* ⓜ re
kiss *bacio* ⓜ *ba*·cho
kiss *baciare* ba·*cha*·re
kitchen *cucina* ⓕ koo·*chee*·na
kitten *gattino* ⓜ ga·*tee*·no
kiwifruit *kiwi* ⓜ *kee*·wee
knapsack *zaino* ⓜ *dzai*·no
knee *ginocchio* ⓜ jee·*no*·kyo
knife *coltello* ⓜ kol·*te*·lo
know (a person) *conoscere* ko·*no*·she·re
know (how to) *sapere* sa·*pe*·re
kosher *kasher* ka·*sher*

L

labourer *lavoratore/lavoratrice* ⓜ/ⓕ
la·vo·ra·*to*·re/la·vo·ra·*tree*·che
lace *merletto* ⓜ mer·*le*·to
lager *birra* ⓕ *chiara* bee·ra *kya*·ra
lake *lago* ⓜ *la*·go
lamb *agnello* ⓜ a·*nye*·lo
land *terra* ⓕ *te*·ra
lane *vicolo* ⓜ *vee*·ko·lo
landlady *padrona* ⓕ *di casa*
pa·*dro*·na dee *ka*·za
landlord *padrone* ⓜ *di casa*
pa·*dro*·ne dee *ka*·za
language *lingua* ⓕ *leen*·gwa
laptop (computer) *portatile* ⓜ
(kom·*pyoo*·ter) por·ta·*tee*·le
lard *lardo* ⓜ *lar*·do
large *grande* *gran*·de
last *ultimo/a* ⓜ/ⓕ *ool*·tee·mo/a
late *in ritardo* een ree·*tar*·do
laugh *ridere* *ree*·de·re
laundrette *lavanderia* ⓕ *a gettone*
la·van·de·*ree*·a je·*to*·ne
laundry *lavanderia* ⓕ la·van·de·*ree*·a

law *legge* ① *le·*je
lawyer *avvocato/a* ⓜ/① a·vo·*ka·*to/a
laxatives *lassativi* ⓜ pl la·sa·*tee·*vee
lazy *pigro/a* ⓜ/① *pee·*gro/a
leader *capo* ⓜ *ka·*po
leaf *foglia* ① *fo·*lya
learn *imparare* eem·pa·*ra·*re
leather *cuoio* ⓜ *kwo·*yo
leave *partire* par·*tee·*re
leek *porro* ⓜ *po·*ro
left (direction) *sinistra* ① see·*nee·*stra
left luggage (office) *deposito* ⓜ *bagagli*
de·*po·*zee·to ba·*ga·*lyee
left wing (di) *sinistra* (dee) see·*nee·*stra
leg (body part) *gamba* ① *gam·*ba
leg (in race) *tappa* ① *ta·*pa
legal *legale* le·*ga·*le
legume *legume* ⓜ le·*goo·*me
lemon *limone* ⓜ lee·*mo·*ne
lemonade *limonata* ① lee·mo·*na·*ta
lens *obiettivo* ⓜ o·bye·*tee·*vo
Lent *quaresima* ① kwa·re·zee·ma
lentil *lenticchia* ① len·*tee·*kya
lesbian *lesbica* ① *lez·*bee·ka
less (di) *meno* (dee) *me·*no
letter *lettera* ① *le·*te·ra
lettuce *lattuga* ① la·*too·*ga
level (tier) *livello* ⓜ lee·*ve·*lo
liar *bugiardo/a* ⓜ/① boo·*jar·*do/a
library *biblioteca* ① bee·blyo·*te·*ka
lice *pidocchi* ⓜ pl pee·*do·*kee
licence plate number *numero* ⓜ *di targa*
*noo·*me·ro dee *tar·*ga
lie (not stand) *stendersi* sten·*der·*see
life *vita* ① *vee·*ta
life jacket *giubbotto* ⓜ *di salvataggio*
joo·*bo·*to dee sal·va·*ta·*jo
lift (elevator) *ascensore* ⓜ a·shen·*so·*re
light *luce* ① *loo·*che
light (colour) *chiaro/a* ⓜ/① *kya·*ro/a
light (not heavy) *leggero/a* ⓜ/①
*le·*je·ro/a
light bulb *lampadina* ① lam·pa·*dee·*na
light meter *esposimetro* ⓜ
es·po·zee·me·tro
lighter *accendino* ⓜ a·chen·*dee·*no
lights (on car) *fari* ⓜ pl *fa·*ree
like *piacere* pya·*che·*re
lime *limetta* ① lee·*me·*ta

line *linea* ① *lee·*ne·a
lip balm *burro* ⓜ *per le labbra* boo·ro
per le *la·*bra
lips *labbra* ① pl *la·*bra
lipstick *rossetto* ⓜ ro·se·to
liquor store *bottiglieria* ①
bo·tee·lye·*ree·*a
list *elenco* ⓜ e·*len·*ko
listen *ascoltare* as·kol·*ta·*re
litre *litro* ⓜ *lee·*tro
(a) little *un po'* oon po
live *vivere* vee·*ve·*re
liver *fegato* ① *fe·*ga·to
lizard *lucertola* ① loo·*cher·*to·la
local *locale* lo·*ka·*le
lock (door) *serratura* ① se·ra·*too·*ra
locked *chiuso/a* ⓜ/① *(a chiave)*
*kyoo·*zo/a (a *kya·*ve)
locker *armadietto* ⓜ ar·ma·*dye·*to
lollies *caramelle* ① pl ka·ra·*me·*le
long *lungo/a* ⓜ/① *loon·*go/a
long-distance (bus) *interurbano/a* ⓜ/①
een·ter·oor·ba·no/a
look *guardare* gwar·*da·*re
look after *curare* koo·*ra·*re
look for *cercare* cher·*ka·*re
lookout *veduta* ① ve·*doo·*ta
loose change *spiccioli* ⓜ pl *spee·*cho·lee
lose *perdere* per·*de·*re
lost *perso/a* ⓜ/① *per·*so/a
lost-property office *ufficio* ⓜ *oggetti*
smarriti oo·*fee·*cho o·*je·*tee sma·*ree·*tee
a lot (of) *molto/a* ⓜ/① *mol·*to/a
loud *forte* ① *for·*te
love *amare* a·*ma·*re
lover *amante* ① a·*man·*te
low *basso/a* ⓜ/① *ba·*so/a
lubricant *lubrificante* ⓜ
loo·bree·fee·*kan·*te
luck *fortuna* ① for·*too·*na
lucky *fortunato/a* ⓜ/① for·too·*na·*to/a
luggage *bagaglio* ⓜ ba·*ga·*lyo
luggage lockers *armadietti* ⓜ pl *per i*
bagagli ar·ma·*dye·*tee per ee ba·*ga·*lyee
luggage tag *etichetta* ① e·tee·*ke·*ta
lump *nodulo* ⓜ *no·*doo·lo
lunch *pranzo* ⓜ *pran·*dzo
lungs *polmoni* ⓜ pl pol·*mo·*nee
luxurious *di lusso* dee *loo·*so

M

machine *macchina* ① ma·kee·na
made of (cotton) *fatto/a* ⑩/① *di (cotone)* fa·to/a dee (ko·to·ne)
magazine *rivista* ① ree·vee·sta
mail *posta* ① pos·ta
mail box *buca* ① *delle lettere* boo·ka de·le *le*·te·re
main *principale* preen·chee·*pa*·le
make *fare* fa·re
make-up *trucco* ⑩ troo·ko
mallet *mazzuolo* ⑩ ma·*tswo*·lo
mammogram *mammografia* ① ma·mo·gra·*fee*·a
man *uomo* ⑩ *wo*·mo
manager *manager* ⑩ me·nee·je
mandarin *mandarino* ⑩ man·da·*ree*·no
mango *mango* ⑩ *man*·go
manual *manuale* ma·noo·*a*·le
manual worker *manovale* ⑩&① ma·no·*va*·le
many *molti/e* ⑩/① pl *mol*·tee/*mol*·te
map *pianta* ① *pyan*·ta
marble *marmo* ⑩ *mar*·mo
margarine *margarina* ① mar·ga·*ree*·na
marijuana *marijuana* ① ma·ree·wa·na
marital status *stato* ⑩ *civile* *sta*·to chee·*vee*·le
market *mercato* ⑩ mer·*ka*·to
marmalade *marmellata* ① mar·me·*la*·ta
marriage *matrimonio* ⑩ ma·tree·*mo*·nyo
married *sposato/a* ⑩/① spo·*za*·to/a
marry *sposare* spo·*za*·re
martial arts *arti* ① pl *marziali* ar·tee mar·*tsya*·lee
mass (Catholic) *messa* ① *me*·sa
massage *massaggio* ⑩ ma·*sa*·jo
mat *tappeto* ⑩ ta·*pe*·to
match (sport) *partita* ① par·*tee*·ta
matches *fiammiferi* ⑩ pl fya·me·*fe*·ree
mattress *materasso* ⑩ ma·te·*ra*·so
maybe *forse* *for*·se
mayonnaise *maionese* ① ma·yo·*ne*·ze
mayor *sindaco* ⑩ *seen*·da·ko
measles *morbillo* ⑩ mor·*bee*·lo
meat *carne* ① *kar*·ne

mechanic *meccanico* ⑩&① me·*ka*·nee·ko
media *mezzi* ⑩ pl *di comunicazione* *me*·tsee dee ko·moo·nee·ka·*tsyo*·ne
medicine *medicina* ① me·dee·*chee*·na
meditation *meditazione* ① me·dee·ta·*tsyo*·ne
meet *incontrare* een·kon·*tra*·re
melon *melone* ⑩ me·*lo*·ne
member *socio/a* ⑩/① *so*·cho/a
menstruation *mestruazione* ① me·stroo·a·*tsyo*·ne
menu *menu* ⑩ me·*noo*
message *messaggio* ⑩ me·*sa*·jo
metal *metallo* ⑩ me·*ta*·lo
metre (distance) *metro* ⑩ *me*·tro
metro station *stazione* ① *della metropolitana* sta·*tsyo*·ne de·la me·tro·po·lee·*ta*·na
microwave oven *forno* ⑩ *a microonde* *for*·no a mee·kro·on·de
midnight *mezzanotte* ① me·dza no·te
migraine *emicrania* ① e·mee·*kra*·nya
military *le forze* ① pl *armate* le *for*·tse ar·*ma*·te
military service *servizio* ⑩ *militare* ser·vee·tsyo mee·lee·*ta*·re
milk *latte* ⑩ *la*·te
millimetre *millimetro* ⑩ mee·*lee*·me·tro
mince *carne* ① *tritata* *kar*·ne tree·*ta*·ta
mineral water *acqua* ① *minerale* *a*·kwa mee·ne·*ra*·le
mini-bar *frigobar* ⑩ *free*·go·bar
mints *caramelle* ① pl *alla menta* ka·ra·*me*·le a·la *men*·ta
minute *minuto* ⑩ mee·*noo*·to
mirror *specchio* ⑩ *spe*·kyo
miscarriage *aborto* ⑩ *spontaneo* a·*bor*·to spon·*ta*·ne·o
miss (feel absence of) *mancare* man·*ka*·re
mistake *sbaglio* ⑩ *sba*·lyo
mix *mescolare* mes·ko·*la*·re
mobile phone (telefono) *cellulare* (te·*le*·fo·no) che·loo·*la*·re
modem *modem* ⑩ *mo*·dem
modern *moderno/a* ⑩/① mo·*der*·no/a
moisturiser *idratante* ⑩ ee·dra·*tan*·te

monastery *monastero* ⓜ mon·as·te·ro
money *denaro* ⓜ de·na·ro
month *mese* ⓜ me·ze
monument *monumento* ⓜ
  mo·noo·men·to
(full) moon *luna* ⓕ *(piena)*
  loo·na (pye·na)
more *(di) più* (dee) pyoo
morning *mattina* ⓕ ma·tee·na
morning after pill
  la pillola ⓕ *del mattino dopo*
  la pee·lo·la del ma·tee·no do·po
morning sickness *nausea* ⓕ *mattutina*
  now·ze·a ma·too·tee·na
mosque *moschea* ⓕ mos·ke·a
mosquito *zanzara* ⓕ tsan·tsa·ra
mother *madre* ⓕ ma·dre
mother-in-law *suocera* ⓕ swo·che·ra
motorboat *motoscafo* ⓜ mo·to·ska·fo
motorbike *moto* ⓕ mo·to
motorway (tollway) *autostrada* ⓕ
  ow·to·stra·da
mountain *montagna* ⓕ mon·ta·nya
mountain bike *mountain bike* ⓜ
  mown·tayn baik
mountain path *sentiero* ⓜ *di montagna*
  sen·tye·ro dee mon·ta·nya
mountain range *catena* ⓕ *di montagne*
  ka·te·na dee mon·ta·nye
mountaineering *alpinismo* ⓜ
  al·pee·neez·mo
mouse (computer) *mouse* ⓜ mows
mouse (rodent) *topo* ⓜ to·po
mouth *bocca* ⓕ bo·ka
movie *film* ⓜ feelm
mud *fango* ⓜ fan·go
muesli *muesli* ⓜ moos·lee
mum *mamma* ⓕ ma·ma
muscle *muscolo* ⓜ moo·sko·lo
museum *museo* ⓜ moo·ze·o
mushroom *fungo* ⓜ foon·go
music *musica* ⓕ moo·zee·ka
musician *musicista* ⓜ&ⓕ
  moo·zee·chee·sta
Muslim *musulmano/a* ⓜ/ⓕ
  moo·sool·ma·no/a
mussels *cozze* ⓕ pl ko·tse
mustard *senape* ⓕ se·na·pe
mute *muto/a* ⓜ/ⓕ moo·to/a

N

nail clippers *tagliaunghie* ⓜ
  ta·lya·oon·gye
name *nome* ⓜ no·me
napkin *tovagliolo* ⓜ to·va·lyo·lo
nappy *pannolino* ⓜ pa·no·lee·no
nappy rash *sfogo* ⓜ *da pannolino*
  sfo·go da pa·no·lee·no
national *nazionale* na·tsyo·na·le
national park *parco* ⓜ *nazionale*
  par·ko na·tsyo·na·le
nationality *nazionalità* ⓕ
  na·tsyo·na·lee·ta
nature *natura* ⓕ na·too·ra
naturopathy *naturopatia* ⓕ
  na·too·ro·pa·tee·a
near (to) *vicino (a)* vee·chee·no (a)
nearby *vicino/a* ⓜ/ⓕ vee·chee·no/a
necessary *necessario/a* ⓜ/ⓕ
  ne·che·sa·ryo/a
neck *collo* ⓜ ko·lo
need *avere bisogno di*
  a·ve·re bee·zo·nyo dee
needle (sewing) *ago* ⓜ a·go
needle (syringe) *ago* ⓜ *da siringa*
  a·go da see·reen·ga
neither *nessuno/a* ⓜ/ⓕ ne·soo·no/a
net *rete* ⓕ re·te
Netherlands *Paesi Bassi* ⓜ pl
  pa·e·zee ba·see
never *mai* mai
new *nuovo/a* ⓜ/ⓕ nwo·vo/a
New Year's Day *Capodanno* ⓜ
  ka·po da·no
New Year's Eve *san Silvestro* ⓜ
  san seel·ves·tro
New Zealand *Nuova Zelanda* ⓕ
  nwo·va dze·lan·da
news *notizie* ⓕ pl no·tee·tsye
newsagency *edicola* ⓕ e·dee·ko·la
newspaper *giornale* ⓜ jor·na·le
next *prossimo/a* ⓜ/ⓕ pro·see·mo/a
next to *accanto a* a·kan·to a
nice (meal) *buono/a* ⓜ/ⓕ bwo·no/a
nice (person) *gentile* jen·tee·le
nice (weather) *bello/a* ⓜ/ⓕ be·lo/a
nickname *soprannome* ⓜ so·pra·no·me
night *notte* ⓕ no·te

no *no* no
noisy *rumoroso/a* ⓜ/ⓕ roo·mo·ro·zo/a
non-direct *non-diretto/a* ⓜ/ⓕ non·dee·re·to/a
none *niente* nyen·te
non-smoking *non fumatore* non foo·ma·to·re
noodles *pasta* ⓕ pas·ta
noon *mezzogiorno* ⓜ me·dzo jor·no
north *nord* ⓜ nord
nose *naso* ⓜ na·zo
notebook *quaderno* ⓜ kwa·der·no
nothing *niente* nyen·te
novel *romanzo* ⓜ ro·man·dzo
now *adesso* a·de·so
nuclear energy *energia* ⓕ *nucleare* en·er·jee·a noo·kle·a·re
nuclear testing *esperimenti* ⓜ pl *nucleari* es·pe·ree·men·tee noo·kle·a·ree
nuclear waste *scorie* ⓕ pl *radioattive* sko·rye ra·dyo·a·tee·ve
number *numero* ⓜ noo·me·ro
number plate *targa* ⓕ tar·ga
nun *suora* ⓕ swo·ra
nurse *infermiere/a* ⓜ/ⓕ een·fer·mye·re/a

O

oats *avena* ⓕ a·ve·na
occupation (work) *mestiere* ⓜ mes·tye·re
ocean *oceano* ⓜ o·che·a·no
off (spoiled) *guasto/a* ⓜ/ⓕ gwa·sto/a
office *ufficio* ⓜ oo·fee·cho
office worker *impiegato/a* ⓜ/ⓕ eem·pye·ga·to/a
often *spesso* spe·so
oil *olio* ⓜ o·lyo
old *vecchio/a* ⓜ/ⓕ ve·kyo/a
old city *centro* ⓜ *storico* chen·tro sto·ree·ko
olive *oliva* ⓕ o·lee·va
olive oil *olio* ⓜ *d'oliva* o·lyo do·lee·va
on *su* soo
once *una volta* ⓕ oo·na vol·ta
one-way (ticket) *(un biglietto di) solo andata* (oon bee·lye·to dee) so·lo an·da·ta

onion *cipolla* ⓕ chee·po·la
only *solo* so·lo
open *aperto/a* ⓜ/ⓕ a·per·to/a
open *aprire* a·pree·re
opening hours *orario* ⓜ *di apertura* o·ra·ryo dee a·per·too·ra
opera *opera* ⓕ *lirica* o·pe·ra lee·ree·ka
opera house *teatro* ⓜ *dell'opera* te·a·tro del·o·pe·ra
operation (medical) *intervento* ⓜ een·ter·ven·to
operator *operatore/operatrice* ⓜ/ⓕ o·pe·ra·to·re/o·pe·ra·tree·che
opinion *opinione* ⓕ o·pee·nyo·ne
opposite *di fronte a* dee fron·te a
or *o* o
orange (colour) *arancione* a·ran·cho·ne
orange (fruit) *arancia* ⓕ a·ran·cha
orange juice (bottled) *succo* ⓜ *d'arancia* soo·ko da·ran·cha
orange juice (fresh) *spremuta* ⓜ *d'arancia* spre·moo·ta da·ran·cha
orchestra *orchestra* ⓕ or·kes·tra
order *ordine* ⓜ or·dee·ne
order *ordinare* or·dee·na·re
ordinary *ordinario/a* ⓜ/ⓕ or·dee·na·ryo/a
original *originale* ⓜ/ⓕ o·ree·jee·na·le
other *altro/a* ⓜ/ⓕ al·tro/a
outside *fuori* fwo·ree
ovarian cyst *cisti* ⓕ *ovarica* chee·stee o·va·ree·ka
oven *forno* ⓜ for·no
over (above) *sopra* so·pra
overdose *dose* ⓕ *eccessiva* do·ze e·che·see·va
owner *proprietario/a* ⓜ/ⓕ pro·prye·ta·ryo/a
oxygen *ossigeno* ⓜ o·see·je·no
oyster *ostrica* ⓕ o·stree·ka
ozone layer *strato* ⓜ *d'ozono* stra·to do·dzo·no

P

pacemaker *pacemaker* ⓜ pays·may·ke
pacifier *ciucciotto* ⓜ choo·cho·to
package *pacchetto* ⓜ pa·ke·to
packet (general) *pacchetto* ⓜ pa·ke·to

padded envelope *busta* ① *imbottita*
boos·ta eem·bo·tee·ta
padlock *lucchetto* ⓜ loo·ke·to
page *pagina* ① pa·jee·na
pain *dolore* ⓜ do·lo·re
painful *doloroso/a* ⓜ/① do·lo·ro·zo/a
painkillers *analgesico* ⓜ an·al·je·zee·ko
paint *dipingere* dee·peen·je·re
painter *pittore/pittrice* ⓜ/①
pee·to·re/pee·tree·che
painting (the art) *pittura* ① pee·too·ra
painting (canvas) *quadro* ⓜ kwa·dro
pair *paio* ⓜ pa·yo
palace *palazzo* ⓜ pa·la·tso
pan *pentola* ① pen·to·la
pants *pantaloni* ⓜ pl pan·ta·lo·nee
panty liners *salva slip* ① pl sal·va sleep
pantyhose *collant* ① pl ko·lant
pap smear *pap test* ⓜ pap test
paper *carta* ① kar·ta
papers *documenti* ⓜ pl do·koo·men·tee
paperwork *moduli* ⓜ pl mo·doo·lee
parcel *pacchetto* ⓜ pa·ke·to
parents *genitori* ⓜ pl je·nee·to·ree
park *parco* ⓜ par·ko
parliament *parlamento* ⓜ par·la·men·to
part *parte* ① par·te
part-time *ad orario ridotto*
ad o·ra·ryo ree·do·to
partner (intimate) *compagno/a* ⓜ/①
kom·pa·nyo/a
party (celebration) *festa* ① fes·ta
party (politics) *partito* ⓜ par·tee·to
pass (document) *tessera* ① te·se·ra
pass (mountain) *passo* ⓜ pa·so
pass (sport) *passaggio* ⓜ pa·sa·jo
passenger *passeggero/a* ⓜ/①
pa·se·je·ro/a
passport *passaporto* ⓜ pa·sa·por·to
past *passato* ⓜ pa·sa·to
pate (food) *paté* ⓜ pa·te
path *sentiero* ⓜ sen·tye·ro
pay *pagare* pa·ga·re
payment *pagamento* ⓜ pa·ga·men·to
pea *pisello* ⓜ pee·ze·lo
peace *pace* ① pa·che
peach *pesca* ① pe·ska
peak *cima* ① chee·ma

peanuts *arachidi* ① pl a·ra·kee·dee
pear *pera* ① pe·ra
pedal *pedale* ⓜ pe·da·le
pedestrian *pedone* ⓜ/① pe·do·ne
pegs (tent) *picchetti* ⓜ pl pee·ke·tee
pen (ballpoint) *penna* ① *(a sfera)*
pe·na (a sfe·ra)
pencil *matita* ① ma·tee·ta
penis *pene* ⓜ pe·ne
penicillin *penicillina* ①
pe·nee·chee·lee·na
penknife *temperino* ⓜ tem·pe·ree·no
pensioner *pensionato/a* ⓜ/①
pen·syo·na·to/a
people *gente* ① jen·te
pepper *pepe* ⓜ pe·pe
per (day) *al (giorno)* al (jor·no)
per cent *per cento* ① per·chen·to
performance *spettacolo* ⓜ spe·ta·ko·lo
perfume *profumo* ⓜ pro·foo·mo
period pain *dolori* ⓜ pl *mestruali*
do·lo·ree me·stroo·a·lee
permanent *permanente* ⓜ/①
per·ma·nen·te
permission *permesso* ⓜ per·me·so
permit *permesso* ⓜ per·me·so
person *persona* ① per·so·na
personal *personale* ⓜ/① per·so·na·le
petition *petizione* ① pe·tee·tsyo·ne
petrol *benzina* ① ben·dzee·na
petrol station *distributore* ⓜ
dee·stree·boo·to·re
pharmacy *farmacia* ① far·ma·chee·a
phone book *elenco* ⓜ *telefonico*
e·len·ko te·le·fo·nee·ko
phone box *cabina* ① *telefonica*
ka·bee·na te·le·fo·nee·ka
phone call *chiamata* ① kya·ma·ta
phonecard *scheda* ① *telefonica*
ske·da te·le·fo·nee·ka
photo *foto* ① fo·to
photographer *fotografo* ⓜ fo·to·gra·fo
photography *fotografia* ① fo·to·gra·fee·a
phrasebook *vocabolarietto* ⓜ
vo·ka·bo·la·rye·to
pick (up) *raccogliere* ra·ko·lye·re
pickaxe *piccone* ⓜ pee·ko·ne
pickles *sottoaceti* ⓜ pl so·to·a·che·tee

picnic *picnic* ⓜ peek·neek

pie *torta* ① tor·ta

piece *pezzo* ⓜ pe·tso

pig *maiale* ⓜ ma·ya·le

pill *pillola* ① pee·lo·la

the Pill *la pillola* ① *(anticoncezionale)* la pee·lo·la (an·tee·kon·che·tsyo·na·le)

pillow *cuscino* ⓜ koo·shee·no

pillowcase *federa* ① fe·de·ra

pineapple *ananas* ⓜ a·na·nas

pink *rosa* ⓜ/① ro·za

pistachio *pistacchio* ⓜ pee·sta·kyo

place (location) *luogo* ⓜ lwo·go

place (seat) *posto* ⓜ pos·to

place of birth *luogo* ⓜ *di nascita* lwo·go dee na·shee·ta

plane *aereo* ⓜ a·e·re·o

planet *pianeta* ① pya·ne·ta

plant *pianta* ① pyan·ta

plastic *plastica* ① pla·stee·ka

plate *piatto* ⓜ pya·to

plateau *altopiano* ⓜ al·to·pya·no

platform *binario* ⓜ bee·na·ryo

play (a game) *giocare* jo·ka·re

play (guitar) *suonare (la chitarra)* swo·na·re (la kee·ta·ra)

play (soccer) *giocare (a calcio)* jo·ka·re (a kal·cho)

play (sport) *praticare* pra·tee·ka·re

play (theatre) *commedia* ① ko·me·dya

playground *parco* ⓜ *giochi* par·ko jo·kee

plug (bath) *tappo* ⓜ ta·po

plug (electricity) *spina* ① spee·na

plum *prugna* ① proo·nya

pocket *tasca* ① tas·ka

poetry *poesia* ① po·e·zee·a

point *punto* ⓜ poon·to

point *indicare* een·dee·ka·re

poisonous *velenoso/a* ⓜ/① ve·le·no·zo/a

police (civilian) *polizia* ① po·lee·tsee·a

police (military) *carabinieri* ⓜ pl ka·ra·bee·nye·ree

police station *posto* ⓜ *di polizia* pos·to dee po·lee·tsee·a

politician *politico* ⓜ po·lee·tee·ko

politics *politica* ① po·lee·tee·ka

pollen *polline* ① po·lee·ne

polls *elezioni* ① pl e·le·tsyo·nee

pollution *inquinamento* ⓜ een·kwee·na·men·to

pony *cavallino* ⓜ ka·va·lee·no

pool (game) *biliardo* ⓜ beel·yar·do

pool (swimming) *piscina* ① pee·shee·na

poor *povero/a* ⓜ/① po·ve·ro/a

popular *popolare* po·po·la·re

pork *maiale* ⓜ ma·ya·le

port *porto* ⓜ por·to

possible *possibile* po·see·bee·le

post code *codice* ⓜ *postale* ko·dee·che pos·ta·le

poste restante *fermo* ⓜ *posta* fer·mo pos·ta

post office *ufficio* ⓜ *postale* oo·fee·cho pos·ta·le

postage *tariffa* ① *postale* ta·ree·fa pos·ta·le

postcard *cartolina* ① kar·to·lee·na

pot (ceramics) *pignatta* ① pee·nya·ta

pot (dope) *erba* ① er·ba

pot (cooking) *pentola* ① pen·to·la

potato *patata* ① pa·ta·ta

pottery *oggetti* ⓜ pl *in ceramica* o·je·tee een che·ra·mee·ka

pound (money) *sterlina* ① ster·lee·na

poverty *povertà* ① po·ver·ta

power *potere* ⓜ po·te·re

prawn *gambero* ⓜ gam·be·ro

prayer *preghiera* ① pre·gye·ra

prefer *preferire* pre·fe·ree·re

pregnancy test kit *test* ⓜ *di gravidanza* test dee gra·vee·dan·tsa

pregnant *incinta* een·cheen·ta

premenstrual tension *tensione* ① *premestruale* ten·syo·ne pre·me·stroo·a·le

prepare *preparare* pre·pa·ra·re

prescription *ricetta* ① ree·che·ta

present (gift) *regalo* ⓜ re·ga·lo

president *presidente* ⓜ/① pre·zee·den·te

pressure *pressione* ① pre·syo·ne

pretty *carino/a* ⓜ/① ka·ree·no/a

previous *precedente* pre·che·den·te

price *prezzo* ⓜ pre·tso

priest *prete* ⓜ pre·te

prime minister *primo ministro* ⓜ/① pree·mo mee·nee·stro

printer (computer) *stampante* ①
stam·*pan*·te

prison *prigione* ① pree·*jo*·ne

prisoner *prigioniero/a* ⓜ/①
pree·jo·*nye*·ro/a

private *privato/a* ⓜ/① pree·*va*·to/a

produce *produrre* pro·*doo*·re

profit *profitto* ⓜ pro·*fee*·to

program *programma* ⓜ pro·*gra*·ma

projector *proiettore* ⓜ pro·ye·*to*·re

promise *promessa* ① pro·*me*·sa

protect *proteggere* pro·*te*·je·re

protected (species) *(specie)* ① *protetta*
(*spe*·che) pro·*te*·ta

protest *manifestazione* ①
ma·ne·fes·ta·*tsyo*·ne

protest *protestare* pro·tes·*ta*·re

provisions *provviste* ① pl pro·*vee*·ste

prune *prugna* ① *proo*·nya

pub *pub* ⓜ poob

public holiday *festa* ① *fes*·ta

public telephone *telefono* ⓜ *pubblico*
te·*le*·fo·no *poo*·blee·ko

public toilet *gabinetto* ⓜ *pubblico*
ga·bee·*ne*·to *poo*·blee·ko

pull *tirare* tee·*ra*·re

pump *pompa* ① *pom*·pa

pumpkin *zucca* ① *tsoo*·ka

puncture *bucatura* ① boo·ka·*too*·ra

puppy *cucciolo* ⓜ *koo*·cho·lo

pure *puro/a* ⓜ/① *poo*·ro/a

purple *viola* vee·*o*·la

push *spingere* *speen*·je·re

put *mettere* *me*·te·re

Q

qualifications *titoli* ⓜ pl *di studio*
tee·to·lee dee *stoo*·dee·o

quality *qualità* ① kwa·lee·*ta*

quantity *quantità* ① kwan·tee·*ta*

quarantine *quarantena* ① kwa·ran·*te*·na

quarrel *bisticcio* ⓜ bees·*tee*·cho

quarter *quarto* ⓜ *kwar*·to

queen *regina* ① re·*jee*·na

question *domanda* ① do·*man*·da

queue *coda* ① *ko*·da

quick *rapido/a* ⓜ/① *ra*·pee·do/a

quiet *tranquillo/a* ⓜ/① tran·*kwee*·lo/a

R

rabbit *coniglio* ⓜ ko·*nee*·lyo

race (sport) *gara* ① *ga*·ra

racetrack *pista* ① *pee*·sta

racing bike *bici* ① *da corsa*
bee·chee da *kor*·sa

racism *razzismo* ⓜ ra·*tseez*·mo

racquet *racchetta* ① ra·*ke*·ta

radiator *radiatore* ⓜ ra·dya·*to*·re

(railway) station *stazione* ① *(ferroviaria)*
sta·*tsyo*·ne fe·ro·vee·a·*ree*·a

rain *pioggia* ⓜ *pyo*·ja

raincoat *impermeabile* ⓜ
eem·per·me·a·*bee*·le

raisin *uva* ① *passa* oo·va *pa*·sa

rape *stupro* ⓜ *stoo*·pro

rare *raro/a* ⓜ/① *ra*·ro/a

rash *sfogo* ⓜ *sfo*·go

raspberry *lampone* ⓜ lam·*po*·ne

rat *topo* ⓜ *to*·po

raw *crudo/a* ⓜ/① *kroo*·do/a

razor *rasoio* ⓜ ra·*zo*·yo

razor blades *lamette* ① pl *(da barba)*
la·*me*·te (da *bar*·ba)

read *leggere* *le*·je·re

ready *pronto/a* ⓜ/① *pron*·to/a

realistic *realistico/a* ⓜ/①
re·a·*lee*·stee·ko/a

reason *ragione* ① ra·*jo*·ne

receipt *ricevuta* ① ree·che·*voo*·ta

receive *ricevere* ree·*che*·ve·re

recently *di recente* dee re·*chen*·te

recommend *raccomandare*
ra·ko·man·*da*·re

recyclable *riciclabile* ree·chee·*kla*·bee·le

recycle *riciclare* ree·chee·*kla*·re

red *rosso/a* ⓜ/① *ro*·so/a

referee *arbitro* ⓜ *ar*·bee·tro

reflexology *riflessologia* ①
ree·fle·so·lo·*jee*·a

refrigerator *frigo* ⓜ *free*·go

refugee *rifugiato/a* ⓜ/① ree·foo·*gya*·to/a

refund *rimborso* ⓜ reem·*bor*·so

refuse *rifiutare* ree·fyoo·*ta*·re

region *regione* ① re·*jo*·ne

registered mail (posta) *raccomandata* ①
(*pos*·ta) ra·ko·man·*da*·ta

regular *normale* nor·ma·le
relationship *rapporto* ⓜ ra·por·to
relax *rilassarsi* ree·la·sar·see
relic *reliquia* ⓕ re·lee·kwee·a
religion *religione* ⓕ re·lee·jo·ne
religious *religioso/a* ⓜ/ⓕ re·lee·jo·zo/a
remote *remoto/a* ⓜ/ⓕ re·mo·to/a
remote control *telecomando* ⓜ
te·le·ko·man·do
rent *affitto* ⓜ a·fee·to
rent *prendere in affitto*
pren·de·re een a·fee·to
repair *riparare* ree·pa·ra·re
reservation *prenotazione* ⓕ
pre·no·ta·tsyo·ne
rest *riposare* ree·po·za·re
restaurant *ristorante* ⓜ rees·to·ran·te
resume *curriculum vitae* ⓜ
koo·ree·koo·loom vee·tay
retired *pensionato/a* ⓜ/ⓕ
pen·syo·na·to/a
return *ritornare* ree·tor·na·re
return (ticket)
(biglietto) di andata e ritorno
(bee·lye·to) dee an·da·ta e ree·tor·no
reverse-charges call *chiamata* ⓕ *a
carico del destinatario* kya·ma·ta a
ka·ree·ko del des·tee·na·ta·ryo
rhythm *ritmo* ⓜ reet·mo
rice *riso* ⓜ ree·zo
brown rice *riso* ⓜ *integrale*
ree·zo een·te·gra·le
rich (wealthy) *ricco/a* ⓜ/ⓕ ree·ko/a
ride *corsa* ⓕ kor·sa
ride (a bike) *andare in bicicletta*
an·da·re een bee·chee·kle·ta
ride (a horse) *cavalcare* ka·val·ka·re
right (correct) *giusto/a* ⓜ/ⓕ joo·sto/a
right (direction) *a destra* a de·stra
right-wing *(di) destra* (dee) de·stra
ring (on finger) *anello* ⓜ a·ne·lo
ring (by phone) *telefonare* te·le·fo·na·re
rip-off *bidone* ⓜ bee·do·ne
risk *rischio* ⓜ rees·kyo
river *fiume* ⓜ fyoo·me
road *strada* ⓕ stra·da
rob *derubare* de·roo·ba·re
rock *roccia* ⓕ ro·cha

rock (music) *(musica)* ⓕ *rock*
(moo·zee·ka) rok
rock climbing *(andare su) roccia* ⓕ
(an·da·re soo) ro·cha
rock group *gruppo* ⓜ *rock*
groo·po rok
roll (bread) *panino* ⓜ pa·nee·no
romantic *romantico/a* ⓜ/ⓕ
ro·man·tee·ko/a
room *camera* ⓕ ka·me·ra
rope *corda* ⓕ kor·da
round *rotondo/a* ⓜ/ⓕ ro·ton·do/a
roundabout *rotonda* ⓕ ro·ton·da
route *itinerario* ⓜ ee·tee·ne·ra·ryo
rowing *canottaggio* ⓜ ka·no·ta·jo
rubbish *spazzatura* ⓕ spa·tsa·too·ra
rug *tappeto* ⓜ ta·pe·to
rugby *rugby* ⓜ roog·bee
ruins *rovine* ⓕ pl ro·vee·ne
rules *regole* ⓕ pl re·go·le
run *correre* ko·re·re
running (sport) *footing* ⓜ foo·teeng

S

Sabbath *sabato* ⓜ sa·ba·to
sad *triste* tree·ste
saddle *sella* ⓕ se·la
safe *cassaforte* ⓕ ka·sa·for·te
safe *sicuro/a* ⓜ/ⓕ see·koo·ro/a
safe sex *rapporti* ⓜ pl *protetti*
ra·por·tee pro·te·tee
safety gear *corredo* ⓜ *antinfortunistico*
ko·re·do an·teen·for·too·nee·stee·ko
saint *santo/a* ⓜ/ⓕ san·to/a
salad *insalata* ⓕ een·sa·la·ta
salami *salame* ⓜ sa·la·me
salary *stipendio* ⓜ stee·pen·dyo
(on) sale *in vendita* een ven·dee·ta
sales tax *IVA* ⓕ ee·va
salmon *salmone* ⓜ sal·mo·ne
salt *sale* ⓜ sa·le
same *stesso/a* ⓜ/ⓕ ste·so/a
sand *sabbia* ⓕ sa·bya
sandals *sandali* ⓜ pl san·da·lee
sandwich *tramezzino* ⓜ tra·me·dzee·no
sanitary napkins *assorbenti* ⓜ pl *igienici*
as·or·ben·tee ee·je·nee·chee

sardines *sardine* ⓕ pl sar·*dee*·ne
sauce *sugo* ⓜ *soo*·go
sauna *sauna* ⓕ *sow*·na
sausage *salsiccia* ⓕ sal·*see*·cha
say *dire* *dee*·re
scanner *scanner* ⓜ *ska*·ner
scarf *sciarpa* ⓕ *shar*·pa
school *scuola* ⓕ *skwo*·la
science *scienza* ⓕ *shen*·tsa
scissors *forbici* ⓕ pl *for*·bee·chee
score *punteggio* ⓜ poon·*te*·jo
score *segnare* se·*nya*·re
scoreboard *tabellone* ⓜ *segnapunti*
  ta·be·*lo*·ne se·nya·*poon*·tee
Scotland *Scozia* ⓕ *sko*·tsya
sculpture *scultura* ⓕ skool·*too*·ra
sea *mare* ⓜ *ma*·re
seasickness *mal* ⓜ *di mare*
  mal dee *ma*·re
seaside *al mare* al *ma*·re
season *stagione* ⓕ sta·*jo*·ne
seat (chair) *sedile* ⓜ se·*dee*·le
seat (place) *posto* ⓜ *pos*·to
seatbelt *cintura* ⓕ *di sicurezza*
  cheen·*too*·ra dee see·koo·*re*·tsa
second *secondo* ⓜ se·*kon*·do
second *secondo/a* ⓜ/ⓕ se·*kon*·do/a
second class *seconda classe* ⓕ
  se·*kon*·da *kla*·se
second-hand *di seconda mano* ⓜ/ⓕ
  dee se·*kon*·da *ma*·no
secretary *segretario/a* ⓜ/ⓕ
  se·gre·*ta*·ryo/a
see *vedere* ve·*de*·re
(to be) self-employed *lavorare in*
  proprio la·vo·*ra*·re een *pro*·pryo
selfish *egoista* ⓜ/ⓕ e·go·*ee*·sta
self-service *self-service* self·*ser*·vees
sell *vendere* *ven*·de·re
send *mandare* man·*da*·re
sensual *sensuale* ⓜ/ⓕ sen·soo·*a*·le
separate *separato/a* ⓜ/ⓕ se·pa·*ra*·to/a
(TV) series *serie* ⓕ *(televisiva)*
  se·ree·e (te·le·vee·*see*·va)
serious *serio/a* ⓜ/ⓕ *se*·ryo/a
service *servizio* ⓜ ser·*vee*·tsyo
service charge *servizio* ⓜ ser·*vee*·tsyo

service station *stazione* ⓕ *di servizio*
  sta·*tsyo*·ne dee ser·*vee*·tsyo
several *diversi/e* ⓜ/ⓕ pl
  dee·*ver*·see/dee·*ver*·se
sew *cucire* koo·*chee*·re
sex *sesso* ⓜ *se*·so
sexism *sessismo* ⓜ se·*seez*·mo
sexy *erotico/a* ⓜ/ⓕ e·ro·*tee*·ko/a
shade *ombra* ⓕ *om*·bra
shadow *ombra* ⓕ *om*·bra
shampoo *shampoo* ⓜ *sham*·poo
shape *forma* ⓕ *for*·ma
share (with) *condividere*
  kon·dee·*vee*·de·re
sharp *affilato/a* ⓜ/ⓕ a·fee·*la*·to/a
shave *rasatura* ⓕ ra·za·*too*·ra
shave *fare la barba* fa·re la *bar*·ba
shaving cream *crema* ⓕ *da barba*
  kre·ma da *bar*·ba
she *lei* lay
sheep *pecora* ⓕ *pe*·ko·ra
sheet (bed) *lenzuolo* ⓜ len·*tswo*·lo
ship *nave* ⓕ *na*·ve
shirt *camicia* ⓕ ka·*mee*·cha
shoe shop *negozio* ⓜ *di scarpe*
  ne·*go*·tsyo dee *skar*·pe
shoes *scarpe* ⓕ pl *skar*·pe
shop *negozio* ⓜ ne·*go*·tsyo
shopping centre *centro* ⓜ *commerciale*
  chen·tro ko·mer·*cha*·le
short (height) *basso/a* ⓜ/ⓕ *ba*·so/a
short (length) *corto/a* ⓜ/ⓕ *kor*·to/a
shorts *pantaloncini* ⓜ pl
  pan·ta·lon·*chee*·nee
shoulder *spalla* ⓕ *spa*·la
shout *urlare* oor·*la*·re
show *spettacolo* ⓜ spe·*ta*·ko·lo
show *mostrare* mos·*tra*·re
shower *doccia* ⓕ *do*·cha
shrine *santuario* ⓜ san·too·*a*·ryo
shut *chiuso/a* ⓜ/ⓕ *kyoo*·zo/a
shy *timido/a* ⓜ/ⓕ *tee*·mee·do/a
sick *malato/a* ⓜ/ⓕ ma·*la*·to/a
side *lato* ⓜ *la*·to
sign *segno* ⓜ *se*·nyo
signature *firma* ⓕ *feer*·ma
silk *seta* ⓕ *se*·ta

S

english–italian

219

silver *argento* ⓜ ar·*jen*·to
similar *simile* ⓜ/ⓕ *see*·mee·le
simple *semplice* ⓜ/ⓕ *sem*·plee·che
since (time) *da* da
sing *cantare* kan·*ta*·re
singer *cantante* ⓜ/ⓕ kan·*tan*·te
single (man) *celibe* ⓜ *che*·lee·be
single (woman) *nubile* ⓕ *noo*·bee·le
single room *camera* ⓕ *singola*
ⓜ *ka*·me·ra *seen*·go·la
singlet *canottiera* ⓕ ka·no·*tye*·ra
sister *sorella* ⓕ so·*re*·la
sit *sedere* se·*de*·re
size (clothes) *taglia* ⓕ *ta*·lya
size (general) *dimensioni* ⓕ pl
dee·men·*syo*·nee
ski *sciare* shee·*a*·re
ski lift *sciovia* ⓕ shee·o·*vee*·a
skiing *sci* ⓜ shee
ski(s) *sci* ⓜ sg&pl shee
skimmed milk *latte* ⓜ *scremato*
la·te skre·*ma*·to
skin *pelle* ⓕ *pe*·le
skirt *gonna* ⓕ *go*·na
sky *cielo* ⓜ *che*·lo
sleep *dormire* dor·*mee*·re
sleeping bag *sacco* ⓜ *a pelo*
sa·ko a *pe*·lo
sleeping car *vagone* ⓜ *letto*
va·*go*·ne *le*·to
sleeping pills *sonniferi* ⓜ pl
so·*nee*·fe·ree
(to be) **sleepy** *avere sonno* ⓜ
a·*ve*·re *so*·no
slice *fetta* ⓕ *fe*·ta
slide (film) *diapositiva* ⓕ
dee·a·po·zee·*tee*·va
slope *pista* ⓕ *pee*·sta
Slovenia *Slovenia* ⓕ slo·*ve*·nya
slow *lento/a* ⓜ/ⓕ *len*·to/a
slowly *lentamente* len·ta·*men*·te
small *piccolo/a* ⓜ/ⓕ *pee*·ko·lo/a
smell *odore* ⓜ o·*do*·re
smile *sorridere* so·*ree*·de·re
smoke *fumare* foo·*ma*·re
snack *spuntino* ⓜ spoon·*tee*·no
snail *lumaca* ⓕ loo·*ma*·ka

snake *serpente* ⓜ ser·*pen*·te
snorkel *boccaglio* ⓜ bo·*ka*·lyo
snorkelling *snorkelling* snor·ke·*leeng*
snow *neve* ⓕ *ne*·ve
snow boarding *surf* ⓜ *da neve*
soorf da *ne*·ve
snow chains *catene* ⓕ pl *da neve*
ka·*te*·ne da *ne*·ve
soap *sapone* ⓜ sa·*po*·ne
soap opera *telenovela* ⓕ te·le·no·*ve*·la
soccer *calcio* ⓜ *kal*·cho
social welfare *assistenza* ⓕ *sociale*
a·sees·*ten*·tsa so·*cha*·le
socialist *socialista* ⓜ&ⓕ so·cha·*lee*·sta
socks *calzini* ⓜ pl cal·*tsee*·nee
soft *morbido/a* ⓜ/ⓕ mor·*bee*·do/a
soft drink *bibita* ⓕ *bee*·bee·ta
soldier *soldato* ⓜ sol·*da*·to
some *alcuni/e* ⓜ/ⓕ pl
al·*koo*·nee/al·*koo*·ne
someone *qualcuno/a* ⓜ/ⓕ
kwal·*koo*·no/a
something *qualcosa* kwal·*ko*·za
sometimes *a volte* a *vol*·te
son *figlio* ⓜ *fee*·lyo
song *canzone* ⓕ kan·*tso*·ne
soon *fra poco* fra *po*·ko
sore *doloroso/a* ⓜ/ⓕ do·lo·*ro*·zo/a
soup *minestra* ⓕ mee·*nes*·tra
sour cream *panna* ⓕ *acida*
pa·na a·*chee*·da
south *sud* ⓜ sood
souvenir *ricordino* ⓜ ree·kor·*dee*·no
souvenir shop *negozio* ⓜ *di souvenir*
ne·*go*·tsyo dee soo·ve·*neer*
soy milk *latte* ⓜ *di soia* *la*·te dee so·ya
soy sauce *salsa* ⓕ *di soia*
sal·sa dee so·ya
space *spazio* ⓜ *spa*·tsyo
spade *vanga* ⓕ *van*·ga
Spain *Spagna* ⓕ *spa*·nya
speak *parlare* par·*la*·re
special *speciale* spe·*cha*·le
specialist *specialista* ⓜ&ⓕ
spe·cha·*lee*·sta
speed *velocità* ⓕ ve·lo·chee·*ta*

speed limit *limite* ⑩ *di velocità*
lee·mee·te dee ve·lo·chee·ta

speedometer *tachimetro* ⑩
ta·kee·me·tro

spermicide *spermicida* ①
sper·mee·chee·da

spider *ragno* ⑩ ra·nyo

spinach *spinaci* ⑩ pl spee·na·chee

spoke(s) *raggio/raggi* ⑩ ra·jo/ra·jee

spoon *cucchiaio* ⑩ koo·kya·yo

sport *sport* ⑩ sport

sports store *negozio* ⑩ *di articoli*
sportivi ne·go·tsyo dee ar·tee·ko·lee
spor·tee·vee

sportsperson *sportivo/a* ⑩/①
spor·tee·vo/a

sprain *storta* ① stor·ta

spring (season) *primavera* ①
pree·ma·ve·ra

square (town) *piazza* ① pya·tsa

stadium *stadio* ⑩ sta·dyo

stage (theatre) *palcoscenico* ⑩
pal·ko·she·nee·ko

stage (in race) *tappa* ① ta·pa

stairway *scale* ① pl ska·le

stamp *francobollo* ⑩ fran·ko·bo·lo

standby (ticket) *(in lista) d'attesa*
(een lee·sta) da·te·za

(four-)star *(a quattro) stelle*
(a kwa·tro) ste·le

stars *stelle* ① pl ste·le

start *inizio* ⑩ ee·nee·tsyo

start *cominciare* ko·meen·cha·re

station *stazione* ① sta·tsyo·ne

stationer *cartolaio* ⑩ kar·to·la·yo

statue *statua* ① sta·too·a

stay (at a hotel) *fermarsi* fer·mar·see

steak (beef) *bistecca* ① bees·te·ka

steal *rubare* roo·ba·re

steep *ripido/a* ⑩/① ree·pee·do/a

stingy *avaro/a* ⑩/① a·va·ro/a

stockings *calze* ① pl kal·tse

stolen *rubato/a* ⑩/① roo·ba·to/a

stomach *stomaco* ⑩ sto·ma·ko

stomachache *mal* ⑩ *di pancia*
mal dee pan·cha

stone *pietra* ① pye·tra

stoned (drugged) *fumato/a* ⑩/①
foo·ma·to/a

stop *fermata* ① fer·ma·ta

stop *fermare* fer·ma·re

storm *temporale* ⑩ tem·po·ra·le

story *racconto* ⑩ ra·kon·to

stove *stufa* ① *(a gas)* stoo·fa a gaz

straight *diritto/a* ⑩/① dee·ree·to/a

strange *strano/a* ⑩/① stra·no/a

stranger *sconosciuto/a* ⑩/①
sko·no·shoo·to/a

strawberry *fragola* ① fra·go·la

stream *ruscello* ⑩ roo·she·lo

street *strada* ① stra·da

(on) strike *(in) sciopero* ⑩ een sho·pe·ro

string *spago* ⑩ spa·go

strong *forte* ⑩/① for·te

student *studente/studentessa* ⑩/①
stoo·den·te/stoo·den·te·sa

stupid *stupido/a* ⑩/① stoo·pee·do/a

style *stile* ① stee·le

subtitles *sottotitoli* ⑩ pl so·to·tee·to·lee

suburb *quartiere* ⑩ kwar·tye·re

subway *metropolitana* ①
me·tro·po·lee·ta·na

sugar *zucchero* ⑩ tsoo·ke·ro

suitcase *valigia* ① va·lee·ja

summer *estate* ① es·ta·te

sun *sole* ⑩ so·le

sunblock *crema* ① *solare* kre·ma so·la·re

sunburn *scottatura* ① sko·ta·too·ra

sunglasses *occhiali* ⑩ pl *da sole*
o·kya·lee da so·le

sunny *soleggiato/a* ⑩/① so·le·ja·to/a

sunrise *alba* ① al·ba

sunscreen *crema* ① *solare* kre·ma so·la·re

sunset *tramonto* ⑩ tra·mon·to

supermarket *supermercato* ⑩
soo·per·mer·ka·to

superstition *superstizione* ①
soo·per·stee·tsyo·ne

supplies *provviste* ⑩ pl pro·vee·ste

support (cheer on) *fare il tifo*
fa·re eel tee·fo

supporters *tifosi* ⑩ pl tee·fo·zee

surf *praticare il surf* pra·tee·ka·re eel soorf

surface mail *posta* ① *ordinaria*
pos·ta or·dee·na·rya

surfboard *tavola da surf* ta·vo·la da soorf
surname *cognome* ⓜ ko·nyo·me
surprise *sorpresa* ⓕ sor·pre·sa
sweater *maglione* ⓜ ma·lyo·ne
Sweden *Svezia* ⓕ sve·tsee·a
sweet *dolce* dol·che
swelling *gonfiore* ⓜ gon·fyo·re
swim *nuotare* nwo·ta·re
swimming *nuoto* ⓜ nwo·to
swimming pool *piscina* ⓕ pee·shee·na
swimsuit *costume* ⓜ *da bagno*
ko·stoo·me da ba·nyo
Switzerland *Svizzera* ⓕ svee·tse·ra
synagogue *sinagoga* ⓕ see·na·go·ga
synthetic *sintetico/a* ⓜ/ⓕ
seen·te·tee·ko/a
syringe *siringa* ⓕ see·reen·ga

T

table *tavola* ⓕ ta·vo·la
table tennis *ping-pong* ⓜ peeng·pong
tablecloth *tovaglia* ⓕ to·va·lya
tailor *sarto* ⓜ sar·to
take *prendere* pren·de·re
take (photo) *fare* fa·re
talk *parlare* par·la·re
tall *alto/a* ⓜ/ⓕ al·to/a
tampons *tamponi* ⓜ pl tam·po·nee
tanning lotion *lozione* ⓕ *abbronzante*
lo·tsyo·ne a·bron·dzan·te
tap (faucet) *rubinetto* ⓜ roo·bee·ne·to
tasty *gustoso/a* ⓜ/ⓕ goo·sto·zo/a
tax *tassa* ⓕ ta·sa
taxi *tassì* ta·see
taxi stand *posteggio* ⓜ *di tassì*
po·ste·jo dee ta·see
tea *tè* ⓜ te
teacher (general) *insegnante* ⓜ&ⓕ
een·sen·yan·te
teacher (primary) *maestro/a* ⓜ/ⓕ
ma·es·tro/a
teacher (secondary)
professore/professoressa ⓜ/ⓕ
pro·fe·so·re/pro·fe·so·re·sa
team *squadra* ⓕ skwa·dra
teaspoon *cucchiaino* ⓜ koo·kya·ee·no

teeth *denti* ⓜ pl den·tee
telegram *telegramma* ⓜ te·le·gra·ma
telephone *telefono* ⓜ te·le·fo·no
telephone *telefonare* te·le·fo·na·re
telephone centre *centro* ⓜ *telefonico*
chen·tro te·le·fo·nee·ko
telephoto lens *teleobiettivo* ⓜ
te·le·o·bye·tee·vo
television *televisione* ⓕ te·le·vee·zyo·ne
tell *raccontare* ra·kon·ta·re
temperature (fever) *febbre* ⓕ fe·bre
temperature (weather) *temperatura* ⓕ
tem·pe·ra·too·ra
temple *tempio* ⓜ tem·pyo
tennis *tennis* ⓜ te·nees
tennis court *campo* ⓜ *da tennis*
kam·po da te·nees
tent *tenda* ⓕ ten·da
tent pegs *picchetti* ⓜ pl *(per la tenda)*
pee·ke·tee (per la ten·da)
terrible *terribile* ⓜ/ⓕ te·ree·bee·le
test *esame* ⓜ e·za·me
thank *ringraziare* reen·gra·tsya·re
theatre *teatro* ⓜ te·a·tro
there *là* la
they *loro* lo·ro
thick *spesso/a* ⓜ/ⓕ spe·so/a
thief *ladro/a* ⓜ/ⓕ la·dro/a
thin *magro/a* ⓜ/ⓕ ma·gro/a
think *pensare* pen·sa·re
third *terzo/a* ⓜ/ⓕ ter·tso/a
(to be) thirsty *avere sete* ⓜ a·ve·re se·te
this (one) *questo/a* ⓜ/ⓕ kwe·sto/a
thread (sewing) *filo* ⓜ fee·lo
throat *gola* ⓕ go·la
thrush (medical) *mughetto* ⓜ moo·ge·to
ticket *biglietto* ⓜ bee·lye·to
ticket collector *controllore* ⓜ
kon·tro·lo·re
ticket machine *distributore* ⓜ
automatico di biglietti
dee·stree·boo·to·re ow·to·ma·tee·ko
dee bee·lye·tee
ticket office *biglietteria* ⓕ
bee·lye·te·ree·a
tide *marea* ⓕ ma·re·a
tight *stretto/a* ⓜ/ⓕ stre·to/a

time *tempo* ⓜ tem·po
time difference
  differenza ① *di fuso orario*
  dee·fe·ren·tsa dee foo·zo o·ra·ryo
timetable *orario* ⓜ o·ra·ryo
tin (can) *scatoletta* ① ska·to·le·ta
tin opener *apriscatole* ⓜ a·pree·ska·to·le
tiny *minuscolo/a* ⓜ/① mee·noos·ko·lo/a
tip (gratuity) *mancia* ① man·cha
tired *stanco/a* ⓜ/① stan·ko/a
tissues *fazzolettini* ⓜ pl *di carta*
  fa·tso·le·tee·nee dee kar·ta
toast *pane* ⓜ *tostato* pa·ne tos·ta·to
toaster *tostapane* ⓜ tos·ta·pa·ne
tobacco *tabacco* ⓜ ta·ba·ko
tobacconist *tabaccheria* ① ta·ba·ke·ree·a
tobogganing *andare in slitta*
  an·da·re een slee·ta
today *oggi* o·jee
toe *dito* ⓜ *del piede* dee·to del pye·de
together *insieme* een·sye·me
toilet *gabinetto* ⓜ ga·bee·ne·to
toilet paper *carta* ① *igienica*
  kar·ta ee·je·nee·ka
toilets *servizi* ⓜ pl *igienici*
  ser·vee·tse ee·je·nee·chee
token *gettone* ⓜ je·to·ne
tomato *pomodoro* ⓜ po·mo·do·ro
tomato sauce *salsa* ① *di pomodoro*
  sal·sa dee po·mo·do·ro
tomorrow *domani* do·ma·nee
tonight *stasera* sta·se·ra
too (expensive) *troppo (caro/a)*
  tro·po (ka·ro/a)
too many *troppi/e* ⓜ/① pl
  tro·pee/tro·pe
too much *troppo/a* ⓜ/① sg tro·po/a
tooth (front) *dente* ⓜ den·te
toothache *mal* ⓜ *di denti*
  mal dee den·tee
toothbrush *spazzolino* ⓜ *da denti*
  spa·tso·lee·no da den·tee
toothpaste *dentifricio* ⓜ
  den·tee·free·cho
toothpick *stuzzicadenti* ⓜ
  stoo·tsee·ka·den·tee
torch (flashlight) *torcia* ① *elettrica*
  tor·cha e·le·tree·ka

touch *toccare* to·ka·re
tour *gita* ① jee·ta
tourist *turista* ⓜ&① too·ree·sta
tourist office *ufficio* ⓜ *del turismo*
  oo·fee·cho del too·reez·mo
towel *asciugamano* ⓜ a·shoo·ga·ma·no
tower *torre* ① to·re
toxic waste *rifiuti* ⓜ pl *tossici*
  ree·fyoo·tee to·see·chee
toyshop *negozio* ⓜ *di giocattoli*
  ne·go·tsyo dee jo·ka·to·lee
track (path) *sentiero* ⓜ sen·tye·ro
track (sports) *pista* ① pee·sta
trade *commercio* ⓜ ko·mer·cho
traffic *traffico* ⓜ tra·fee·ko
traffic jam *ingorgo* ⓜ een·gor·go
traffic lights *semaforo* ⓜ se·ma·fo·ro
trail *pista* ① pee·sta
train *treno* ⓜ tre·no
train station *stazione* ① *(ferroviaria)*
  sta·tsyo·ne (fe·ro·vyar·ya)
tram *tram* ⓜ tram
transit lounge *sala* ① *di transito*
  sa·la dee tran·zee·to
translate *tradurre* tra·doo·re
transport *trasporto* ⓜ tras·por·to
travel *viaggiare* vee·a·ja·re
travel agency *agenzia* ① *di viaggio*
  a·jen·tsee·a dee vee·a·jo
travel sickness (air) *mal* ⓜ *di aereo*
  mal dee a·e·re·o
travel sickness (car) *mal* ⓜ *di macchina*
  mal dee ma·kee·na
travel sickness (sea) *mal* ⓜ *di mare*
  mal dee ma·re
travellers cheque *assegno* ⓜ *di viaggio*
  a·se·nyo dee vee·a·jo
tree *albero* ⓜ al·be·ro
trip *gita* ① jee·ta
trolley (luggage) *carrello* ⓜ ka·re·lo
trousers *pantaloni* ⓜ pl pan·ta·lo·nee
truck *camion* ⓜ ka·myon
true *vero/a* ⓜ/① ve·ro/a
try (attempt) *provare* pro·va·re
T-shirt *maglietta* ① ma·lye·ta
tube (tyre) *camera* ① *d'aria*
  ka·me·ra da·rya

tuna *tonno* ⓜ *to·no*
tune *melodia* ⓕ *me·lo·dee·a*
turkey *tacchino* ⓜ *ta·kee·no*
turn *girare* *jee·ra·re*
TV *TV* ⓕ *tee·voo*
tweezers *pinzette* ⓕ pl *peen·tse·te*
twice *due volte* *doo·e vol·te*
twin beds *due letti* *doo·e le·tee*
twins *gemelli/e* ⓜ/ⓕ pl
je·me·lee/je·me·le
type *tipo* ⓜ *tee·po*
typical *tipico/a* ⓜ/ⓕ *tee·pee·ko/a*
tyre *gomma* ⓕ *go·ma*

U

ugly *brutto/a* ⓜ/ⓕ *broo·to/a*
ultrasound *ecografia* ⓕ *e·ko·gra·fee·a*
umbrella *ombrello* ⓜ *om·bre·lo*
uncomfortable *scomodo/a* ⓜ/ⓕ
sko·mo·do/a
understand *capire* *ka·pee·re*
underwear *biancheria* ⓕ *intima*
byan·ke·ree·a een·tee·ma
unemployed *disoccupato/a* ⓜ/ⓕ
dee·zo·koo·pa·to/a
uniform *divisa* ⓕ *dee·vee·za*
universe *universo* ⓜ *oo·nee·ver·so*
university *università* ⓕ *oo·nee·ver·see·ta*
unleaded *senza piombo* *sen·tsa pyom·bo*
unsafe *pericoloso/a* ⓜ/ⓕ
pe·ree·ko·lo·zo/a
until *fino a* *fee·no a*
unusual *insolito/a* ⓜ/ⓕ *een·so·lee·to/a*
up *su* *soo*
uphill *in salita* *een sa·lee·ta*
urgent *urgente* ⓜ/ⓕ *oor·jen·te*
USA *Stati* ⓜ pl *Uniti d'America*
sta·tee oo·nee·tee da·me·ree·ka
useful *utile* *oo·tee·le*

V

vacant *libero/a* ⓜ/ⓕ *lee·be·ro/a*
vacation *vacanza* ⓕ *va·kan·tsa*
vaccination *vaccinazione* ⓕ
va·chee·na·tsyo·ne
vagina *vagina* ⓕ *va·jee·na*

validate *convalidare* *kon·va·lee·da·re*
valley *valle* ⓕ *va·le*
valuable *prezioso/a* ⓜ/ⓕ *pre·tsyo·zo/a*
valuables *oggetti* ⓜ pl *di valore*
o·je·tee dee va·lo·re
value (price) *valore* ⓜ *va·lo·re*
van *furgone* ⓜ *foor·go·ne*
veal *vitello* ⓜ *vee·te·lo*
vegetable *verdura* ⓕ *ver·doo·ra*
vegetarian *vegetariano/a* ⓜ/ⓕ
ve·je·ta·rya·no/a
venereal disease *malattia* ⓕ *venerea*
ma·la·tee·a ve·ne·re·a
venue *locale* ⓜ *lo·ka·le*
very *molto* *mol·to*
video *videoregistratore* ⓜ
vee·de·o·re·jee·stra·to·re
video camera *videocamera* ⓕ
vee·de·o·ka·me·ra
video tape *videonastro* ⓜ
vee·de·o·nas·tro
view *vista* ⓕ *vee·sta*
village *villaggio* ⓜ *vee·la·jo*
vinegar *aceto* ⓜ *a·che·to*
vineyard *vigneto* ⓜ *vee·nye·to*
virus *virus* ⓜ *vee·roos*
visa *visto* ⓜ *vee·sto*
visit (person) *andare a trovare*
an·da·re a tro·va·re
visit (place) *fare una visita*
fa·re oo·na vee·see·ta
vitamins *vitamine* ⓕ pl *vee·ta·mee·ne*
voice *voce* ⓕ *vo·che*
volleyball *pallavolo* ⓕ *pa·la·vo·lo*
vomit *vomitare* *vo·mee·ta·re*
vote *votare* *vo·ta·re*

W

wage *salario* ⓜ *sa·la·ryo*
wait *aspettare* *as·pe·ta·re*
waiter *cameriere/a* ⓜ/ⓕ *ka·mer·ye·re/a*
waiting room *sala* ⓕ *d'attesa*
sa·la da·te·sa
wake up *svegliarsi* *sve·lyar·see*
Wales *Galles* ⓜ *ga·les*
walk *passeggiata* ⓕ *pa·se·ja·ta*

walk *camminare* ka·mee·*na*·re
wall (external) *muro* ⓜ *moo*·ro
wall (internal) *parete* ① pa·*re*·te
wallet *portafoglio* ⓜ por·ta·*fo*·lyo
want *volere* vo·*le*·re
war *guerra* ① *gwe*·ra
wardrobe *armadio* ⓜ ar·*ma*·dyo
warm *tiepido/a* ⓜ/① tye·*pee*·do/a
warn *avvertire* a·ver·*tee*·re
wash (oneself) *lavarsi* la·*var*·see
wash (something) *lavare* la·*va*·re
washing machine *lavatrice* ①
  la·va·*tree*·che
washing powder *detersivo* ⓜ
  de·ter·*see*·vo
watch *orologio* ⓜ o·ro·*lo*·jo
watch *guardare* gwar·*da*·re
water *acqua* ① *a*·kwa
  boiled water *acqua* ① *bollita*
  a·kwa bo·*lee*·ta
  still water *acqua* ① *non gassata*
  a·kwa non ga·*sa*·ta
  tap water *acqua* ① *del rubinetto*
  a·kwa del roo·bee·*ne*·to
water bottle *borraccia* ① bo·*ra*·cha
waterfall *cascata* ① kas·*ka*·ta
watermelon *anguria* ① an·*goo*·rya
waterproof *impermeabile* ⓜ
  eem·per·me·*a*·bee·le
water skiing *sci* ⓜ *acquatico*
  shee a·*kwa*·tee·ko
watersports *sport* ⓜ *acquatici*
  sport a·*kwa*·tee·chee
wave *onda* ① *on*·da
way via ① *vee*·a
we *noi* noy
weak *debole* *de*·bo·le
wealthy *ricco/a* ⓜ/① *ree*·ko/a
wear *indossare* een·do·*sa*·re
weather *tempo* ⓜ *tem*·po
wedding *matrimonio* ⓜ ma·tree·*mo*·nyo
wedding present *regalo* ⓜ *di nozze*
  re·*ga*·lo dee *no*·tse
week *settimana* ① se·tee·*ma*·na
weekend *fine settimana* ⓜ
  fee·ne se·tee·*ma*·na
weight *peso* ⓜ *pe*·zo

welcome *dare il benvenuto a*
  da·re eel ben·ve·*noo*·to a
well *in buona salute*
  een *bwo*·na sa·*loo*·te
west *ovest* ⓜ o·vest
wet *bagnato/a* ⓜ/① ba·*nya*·to/a
wetsuit *muta* ① *moo*·ta
what *che (cosa)* ke (*ko*·za)
wheel *ruota* ① *rwo*·ta
wheelchair *sedia* ① *a rotelle*
  se·dya a ro·*te*·le
when *quando* *kwan*·do
where *dove* *do*·ve
white *bianco/a* ⓜ/① *byan*·ko/a
who *chi* kee
why *perché* per·*ke*
wide *largo/a* ⓜ/① *lar*·go/a
widow *vedova* ① *ve*·do·va
widower *vedovo* ⓜ *ve*·do·vo
wife *moglie* ① *mo*·lye
win *vincere* *veen*·che·re
wind *vento* ⓜ *ven*·to
window (car, plane) *finestrino* ⓜ
  fee·nes·*tree*·no
window (general) *finestra* ① fee·*nes*·tra
windscreen *parabrezza* ⓜ pa·ra·*bre*·dza
wine *vino* ⓜ *vee*·no
  red wine *vino* ⓜ *rosso* *vee*·no *ro*·so
  sparkling wine *vino* ⓜ *spumante*
  vee·no spoo·*man*·te
  white wine *vino* ⓜ *bianco*
  vee·no *byan*·ko
wine cellar *cantina* ① kan·*tee*·na
wine tasting *degustazione* ① *dei vini*
  de·goos·ta·*tsyo*·ne day *vee*·nee
winery *cantina* ① kan·*tee*·na
wings *ali* ① pl a·*lee*
winner *vincitore/vincitrice* ⓜ/①
  veen·chee·*to*·re/veen·chee·*tree*·che
winter *inverno* ⓜ een·*ver*·no
wish *desiderare* de·see·de·*ra*·re
with *con* kon
within (an hour) *entro (un'ora)*
  en·tro (oon·*o*·ra)
without *senza* *sen*·tsa
woman *donna* ① *do*·na

wonderful *meraviglioso/a* ⓜ/ⓕ
me·ra·vee·lyo·zo/a

wood *legno* ⓜ le·nyo

wool *lana* ⓕ la·na

word *parola* ⓕ pa·ro·la

work (occupation) *lavoro* ⓜ la·vo·ro

work (of art) *opera* ⓕ *(d'arte)*
o·pe·ra *(dar·*te)

work *lavorare* la·vo·ra·re

workout *allenamento* ⓜ a·le·na·men·to

workshop *laboratorio* ⓜ la·bo·ra·to·ryo

world *mondo* ⓜ mon·do

World Cup *Coppa* ⓕ *del Mondo*
ko·pa del mon·do

worried *preoccupato/a* ⓜ/ⓕ
pre·o·koo·pa·to/a

worship (pray) *pregare* pre·ga·re

wrist *polso* ⓜ pol·so

write *scrivere* skree·ve·re

writer *scrittore/scrittrice* ⓜ/ⓕ
skree·to·re/skree·tree·che

wrong *sbagliato/a* ⓜ/ⓕ sba·lya·to/a

Y

year *anno* ⓜ a·no
   this year *quest'anno* ⓜ kwe·sta·no
   last year *l'anno* ⓜ *scorso* la·no skor·so

yellow *giallo/a* ⓜ/ⓕ ja·lo/a

yes *sì* see

yesterday *ieri* ye·ree

(not) yet *(non) ancora* (non) an·ko·ra

yoga *yoga* ⓕ yo·ga

yogurt *yogurt* ⓜ yo·goort

you (polite/informal) *Lei/tu* lay/too

young *giovane* jo·va·ne

youth hostel *ostello* ⓜ *della gioventù*
os·te·lo de·la jo·ven·too

Z

zoo *giardino* ⓜ *zoologico*
jar·dee·no dzo·o·lo·jee·ko

zoom lens *zoom* ⓜ zoom

zucchini *zucchini* ⓜ pl tsoo·kee·nee

A

Nouns in this dictionary, and adjectives affected by gender, have their gender indicated by ⓜ and/or ⓕ. If it's a plural noun, you'll also see pl. Where a word that could be either a noun or a verb has no gender indicated, it's a verb.

A

a a *in • at • to • until • per*
a bordo a bor·do *aboard*
abbastanza a·bas·tan·tsa *enough*
abbigliamento ⓜ a·bee·lya·men·to *clothing*
abbracciare a·bra·cha·re *hug*
abitare a·bee·ta·re *live (somewhere)*
abito ⓜ a·bee·to *dress*
aborto ⓜ a·bor·to *abortion*
— **spontaneo** spon·ta·ne·o *miscarriage*
accanto a·kan·to *nearby*
accanto a a·kan·to a *next to*
accendino a·chen·dee·no *(cigarette) lighter*
accetazione ⓕ a·che·ta·tsyo·ne *check-in (airport)*
aceto ⓜ a·che·to *vinegar*
acqua ⓕ a·kwa *water*
— **bollita** bo·lee·ta *boiled water*
— **calda** kal·da *hot water*
— **del rubinetto** del roo·bee·ne·to *tap water*
— **minerale** mee·ne·ra·le *mineral water*
— **non gassata** non ga·sa·ta *still water*
adesso a·de·so *now*
adulto/a ⓜ/ⓕ a·dool·to/a *adult*
aereo ⓜ a·e·re·o *plane*
aerobica ⓕ a·e·ro·bee·ka *aerobics*
aeroporto ⓜ a·e·ro·por·to *airport*
affari ⓜ pl a·fa·ree *business*
affascinante a·fa·shee·nan·te *charming • attractive*
affilato/a ⓜ/ⓕ a·fee·la·to/a *sharp*
affitto a·fee·to *rent*
affollato/a ⓜ/ⓕ a·fo·la·to/a *crowded*

agenda ⓕ a·jen·da *diary*
agenzia ⓕ a·jen·tsee·a *agency*
— **di viaggio** dee vee·a·jo *travel agency*
agganciare a·gan·cha·re *chat up*
aggiustare a·joo·sta·re *repair*
aggressivo/a ⓜ/ⓕ a·gre·see·vo/a *aggressive*
aglio ⓜ a·lyo *garlic*
agnello ⓜ a·nye·lo *lamb*
ago ⓜ a·go *needle (sewing)*
agopuntura ⓕ a·go·poon·too·ra *acupuncture*
agricoltore/agricoltrice ⓜ/ⓕ a·gree·kol·to·re/a·gree·kol·tree·che *farmer*
agricoltura ⓕ a·gree·kol·too·ra *agriculture*
AIDS ⓜ a·ee·dee·e·se (or a·eedz) *AIDS*
aiutare a·yoo·ta·re *help*
alba ⓕ al·ba *sunrise*
albergo ⓜ al·ber·go *hotel*
albero ⓜ al·be·ro *tree*
albicocca ⓕ al·bee·ko·ka *apricot*
alcuni/e ⓜ/ⓕ pl al·koo·nee/al·koo·ne *some*
ali ⓕ pl a·lee *wings*
alimentari ⓜ a·lee·men·ta·ree *grocery store • convenience store*
alimento ⓜ a·lee·men·to *food*
al giorno al jor·no *per (day)*
al mare al ma·re *seaside*
all'estero a·les·te·ro *abroad*
allenamento ⓜ a·le·na·men·to *workout*
allergia ⓕ a·ler·jee·a *allergy*
alloggio ⓜ a·lo·jo *accommodation*
allucinare a·loo·chee·na·re *hallucinate*
alpinismo ⓜ al·pee·neez·mo *mountaineering*
altare ⓜ al·ta·re *altar*

altezza ① al·te·tsa *height*

alto/a ⓜ/① al·to/a *high • tall*

altopiano ⓜ al·to·pya·no *plateau*

altro/a ⓜ/① al·tro/a *other*

— **ieri** ⓜ ye·ree *day before yesterday*

amaca ① a·ma·ka *hammock*

amante ⓜ/① a·man·te *lover*

amare a·ma·re *love*

ambasciata ① am·ba·sha·ta *embassy*

ambasciatore/ambasciatrice ⓜ/①
am·ba·sha·to·re/am·ba·sha·tree·che
ambassador

ambiente ⓜ am·byen·te *environment*

ambulanza ① am·boo·lan·tsa *ambulance*

amico/a ⓜ/① a·mee·ko/a *friend*

ammazzare a·ma·tsa·re *kill*

amministrazione ①
a·mee·nee·stra·tsyo·ne *administration*

analgesico ⓜ an·al·je·zee·ko *painkillers*

analisi ① **del sangue** a·na·lee·zee del
san·gwe *blood test*

ananas ⓜ a·na·nas *pineapple*

anatra ① a·na·tra *duck*

anche an·ke *also*

ancora an·ko·ra *still • yet*

andare an·da·re *go*

— **a cavallo** a ka·va·lo *horse riding*

— **a vedere** a ve·de·re *visit*

— **in bicicletta** een bee·chee·kle·ta
cycle • ride (a bike)

— **in slitta** een slee·ta *tobogganing*

— **su roccia** soo ro·cha *rock climbing*

andata ① an·da·ta *outward journey*

anello ⓜ a·ne·lo *ring (on finger)*

angolo ⓜ an·go·lo *corner*

anguria ① an·goo·rya *watermelon*

animale ⓜ a·nee·ma·le *animal*

anno ⓜ a·no *year*

annoiato/a ⓜ/① a·no·ya·to/a *bored*

annuale a·noo·a·le *annual*

annuncio ⓜ a·noon·cho *advertisement*

antibiotici ⓜ pl an·tee·bee·o·tee·chee
antibiotics

antico/a ⓜ/① an·tee·ko/a *ancient*

antinucleare an·tee·noo·kle·a·re
antinuclear

antisettico ⓜ an·tee·se·tee·ko *antiseptic*

antistaminici ⓜ pl an·tee·sta·mee·
nee·chee *antihistamines*

ape ① a·pe *bee*

aperto/a ⓜ/① a·per·to/a *open*

apparecchio ⓜ **acustico** a·pa·re·kyo
a·koos·tee·ko *hearing aid*

appartamento ⓜ a·par·ta·men·to *flat*

appendice ① a·pen·dee·che *appendix*

appuntamento ⓜ a·poon·ta·men·to
appointment • date

apribottiglie ⓜ a·pree·bo·tee·lye
bottle opener

aprire a·pree·re *open*

apriscatole ⓜ a·pree·ska·to·le *can opener*

arachidi ① pl a·ra·kee·dee
peanuts • groundnuts

arancia ① a·ran·cha *orange (fruit)*

arancione a·ran·cho·ne *orange (colour)*

arbitro ⓜ ar·bee·tro *referee*

archeologico/a ⓜ/① ar·ke·o·lo·jee·ko/a
archaeological

architetto ⓜ ar·kee·te·to *architect*

architettura ① ar·kee·te·too·ra
architecture

argento ⓜ ar·jen·to *silver*

aria ① a·rya *air*

— **condizionata** kon·dee·tsyo·na·ta
air·conditioning

aringa ① a·reen·ga *herring*

armadietti ⓜ pl ar·ma·dye·tee *lockers*

— **per i bagagli** per ee ba·ga·lyee
luggage lockers

armadio ⓜ ar·ma·dyo *wardrobe*

arrabbiato/a ⓜ/① a·ra·bya·to/a *angry*

arrestare a·res·ta·re *arrest*

arrivare a·ree·va·re *arrive*

arrivi ⓜ pl a·ree·vee *arrivals*

arte ① ar·te *art*

arti ① pl **marziali** ar·tee mar·tsya·lee
martial arts

artista ⓜ&① ar·tee·sta *artist*

ASA a·za *film speed*

ascensore ⓜ a·shen·so·re *elevator*

asciugamano ⓜ a·shoo·ga·ma·no *towel*

asciugare a·shoo·ga·re *dry*

ascoltare as·kol·ta·re *listen*

asilo ⓜ a·zee·lo *kindergarten*

— **nido** nee·do *creche*

asma ① az·ma *asthma*

asparagi ⓜ pl as·pa·ra·jee *asparagus*

aspettare as·pe·ta·re *wait*

aspirina ① as·pee·ree·na *aspirin*
assegno ⓜ a·se·nyo *cheque*
 — **di viaggio** dee vee·a·jo
  travellers cheque
assicurazione ① a·see·koo·ra·tsyo·ne
  insurance
assistenza ① **sociale** a·sees·ten·tsa
  so·cha·le *(social) welfare*
assorbenti ⓜ pl **igienici** as·or·ben·tee
  ee·je·nee·chee *sanitary napkins*
atletica ① at·le·tee·ka *athletics*
atrio ⓜ a·tryo *foyer*
attesa ① a·te·sa *wait*
attrezzatura ① a·tre·tsa·too·ra *equipment*
attualità ① a·too·a·lee·ta *current affairs*
autobus ⓜ ow·to·boos *bus (city)*
autostop ⓜ ow·to·stop *hitchhiking*
automatico/a ⓜ/① ow·to·ma·tee·ko/a
  automatic
automobilismo ⓜ ow·to·mo·bee·leez·mo
  car racing
autonoleggio ⓜ ow·to·no·le·jo *car hire*
autostrada ① ow·to·stra·da
  motorway • tollway
autunno ⓜ ow·too·no *autumn*
a volte a vol·te *sometimes*
avaro/a ⓜ/① a·va·ro/a *stingy*
avena ① a·ve·na *oats*
avere a·ve·re *have*
 — **bisogno di** bee·zo·nyo dee *need*
 — **fame** ① fa·me *(to be) hungry*
 — **fretta** ① fre·ta *(to be) in a hurry*
 — **mal di mare** mal dee ma·re
  (to be) seasick
 — **sete** ① se·te *(to be) thirsty*
 — **sonno** ⓜ so·no *(to be) sleepy*
avocado ⓜ a·vo·ka·do *avocado*
avventura ① a·ven·too·ra *adventure*
avvertire a·ver·tee·re *warn*
avvocato/a ⓜ/① a·vo·ka·to/a *lawyer*
azzurro/a ⓜ/① a·dzoo·ro/a *blue (light)*

B

baby-sitter ⓜ&① be·bee·see·ter
  babysitter • childminding (private)
baciare ba·cha·re *kiss*
bacio ⓜ ba·cho *kiss*

bagaglio ⓜ ba·ga·lyo *luggage*
 — **a mano** a ma·no *carry-on luggage*
 — **consentito** kon·sen·tee·to
  baggage allowance
 — **in eccedenza** een e·che·den·tsa
  excess bagage
bagnato/a ⓜ/① ba·nya·to/a *wet*
bagno ⓜ ba·nyo *bath • bathroom*
balcone ⓜ bal·ko·ne *balcony*
ballare ba·la·re *dance*
balletto ⓜ ba·le·to *ballet*
ballo ⓜ ba·lo *ball (dancing) • dancing*
balsamo ⓜ **per i capelli** bal·sa·mo per ee
  ka·pe·lee *conditioner*
bambino/a ⓜ/① bam·bee·no/a *child*
bambola ① bam·bo·la *doll*
banca ① ban·ka *bank (money)*
Bancomat ⓜ ban·ko·mat
  automatic teller machine (ATM)
bancone ⓜ ban·ko·ne *counter (at bar)*
banconota ① ban·ko·no·ta *banknote*
bandiera ① ban·dye·ra *flag*
bar ⓜ bar *cafe*
barattolo ① ba·ra·to·lo *jar*
barbabietola ① bar·ba·bye·to·la *beetroot*
barbiere ⓜ bar·bye·re *barber*
barca ① bar·ka *boat*
baseball ⓜ bays·bol *baseball*
basso/a ⓜ/① ba·so/a
  low • short (height)
batteria ① ba·te·ree·a
  battery (for car) • drums
battesimo ⓜ ba·te·zee·mo *baptism*
batuffoli ⓜ pl **di cotone** ba·too·fo·lee dee
  ko·to·ne *cotton balls*
bebé ⓜ&① be·be *baby*
bello/a ⓜ/① be·lo/a
  beautiful • handsome • good (weather)
benessere ⓜ be·ne·se·re
  welfare (well-being)
benzina ① ben·dzee·na
  gas (petrol) • petrol
bere be·re *drink*
bevanda ① be·van·da *drink*
biancheria ① **intima** byan·ke·ree·a
  een·tee·ma *underwear*
bianco/a ⓜ/① byan·ko/a *white*
bibbia ① bee·bya *bible*
bibita ① bee·bee·ta *soft drink*

C

biblioteca ① beeb·lyo·te·ka *library*
bicchiere ⑩ bee·kye·re *glass (drinking)*
bici ① **(da corsa)** bee·chee (da *kor*·sa) *(racing) bike*
bicicletta ① bee·chee·*kle*·ta *bicycle*
bidone ⑩ bee·*do*·ne *rip-off • bin*
biglietteria ① bee·lye·te·*ree*·a *ticket office*
biglietto ⑩ bee·*lye*·to *ticket*
— **di andata e ritorno** dee an·*da*·ta e ree·*tor*·no *return ticket*
— **di solo andata** dee *so*·lo an·*da*·ta *one-way ticket*
bilancio ⑩ bee·*lan*·cho *budget*
biliardo ⑩ beel·*yar*·do *pool (game)*
bimbo/a ⑩/① *beem*·bo/a *baby*
binario ⑩ bee·*na*·ryo *platform*
binocolo ⑩ bee·*no*·ko·lo *binoculars*
biondo/a ⑩/① *byon*·do/a *blonde*
birra ① *bee*·ra *beer*
— **chiara** *kya*·ra *lager*
biscotto ⑩ bees·*ko*·to *biscuit • cookie*
bisogno ⑩ bee·*zo*·nyo *need • necessity*
bistecca ① bees·*te*·ka *steak (beef)*
bisticcio ⑩ bees·*tee*·cho *quarrel*
bloccato/a ⑩/① blo·*ka*·to/a *blocked*
blu bloo *blue (dark)*
bocca ① *bo*·ka *mouth*
boccaglio ⑩ bo·*ka*·lyo *snorkel*
bollo ⑩ *bo*·lo *stamp • seal*
— **di circolazione** dee cheer·ko·la·*tsyo*·ne *car registration*
bordo ⑩ *bor*·do *edge • border*
borotalco ⑩ bo·ro·*tal*·ko *baby powder*
borraccia ① bo·ra·*cha* *water bottle*
borsa ① *bor*·sa *bag (general)*
borsetta ① bor·*se*·ta *handbag*
bottiglia ① bo·*tee*·lya *bottle*
bottiglieria ① bo·tee·lye·*ree*·a *liquor store*
bottone ⑩ bo·*to*·ne *button*
braccio ⑩ *bra*·cho *arm*
Braille ⑩ bray *Braille*
brillante ⑩/① bree·*lan*·te *brilliant*
bronchite ① bron·*kee*·te *bronchitis*
bruciare broo·*cha*·re *burn*
brutto/a ⑩/① *broo*·to/a *ugly*
buca ① *boo*·ka *hole • pit*
— **delle lettere** de·le *le*·te·re *mail box*
bucatura ① boo·ka·*too*·ra *puncture*

buddista ⑩&① boo·*dee*·sta *Buddhist*
bugiardo/a ⑩/① boo·*jar*·do/a *liar*
buono/a ⑩/① *bwo*·no/a *good • nice (meal)*
burro ⑩ *boo*·ro *butter*
— **per le labbra** per le *la*·bra *lip balm*
bussola ① *boo*·so·la *compass*
busta ① **(imbottita)** *boo*·sta (eem·bo·*tee*·ta) *(padded) envelope*

C

cabina ① ka·*bee*·na *cabin • cubicle*
— **telefonica** te·le·*fo*·nee·ka *phone box*
cacao ⑩ ka·*ka*·o *cocoa*
caccia ① *ka*·cha *hunting*
caffè ⑩ ka·*fe* *coffee*
calcio ⑩ *kal*·cho *soccer*
calcolatrice ① kal·ko·la·*tree*·che *calculator*
caldo ⑩ *kal*·do *heat*
caldo/a ⑩/① *kal*·do/a *hot*
calendario ⑩ ka·len·*da*·ryo *calendar*
calze ① pl *kal*·tse *stockings*
calzini ⑩ pl kal·*tsee*·nee *socks*
cambiare kam·*bya*·re *change*
cambio ⑩ *kam*·byo *exchange*
— **valuta** ① va·*loo*·ta *currency exchange*
camera ① *ka*·me·ra *room*
— **d'aria** *da*·rya *tube (tyre)*
— **da letto** da *le*·to *bedroom*
— **doppia** *do*·pya *double room*
— **singola** *seen*·go·la *single room*
cameriere/a ⑩/① ka·mer·*ye*·re/a *waiter*
camicia ① ka·*mee*·cha *shirt*
camion ⑩ *ka*·myon *truck*
camminare ka·mee·*na*·re *walk*
camminata ① ka·mee·*na*·ta *(long) walk*
campagna ① kam·*pa*·nya *countryside*
campeggiare kam·pe·*ja*·re *camp*
campeggio ⑩ kam·*pe*·jo *camp site*
campionato ⑩ kam·pyo·*na*·to *championships*
campo ⑩ *kam*·po *field • pitch • court*
— **da golf** da golf *golf course*
— **da tennis** da *te*·nees *tennis court*
cancellare kan·che·*la*·re *cancel*
cancello ⑩ kan·*che*·lo *gate*

cancro ⓜ kan·kro *cancer*
candela ⓕ kan·de·la *candle • spark plug*
cane ⓜ ka·ne *dog*
— guida gwee·da *guide dog*
canottaggio ⓜ ka·no·ta·jo
rowing • canoeing
canottiera ⓕ ka·no·tye·ra *singlet*
cantante ⓜ/ⓕ kan·tan·te *singer*
cantare kan·ta·re *sing*
cantina ⓕ kan·tee·na
wine cellar • winery
canzone ⓕ kan·tso·ne *song*
caparra ⓕ ka·pa·ra *deposit (refundable)*
capire ka·pee·re *understand*
capo ⓜ ka·po *leader*
Capodanno ⓜ ka·po da·no
New Year's Day
cappello ⓜ ka·pe·lo *hat*
cappotto ⓜ ka·po·to *coat*
capra ⓕ ka·pra *goat*
carabinieri ⓜ pl ka·ra·bee·nye·ree
police (military)
caramelle ⓕ pl ka·ra·me·le *lollies*
— alla menta a·la men·ta *mints*
carcere ⓜ/ⓕ kar·che·re *jail*
carino/a ⓜ/ⓕ ka·ree·no/a *pretty • cute*
carne ⓕ kar·ne *meat*
— tritata tree·ta·ta *mince meat*
caro/a ⓜ/ⓕ ka·ro/a *expensive*
carota ⓕ ka·ro·ta *carrot*
carpentiere ⓜ kar·pen·tye·re *carpenter*
carrello ⓜ ka·re·lo *trolley*
carrozza ⓕ ka·ro·tsa *carriage*
— ristorante rees·to·ran·te *dining car*
carta ⓕ kar·ta *paper*
— d'identità dee·den·tee·ta
identification card (ID)
— d'imbarco deem·bar·ko
boarding pass
— di credito dee kre·dee·to *credit card*
— igienica ee·je·nee·ka *toilet paper*
— telefonica te·le·fo·nee·ka *phone card*
carte ⓕ pl kar·te *cards*
cartolaio ⓜ kar·to·la·yo *stationer*
cartolina ⓕ kar·to·lee·na *postcard*
cartuccia ⓕ kar·too·cha *cartridge*
— di ricambio del gas dee ree·kam·byo
del gaz *gas cartridge*
casa ⓕ ka·za *house • home*

casalingo/a ⓜ/ⓕ ka·za·leen·go/a
homemaker
cascata ⓕ kas·ka·ta *waterfall*
casco ⓜ kas·ko *helmet*
casinò ⓜ ka·zee·no *casino*
cassa ⓕ ka·sa *cash register*
cassaforte ⓕ ka·sa·for·te *safe*
cassetta ⓕ ka·se·ta *cassette*
cassiere/a ⓜ/ⓕ ka·sye·re/a *cashier*
castello ⓜ kas·te·lo *castle*
catena ⓕ ka·te·na *chain*
— di montagne dee mon·ta·nye
mountain range
catene ⓕ pl da neve ka·te·ne da ne·ve
snow chains
cattivo/a ⓜ/ⓕ ka·tee·vo/a *bad*
cattolico/a ⓜ/ⓕ ka·to·lee·ko/a *Catholic*
cavalcare ka·val·ka·re *ride (horse)*
cavallino ⓜ ka·va·lee·no *pony*
cavallo ⓜ ka·va·lo *horse*
cavi ⓜ pl con morsetti ka·vee kon
mor·se·tee *jumper leads*
caviale ⓜ ka·vya·le *caviar*
caviglia ⓕ ka·vee·lya *ankle*
cavo ⓜ ka·vo *cable*
cavoletti ⓜ pl di Bruxelles ka·vo·le·tee
dee brook·sel *Brussels sprouts*
cavolfiore ⓜ ka·vol·fyo·re *cauliflower*
cavolo ⓜ ka·vo·lo *cabbage*
ceci ⓜ pl che·chee *chickpeas*
celebrazione ⓕ che·le·bra·tsyo·ne
celebration
celibe ⓜ che·lee·be *single (man)*
cellulare ⓜ che·loo·la·re *mobile phone*
cena ⓕ che·na *dinner*
centesimo ⓜ chen·te·zee·mo *cent*
centimetro ⓜ chen·tee·me·tro *centimetre*
centro ⓜ chen·tro *centre*
— commerciale ko·mer·cha·le
shopping centre
— storico sto·ree·ko *old city*
— telefonico te·le·fo·nee·ko
telephone centre
cercare cher·ka·re *look for*
cereali ⓜ pl che·re·a·lee *cereal*
cerotti ⓜ pl che·ro·tee *Band-aids*
certificato ⓜ cher·tee·fee·ka·to *certificate*
cestino ⓜ ches·tee·no *basket*
cetriolo ⓜ che·tree·o·lo *cucumber*

C

italian–english

231

che (cosa) ke (ko·za) *what*
chi kee *who*
chiamata ① kya·ma·ta *phone call*
— **a carico del destinatario**
a ka·ree·ko del des·tee·na·ta·ryo
reverse-charges call • collect call
chiaro/a ⓜ/① kya·ro/a *light (colour)*
chiave ① kya·ve *key*
chiesa ① kye·za *church*
chilo ⓜ kee·lo *kilogram*
chilometro ⓜ kee·lo·me·tro *kilometre*
chitarra ① kee·ta·ra *guitar*
chiudere kyoo·de·re *close*
chiuso/a ⓜ/① kyoo·zo/a
closed • shut • locked
ciascuno/a ⓜ/① chas·koo·no/a *each*
cibo ⓜ chee·bo *food*
— **da bebè** da be·*be baby food*
ciclismo ⓜ chee·kleez·mo *cycling*
ciclista ⓜ&① chee·klee·sta *cyclist*
ciclopista ① chee·klo·pee·sta *bike path*
cidì ⓜ chee·dee *CD*
cieco/a ⓜ/① chye·ko/a *blind*
cielo ⓜ che·lo *sky*
cima ① chee·ma *peak*
cinema ⓜ chee·ne·ma *cinema*
cinghia ① **della ventola** cheen·gya de·la
ven·to·la *fanbelt*
cintura ① **di sicurezza** cheen·too·ra dee
see·koo·re·tsa *seatbelt*
cioccolata ① cho·ko·la·ta *chocolate*
cipolla ① chee·po·la *onion*
circo ⓜ cheer·ko *circus*
cisti ① **ovarica** chee·stee o·va·ree·ka
ovarian cyst
cistite ① chees·tee·te *cystitis*
città ① chee·ta *city*
cittadinanza ① chee·ta·dee·nan·tsa
citizenship
ciuccicotto ⓜ choo·cho·to
dummy (pacifier)
classe ① kla·se *class*
— **business** beez·nes *business class*
— **turistica** too·ree·stee·ka
economy class
classico/a ⓜ/① kla·see·ko/a *classical*
cliente ⓜ&① klee·en·te *client*
cocaina ① ko·ka·ee·na *cocaine*
coda ① ko·da *queue*

codice ⓜ **postale** ko·dee·che pos·ta·le
postcode
cognome ⓜ ko·nyo·me *surname*
coincidenza ① ko·een·chee·den·tsa
coincidence • connection (transport)
collant ① pl ko·lant *pantyhose*
colazione ① ko·la·tsyo·ne *breakfast*
collega ⓜ&① ko·le·ga *colleague*
collegio ⓜ **universitario** ko·le·jo
oo·nee·ver·see·ta·ryo *college*
collina ① ko·lee·na *hill*
collirio ⓜ ko·lee·ryo *eye drops*
collo ⓜ ko·lo *neck*
colloquio ⓜ **(selettivo)** ko·lo·kwyo
(se·le·tee·vo) *interview*
colore ⓜ ko·lo·re *colour*
colpa ① kol·pa *fault (someone's)*
colpevole kol·pe·vo·le *guilty*
coltello ⓜ kol·te·lo *knife*
come ko·me *how*
cominciare ko·meen·cha·re
begin • start
commedia ① ko·me·dya *play (theatre)*
— **comica** ko·mee·ka *comedy*
commercio ⓜ ko·mer·cho
trade • business studies
commissione ① ko·mee·syo·ne
commission
comodo/a ⓜ/① ko·mo·do/a *comfortable*
compagno/a ⓜ/① kom·pa·nyo/a
companion • partner (intimate)
compenso ⓜ kom·pen·so *fee*
compleanno ⓜ kom·ple·a·no *birthday*
complesso ⓜ **rock** kom·ple·so rok
rock group
completo/a ⓜ/① kom·ple·to/a
booked out
comprare kom·pra·re *buy*
compreso/a ⓜ/① kom·pre·zo/a *included*
computer ⓜ kom·pyoo·ter *computer*
— **portatile** ⓜ por·ta·tee·le *laptop*
comunione ① ko·moo·nyo·ne
communion
comunista ⓜ&① ko·moo·nee·sta
communist
con kon *with*
— **filtro** feel·tro *filtered*
concerto ⓜ kon·cher·to *concert*
condividere kon·dee·vee·de·re
share (with)

confermare kon·fer·ma·re
confirm (a booking)

confessione ① kon·fe·syo·ne
confession (religious)

confine ⓜ kon·fee·ne *border*

congelare kon·je·la·re *freeze*

congelato/a ⓜ/① kon·je·la·to/a *frozen*

coniglio ⓜ ko·nee·lyo *rabbit*

conoscere ko·no·she·re *know (a person)*

conservatore/conservatrice ⓜ/①
kon·ser·va·to·re/kon·ser·va·tree·che
conservative

consigliare kon·see·lya·re *recommend*

consolato ⓜ kon·so·la·to *consulate*

contanti ⓜ pl kon·tan·tee *count*

contare kon·ta·re *count*

conto ⓜ kon·to *bill (account)*
— **in banca** een ban·ka *bank account*

contraccettivi ⓜ pl kon·tra·che·tee·vee
contraceptives

contratto ⓜ kon·tra·to *contract*

controllare kon·tro·la·re *check*

controllore ⓜ kon·tro·lo·re
ticket collector

controllare kon·tro·la·re *check*

convalidare kon·va·lee·da·re *validate*

convento ⓜ kon·ven·to *convent*

coperta ① ko·per·ta *blanket*

coperte ① pl **e lenzuola** ① pl ko·per·te e
len·zwo·la *bedding*

coperto ⓜ ko·per·to
cover charge (restaurant)

Coppa ① **del Mondo** ko·pa del mon·do
World Cup

coraggioso/a ⓜ/① ko·ra·jo·zo/a *brave*

corda ① kor·da *rope*
— **del bucato** del boo·ka·to *clothesline*

corpo ⓜ kor·po *body*

corrente ① ko·ren·te *current (electricity)*

correre ko·re·re *run*

corridoio ⓜ ko·ree·do·yo
aisle (in plane, train)

corrompere ko·rom·pe·re *bribe*

corrotto/a ⓜ/① ko·ro·to/a *corrupt*

corsa ① kor·sa *ride • race*

corte ① kor·te *court (legal)*

corto/a ⓜ/① kor·to/a *short (length)*

cosa ① ko·za *thing • object • matter*

costa ① kos·ta *coast*

costare kos·ta·re *cost*

costruire kos·troo·ee·re *build*

costruttore/costruttrice ⓜ/①
kos·troo·to·re/ko·stroo·tree·che *builder*

costume ⓜ **da bagno** kos·too·me da
ba·nyo *bathing suit*

cotone ⓜ ko·to·ne *cotton*

cozza ① ko·tsa *mussel*

crema ① kre·ma *cream*
— **da barba** da bar·ba *shaving cream*
— **solare** so·la·re *sunscreen*

crescere kre·she·re *grow*

criminalità ① kree·mee·na·lee·ta
crime (issue)

cristiano/a ⓜ/① krees·tya·no/a *Christian*

croce ① kro·che *cross (religious)*

crudo/a ⓜ/① kroo·do/a *raw*

cucchiaino ⓜ koo·kya·ee·no *teaspoon*

cucchiaio ⓜ koo·kya·yo *spoon*

cucciolo ⓜ koo·cho·lo *puppy*

cucina ① koo·chee·na *kitchen*

cucinare koo·chee·na·re *cook*

cucire koo·chee·re *sew*

culla ① koo·la *cot*

cuoco/a ⓜ/① kwo·ko/a
cook • chef (restaurant)

cuoio ⓜ kwo·yo *leather*

cuore ⓜ kwo·re *heart*

curare koo·ra·re *look after*

curriculum vitae ⓜ koo·ree·koo·loom
vee·te *CV • resume*

curry ⓜ koo·ree *curry*

cuscino ⓜ koo·shee·no *pillow*

D

da da *from • at • to • since*

da solo/a ⓜ/① da so·lo/a *alone*

danno ⓜ da·no *damage*

dare da·re *give*
— **il benvenuto a** eel ben·ve·noo·to a
welcome
— **un calcio** oon kal·cho *kick*

data ① da·ta *date (day)*
— **di arrivo** dee a·ree·vo *date of arrival*
— **di nascita** dee na·shee·ta
date of birth
— **di partenza** dee par·ten·tsa
date of departure

datore/trice ⑩/① **di lavoro** da·to·re/
da·tree·che dee la·vo·ro *employer*

dea ① *de·a goddess*

debole de·bo·le *weak*

degustazione ① **(dei vini)**
de·goos·ta·tsyo·ne day vee·nee
(wine) tasting

delitto ⑩ de·lee·to *crime (infringement)*

democrazia ① de·mo·kra·tsee·a
democracy

denaro ⑩ de·na·ro *money*

dente ⑩ *den·te tooth (front)*

denti pl *den·tee teeth*

dentifricio ⑩ den·tee·free·cho *toothpaste*

dentista ⑩&① *den·tee·sta dentist*

dentro *den·tro inside*

deodorante ⑩ de·o·do·ran·te *deodorant*

deposito ⑩ de·po·zee·to *deposit (bank)*
— **bagagli** ba·ga·lyee
left luggage (office)

derubare de·roo·ba·re *rob*

desiderare de·see·de·ra·re *wish • desire*

destinazione ① des·tee·na·tsyo·ne
destination

destra *de·stra*
right (direction) • right-wing

detersivo ⑩ de·ter·see·vo
washing powder

di *from • by • of*
— **andata e ritorno** an·da·ta e
ree·tor·no *return (ticket)*
— **destra** *de·stra right-wing*
— **fronte a** *fron·te a opposite*
— **lusso** *loo·so luxurious*
— **meno** *me·no less*
— **nuovo** *nwo·vo again*
— **più** *pyoo more*
— **recente** *re·chen·te recently*
— **seconda mano** se·kon·da ma·no
second-hand
— **sinistra** see·nee·stra *left-wing*
— **solo andata** *so·lo an·da·ta*
one-way ticket

diabete ⑩ dee·a·be·te *diabetes*

diaframma ⑩ dee·a·fra·ma *diaphragm*

diapositiva ① dee·a·po·zee·tee·va
slide (film)

diarrea ① dee·a·re·a *diarrhoea*

diesel ⑩ *dee·zel diesel*

dieta ① *dye·ta diet*

dietro *dye·tro behind*

difettoso/a ⑩/① dee·fe·to·zo/a *faulty*

differente (da) dee·fe·ren·te (da) *different*

differenza ① dee·fe·ren·tsa *difference*
— **di fuso orario** dee foo·zo o·ra·ryo
time difference

difficile dee·fee·chee·le *difficult*

digitale dee·jee·ta·le *digital*

dimensioni ① pl dee·men·syo·nee
size (general)

dimenticare dee·men·tee·ka·re *forget*

dio/dea ⑩/① *dee·o/de·a god (general)*

dipendente ⑩/① dee·pen·den·te
addicted • dependant

dipingere dee·peen·je·re *paint*

dire *dee·re say*

diretto/a ⑩/① dee·re·to/a *direct*

direzione ① dee·re·tsyo·ne *direction*

diritti ⑩ pl **umani** dee·ree·tee oo·ma·nee
human rights

diritto ① dee·ree·to/a
straight • right (prerogative)

disabile de·za·bee·le *disabled*

dischetto ⑩ dees·ke·to *disk (computer)*

discriminazione ①
dees·kree·mee·na·tsyo·ne
discrimination

disinfettante ⑩ deez·een·fe·tan·te
disinfectant

disoccupato/a ⑩/① dee·zo·koo·pa·to/a
unemployed

distributore ⑩ dee·stree·boo·to·re
petrol/service station
— **automatico di biglietti**
ow·to·ma·tee·ko dee bee·lye·tee
ticket machine

disturbo ⑩ dees·toor·bo *trouble*

disturbi ⑩ pl **da fuso orario** dees·toor·bee
da foo·zo o·ra·ryo *jet lag*

dito ⑩ *dee·to finger*
— **del piede** del pye·de *toe*

ditta ① *dee·ta company (firm)*

diversi/e ⑩/① pl dee·ver·see/dee·ver·se
several

diverso/a dee·ver·so/a *different • various*

divertente dee·ver·ten·te
funny • entertaining

divertimento ⑩ dee·ver·tee·men·to *fun*

divertirsi dee·ver·*teer*·see *enjoy (oneself)*

divorziato/a ⓜ/ⓕ dee·vor·*tsya*·to/a *divorced*

divisa ⓕ dee·*vee*·za *uniform*

doccia ⓕ *do*·cha *shower*

documenti pl do·koo·*men*·tee *papers*

documento ⓜ **d'identità** do·koo·*men*·to dee·den·tee·*ta identification*

dogana ⓕ do·*ga*·na *customs*

dolce ⓜ *dol*·che *sweet • dessert*

dolce *dol*·che *sweet • soft*

dolciumi ⓜ pl dol·*choo*·mee *candy*

dollaro ⓜ *do*·la·ro *dollar*

dolore ⓜ do·*lo*·re *pain*

dolori ⓜ pl **mestruali** do·*lo*·ree me·*stroo*·a·lee *period pain*

doloroso/a ⓜ/ⓕ do·lo·ro·zo/a *painful • sore*

domanda ⓕ do·*man*·da *question*

domandare do·man·*da*·re *ask (a question)*

domani do·*ma*·nee *tomorrow*

— **mattina** ma·*tee*·na *tomorrow morning*

— **pomeriggio** po·me·*ree*·jo *tomorrow afternoon*

— **sera** *se*·ra *tomorrow evening*

donna ⓕ *do*·na *woman*

— **d'affari** da·*fa*·ree *businesswoman*

dopo *do*·po *after*

dopobarba ⓜ do·po·*bar*·ba *aftershave*

dopodomani do·po·do·*ma*·nee *day after tomorrow*

doppio/a ⓜ/ⓕ *do*·pyo/a *double*

dormire dor·*mee*·re *sleep*

dose ⓕ *do*·ze *dose*

— **eccessiva** e·che·*see*·va *overdose*

dove *do*·ve *where*

dozzina ⓕ do·*dzee*·na *dozen*

dramma ⓜ *dra*·ma *drama*

droga ⓕ *dro*·ga *drug/ drugs*

drogheria ⓕ dro·ge·*ree*·a *grocery*

due *doo*·e *two*

— **letti** *le*·tee *twin/two beds*

— **volte** *vol*·te *twice*

duomo ⓜ *dwo*·mo *cathedral*

durante doo·*ran*·te *during*

duro/a ⓜ/ⓕ *doo*·ro/a *hard (not soft)*

E

e e *and*

ebreo/a ⓜ/ⓕ e·*bre*·o/a *Jewish*

ecografia ⓕ e·ko·gra·*fee*·a *ultrasound*

economico/a ⓜ/ⓕ e·ko·*no*·mee·ko/a *cheap*

eczema ⓜ ek·*dze*·ma *eczema*

edicola ⓕ e·*dee*·ko·la *newsagency*

edificio ⓜ e·dee·*fee*·cho *building*

egoista ⓜ/ⓕ e·go·*ee*·sta *selfish*

elenco ⓜ **telefonico** e·*len*·ko te·le·*fo*·nee·ko *phone book*

elettricista ⓜ&ⓕ e·le·tree·*chee*·sta *electrician*

elettricità ⓕ e·le·tree·chee·*ta electricity*

elezioni ⓕ pl e·le·*tsyo*·nee *elections • polls*

email ⓜ e·*mayl email*

emergenza ⓕ e·mer·*jen*·tsa *emergency*

emicrania ⓕ e·mee·*kra*·nya *migraine*

emotivo/a ⓜ/ⓕ e·mo·*tee*·vo/a *emotional*

energia ⓕ **(nucleare)** en·er·*jee*·a (noo·kle·*a*·re) *(nuclear) energy*

enorme e·*nor*·me *huge*

entrare en·*tra*·re *enter*

entrata ⓕ en·*tra*·ta *entry*

entro (un'ora) *en*·tro (oon·*o*·ra) *within (an hour)*

epatite ⓕ e·pa·*tee*·te *hepatitis*

epilessia ⓕ e·pee·le·*see*·a *epilepsy*

erba ⓕ *er*·ba *grass • pot (dope)*

erbe ⓕ pl *er*·be *herbs*

erborista ⓜ&ⓕ er·bo·*ree*·sta *herbalist*

eroina ⓕ e·ro·*ee*·na *heroin*

erotico/a ⓜ/ⓕ e·ro·*tee*·ko/a *sexy*

errore ⓜ e·*ro*·re *mistake*

esame ⓜ e·*za*·me *test*

escluso/a ⓜ/ⓕ es·*kloo*·zo/a *excluded*

escursione ⓕ es·koor·*syo*·ne *excursion • trip*

— **a piedi** a *pye*·de *hike*

escursionismo ⓜ es·koor·syo·*neez*·mo *touring*

— **a piedi** a *pye*·de *hiking*

esecuzione ⓕ e·se·koo·*tsyo*·ne *performance*

esempio ⓜ e·*zem*·pyo *example*

esperienza ① es·pe·*ryen*·tsa *experience*

esperimenti ⓜ pl **nucleari**
es·pe·ree·*men*·tee noo·*kle*·a·ree
nuclear testing

esposimetro ⓜ es·po·*zee*·me·tro
light meter

esposizione ① es·po·zee·*tsyo*·ne
exhibition

espresso/a ⓜ/① es·*pre*·so/a *express*

essere *e*·se·re *be*
— **d'accordo** da·*kor*·do *agree*
— **raffreddato/a** ⓜ/① ra·fre·*da*·to/a
have a cold

est ⓜ est *east*

estate ① es·*ta*·te *summer*

estetista ⓜ&① es·te·*tee*·sta *beautician*

estero/a ⓜ/① es·te·*ro*/a *foreign*

età ① e·*ta* *age*

etichetta ① e·tee·*ke*·ta *luggage tag*

etto ⓜ *e*·to *100 grams*

euro ⓜ *e*·oo·ro *euro*

europeo/a ⓜ/① e·oo·ro·*pe*·o/a
European (adj)

eutanasia ① e·oo·ta·na·*zee*·a *euthanasia*

F

fabbrica ① *fa*·bree·ka *factory*

faccia ① *fa*·cha *face*

facile *fa*·chee·le *easy*

fagioli ⓜ pl fa·*jo*·lee *beans*

fame ① *fa*·me *hunger*

famiglia ① fa·*mee*·lya *family*

famoso/a ⓜ/① fa·*mo*·zo/a *famous*

fango ⓜ *fan*·go *mud*

fantastico/a ⓜ/① fan·*tas*·tee·ko/a *great*

fantino ⓜ fan·*tee*·no *jockey*

fare *fa*·re *do* • *make*
— **il tifo** eel *tee*·fo *support* (cheer on)
— **l'autostop** *low*·to·stop *hitchhike*
— **la barba** la *bar*·ba *shave*
— **male** *ma*·le *hurt*
— **una camminata** oo·na ka·mee·*na*·ta
hike
— **una foto** oo·na *fo*·to *take a photo*

farfalla ① far·*fa*·la *butterfly*

fari ⓜ pl fa·ree *headlights*

farina ① fa·*ree*·na *flour*

farmacia ① far·ma·*chee*·a *pharmacy*

farmacista ⓜ&① far·ma·*chee*·sta *chemist*

fascia ① *fa*·sha *bandage*

fatto/a ⓜ/① *fa*·to/a *made*
— **a mano** a *ma*·no *handmade*
— **di (cotone)** dee ko·*to*·ne
made of (cotton)

fattoria ① fa·to·*ree*·a *farm*

fax ⓜ faks *fax*

fazzolettini ⓜ pl **di carta** fa·tso·le·*tee*·nee
dee *kar*·ta *tissues*

fazzoletto ① fa·tso·*le*·to *handkerchief*

febbre ① *fe*·bre *temperature* (fever)
— **da fieno** da *fye*·no *hay fever*

federa ① *fe*·de·ra *pillowcase*

fegato ⓜ *fe*·ga·to *liver*

felice fe·*lee*·che *happy*

ferita ① fe·*ree*·ta *injury*

ferito/a ⓜ/① fe·*ree*·to/a *injured*

fermare fer·*ma*·re *stop*

fermarsi fer·*mar*·see *stay* (at a hotel)

fermata ① fer·*ma*·ta *stop*

fermo ⓜ **posta** *fer*·mo *pos*·ta
poste restante

ferramenta ① fe·ra·*men*·ta
hardware store

ferro ⓜ *fe*·ro *iron*
— **da stiro** da *stee*·ro *iron* (clothes)

festa ① *fes*·ta *festival* • *public holiday* •
party (celebration)

fetta ① *fe*·ta *slice*

fiammiferi ⓜ pl fya·*mee*·fe·ree *matches*

fico ⓜ *fee*·ko *fig*

fidanzamento ⓜ fee·dan·tsa·*men*·to
engagement (couple)

fidanzato/a ⓜ/① fee·dan·*tsa*·to/a
fiance(e)

figlia ① *fee*·lya *daughter*

figlio ⓜ *fee*·lyo *son*

film ⓜ feelm *movie*

filo ⓜ *fee*·lo *thread* (sewing)
— **dentario** den·*ta*·ree·o *dental floss*

fine ① *fee*·ne *end*

fine settimana ① *fee*·ne se·tee·*ma*·na
weekend

finestra ① fee·*nes*·tra *window* (general)

finestrino ⓜ fee·nes·*tree*·no
window (car, plane)

finire fee·*nee*·re
end • *finish* • *run out of*

finito/a ⓜ/ⓕ fee·nee·to *finished*

fino a (giugno) fee·no a (joo·nyo) *until (June)*

fiocchi ⓜ pl **di mais** fyo·kee dee ma·ees *cornflakes*

fioraio ⓜ&ⓕ fyo·ra·yo *florist*

fiore ⓜ fyo·re *flower*

firma ⓕ feer·ma *signature*

fiume ⓜ fyoo·me *river*

flash ⓜ flesh *flash (camera)*

fluido ⓜ **idratante** floo·ee·do ee·dra·tan·te *hydrating fluid*

foglia ⓕ fo·lya *leaf*

fondo ⓜ fon·do *bottom*

fondo/a ⓜ/ⓕ fon·do/a *deep*

footing ⓜ foo·teeng *jogging • running (sport)*

forbici ⓕ pl for·bee·chee *scissors*

forchetta ⓕ for·ke·ta *fork*

foresta ⓕ fo·res·ta *forest*

forma ⓕ for·ma *shape*

formaggio ⓜ for·ma·jo *cheese* — **fresco** fres·ko *cream cheese*

formica ⓕ for·mee·ka *ant*

forno ⓜ for·no *oven* — **a microonde** a mee·kro·on·de *microwave (oven)*

forse for·se *maybe*

forte ⓜ/ⓕ for·te *strong • loud*

fortuna ⓕ for·too·na *chance • luck*

fortunato/a ⓜ/ⓕ for·too·na·to/a *lucky*

foto ⓕ fo·to *photo*

fotografia ⓕ fo·to·gra·fee·a *photography*

fotografo ⓜ fo·to·gra·fo *photographer • camera shop*

fra fra *between* — **poco** po·ko *soon*

fragile fra·jee·le *fragile*

fragola ⓕ fra·go·la *strawberry*

francobollo ⓜ fran·ko·bo·lo *stamp*

fratello ⓜ fra·te·lo *brother*

freccia ⓕ fre·cha *indicator (car)*

freddo/a ⓜ/ⓕ fre·do/a *cold*

freno ⓜ fre·no *brake*

fresco/a ⓜ/ⓕ fres·ko/a *fresh*

fretta ⓕ fre·ta *hurry*

friggere free·je·re *fry*

frigo ⓜ free·go *fridge*

frigobar ⓜ free·go·bar bar *fridge • mini-bar*

frigorifero ⓜ free·go·ree·fe·ro *refrigerator*

frizione ⓕ free·tsyo·ne *clutch*

frutta ⓕ froo·ta *fruit* — **secca** se·ka *dried fruit*

fruttivendolo/a ⓜ/ⓕ froo·tee·ven·do·lo/a *greengrocer*

fumare foo·ma·re *smoke*

fumato/a ⓜ/ⓕ foo·ma·to/a *smoked • stoned (drugged)*

funerale ⓜ foo·ne·ra·le *funeral*

fungo ⓜ foon·go *mushroom*

funivia ⓕ foo·nee·vee·a *cable car*

fuoco ⓜ fwo·ko *fire*

fuori fwo·ree *outside*

furgone ⓜ foor·go·ne *van*

futuro ⓜ foo·too·ro *future*

G

gabinetto ⓜ **(pubblico)** ga·bee·ne·to (poo·blee·ko) *(public) toilet*

galleria ⓕ **d'arte** ga·le·ree·a dar·te *art gallery*

Galles ⓜ ga·les *Wales*

gamba ⓕ gam·ba *leg (body part)*

gambero ⓜ gam·be·ro *prawn*

gara ⓜ ga·ra *race (sport) • competition*

garage ⓜ ga·raj *garage*

gas ⓜ gaz *gas (for cooking)*

gasolio ⓜ ga·zo·lyo *diesel*

gastroenterite ⓕ gas·tro·en·te·ree·te *gastroenteritis*

gattino ⓜ ga·tee·no *kitten*

gatto ⓜ ga·to *cat*

gay gei *gay*

gelateria ⓕ je·la·te·ree·a *ice-cream parlour*

gelato ⓜ je·la·to *ice cream*

geloso/a ⓜ/ⓕ je·lo·zo/a *jealous*

gemelli/e ⓜ/ⓕ pl je·me·lee/je·me·le *twins*

generale je·ne·ra·le *general*

gengiva ⓕ jen·jee·va *gum (mouth)*

genitori ⓜ pl je·nee·to·ree *parents*

gente ⓕ jen·te *people*

gentile jen·tee·le *kind • nice (person)*

germogli ⓜ pl **(di soia)** jer·mo·lyee (dee so·ya) *beansprouts*

gettone ⓜ je·to·ne *token*

ghiaccio ⓜ *gya·cho ice*
già *ja already*
giacca ⓕ *ja·ka jacket*
giallo/a ⓜ/ⓕ *ja·lo/a yellow*
Giappone ⓜ *ja·po·ne Japan*
giardinaggio ⓜ *jar·dee·na·jo gardening*
giardino ⓜ *jar·dee·no garden*
　— zoologico *dzo·o·lo·jee·ko zoo*
ginecologo/a ⓜ/ⓕ *jee·ne·ko·lo·go/a gynaecologist*
ginnastica ⓕ *jee·nas·tee·ka gymnastics*
ginocchio ⓜ *jee·no·kyo knee*
giocare *jo·ka·re play*
　— a calcio *a kal·cho play soccer*
gioco ⓜ *jo·ko game (play)*
　— elettronico *e·le·tro·nee·ko computer game*
gioielli ⓜ pl *jo·ye·lee jewellery*
giornale ⓜ *jor·na·le newspaper*
giornalista ⓜ&ⓕ *jor·na·lee·sta journalist*
giorno ⓜ *jor·no day*
giovane *jo·va·ne young*
girare *jee·ra·re turn*
gita ⓕ *jee·ta tour • trip*
giù *joo down*
giubbotto ⓜ **di salvataggio** *joo·bo·to dee sal·va·ta·jo life jacket*
giudice ⓜ *joo·dee·che judge*
giudò ⓜ *joo·do judo*
giusto/a ⓜ/ⓕ *joo·sto/a right (correct)*
gola ⓕ *go·la throat*
gomma ⓕ *go·ma tyre*
　— da masticare *da ma·stee·ka·re (chewing) gum*
gonfiore ⓜ *gon·fyo·re swelling*
gonna ⓕ *go·na skirt*
governo ⓜ *go·ver·no government*
grammi ⓜ pl *gra·mee grams*
grande *gran·de big • large*
grande magazzino ⓜ *gran·de ma·ga·dzee·no department store*
grandinata ⓕ *gran·dee·na·ta hailstorm*
grandine ⓕ *gran·dee·ne hail*
grasso/a ⓜ/ⓕ *gra·so/a fat*
gratuito/a ⓜ/ⓕ *gra·too·ee·to/a free (gratis) • complimentary (free)*
grigio/a ⓜ/ⓕ *gree·jo/a grey*
grotta ⓕ *gro·ta cave*

gruppo ⓜ *groo·po band (music)*
　— sanguigno *san·gwee·nyo blood group*
guanti ⓜ *gwan·tee gloves*
guardare *gwar·da·re look • watch*
　— le vetrine *le ve·tree·ne go window-shopping*
guardaroba ⓜ *gwar·da·ro·ba cloakroom*
guastarsi *gwas·tar·see break down*
guastato/a ⓜ/ⓕ *gwas·ta·to/a broken down*
guasto/a ⓜ/ⓕ *gwa·sto/a off (food)*
guerra ⓕ *gwe·ra war*
guida ⓕ *gwee·da guide (person) • guidebook*
　— agli spettacoli *a·lyee spe·ta·ko·lee entertainment guide*
　— audio *ow·dyo guide (audio)*
　— turistica *too·ree·stee·ka guidebook*
guidare *gwee·da·re drive*
gustoso/a ⓜ/ⓕ *goo·sto·zo/a tasty*

H

halal *a·lal halal*
hashish ⓜ *a·sheesh hash*
hockey ⓜ *o·kee hockey*
　— su ghiaccio *soo gya·cho ice hockey*

I

idiota ⓜ&ⓕ *ee·dyo·ta idiot*
idratante ⓜ *ee·dra·tan·te moisturiser*
ieri *ye·ree yesterday*
illegale *ee·le·ga·le illegal*
imbarazzato/a ⓜ/ⓕ *eem·ba·ra·tsa·to/a embarrassed*
imbrogliare *eem·bro·lya·re cheat*
immersione ⓕ *ee·mer·syo·ne submersion • dive*
　— in apnea *een ap·ne·a snorkelling*
　— subacquea *soo·ba·kwe·a scuba diving*
immigrazione ⓕ *ee·mee·gra·tsyo·ne immigration*
imparare *eem·pa·ra·re learn*
impermeabile ⓜ *eem·per·me·a·bee·le waterproof*
impermeabile *eem·per·me·a·bee·le waterproof*

impiegato/a ⓜ/ⓕ eem·pye·ga·to/a
employee • office worker

importante eem·por·tan·te *important*

impossibile eem·po·see·bee·le *impossible*

in een *in • to*

— **bianco e nero** byan·ko e ne·ro *B&W*

— **buona salute** bwo·na sa·loo·te
in good health

— **fondo** fon·do
at the bottom • after all

— **fretta** fre·ta *in a hurry*

— **lista d'attesa** lee·sta da·te·za
standby (ticket)

— **omaggio** o·ma·jo
complimentary (free gift)

— **ritardo** ree·tar·do *late* (adv)

— **salita** sa·lee·ta *uphill*

— **sciopero** ⓜ sho·pe·ro *on strike*

— **vendita** ven·dee·ta *on sale*

inalatore ⓜ ee·na·la·to·re *inhaler*

incidente ⓜ een·chee·den·te
accident • crash

incinta een·cheen·ta *pregnant*

incontrare een·kon·tra·re *meet*

incrocio ⓜ een·kro·cho *intersection*

indicare een·dee·ka·re *point*

indigestione ⓕ een·dee·je·styo·ne
indigestion

indirizzo ⓜ een·dee·ree·tso *address*

indossare een·do·sa·re *wear*

indù ⓜ&ⓕ een·doo *Hindu*

industria ⓕ een·doos·trya *industry*

infermiere/a ⓜ/ⓕ een·fer·mye·re/a *nurse*

infezione ⓕ een·fe·tsyo·ne *infection*

infiammazione ⓕ een·fya·ma·tsyo·ne
inflammation

influenza ⓕ een·floo·en·tsa
flu • influenza

informatica ⓕ een·for·ma·tee·ka *IT*

informazioni ⓕ pl een·for·ma·tsyo·nee
information

infortunato/a ⓜ/ⓕ een·for·too·na·to/a
injured

ingegnere ⓜ&ⓕ een·je·nye·re *engineer*

Inghilterra ⓕ een·geel·te·ra *England*

inglese een·gle·ze *English*

ingorgo ⓜ een·gor·go *traffic jam*

ingrediente ⓜ een·gre·dyen·te *ingredient*

ingresso ⓜ een·gre·so
cover charge (venue) • entrance

iniezione ⓕ ee·nye·tsyo·ne *injection*

inizio ⓜ ee·nee·tsyo *start (beginning)*

innocente ee·no·chen·te *innocent*

inquinamento ⓜ een·kwee·na·men·to
pollution

insalata ⓕ een·sa·la·ta *salad*

insegnante ⓜ&ⓕ een·sen·yan·te
teacher (general)

insetto ⓜ een·se·to *insect*

insieme een·sye·me *together*

insolito/a ⓜ/ⓕ een·so·lee·to/a *unusual*

interessante een·te·re·san·te *interesting*

internazionale een·ter·na·tsyo·na·le
international

Internet (point) ⓜ een·ter·net (poynt)
Internet (cafe)

interprete ⓜ/ⓕ een·ter·pre·te *interpreter*

interurbano/a ⓜ/ⓕ een·ter·oor·ba·no/a
long-distance (bus)

intervallo ⓜ een·ter·va·lo *intermission*

intervento ⓜ een·ter·ven·to
*operation (medical) • intervention
(police) • speech*

intossicazione ⓕ **alimentare**
een·to·see·ka·tsyo·ne a·lee·men·ta·re
food poisoning

inverno ⓜ een·ver·no *winter*

invitare een·vee·ta·re *invite*

io ee·o *I*

isola ⓕ ee·zo·la *island*

istruttore/istrutrice ⓜ/ⓕ ee·stroo·to·re/
ee·stroo·tree·che *instructor (general)*

istruzione ⓕ ees·troo·tsyo·ne *education*

itinerario ⓜ ee·tee·ne·ra·ryo
itinerary • route

— **escursionistico**
es·koor·syo·nee·stee·ko *hiking route*

IVA ⓕ ee·va *sales tax*

J

jeans ⓜ pl jeens *jeans*

K

kiwi ⓜ kee·wee *kiwifruit*

kosher ka·sher *kosher*

L

là *la there*
labbra ① pl *la·bra lips*
laboratorio ⓜ *la·bo·ra·to·ryo workshop*
ladro/a ⓜ/① *la·dro/a thief*
lago ⓜ *la·go lake*
lamentarsi *la·men·tar·see complain*
lamette ① pl **(da barba)** *la·me·te (da bar·ba) razor blades*
lampadina ① *lam·pa·dee·na light bulb*
lampone ⓜ *lam·po·ne raspberry*
lana ① *la·na wool*
lardo ⓜ *lar·do lard*
largo/a ⓜ/① *lar·go/a wide*
lassativi ⓜ pl *la·sa·tee·vee laxatives*
lato ⓜ *la·to side*
latte ⓜ *la·te milk*
— **di soia** *dee so·ya soy milk*
— **scremato** *skre·ma·to skimmed milk*
lattuga ① *la·too·ga lettuce*
lavaggio ⓜ **a secco** *la·va·jo a se·ko dry cleaning*
lavanderia *la·van·de·ree·a laundry (room)*
— **a gettone** *je·to·ne laundrette*
lavare *la·va·re wash (something)*
lavarsi *la·var·see wash (oneself)*
lavatrice ① *la·va·tree·che washing machine*
lavorare *la·vo·ra·re work*
— **in proprio** *een pro·pryo (to be) self-employed*
lavoratore/lavoratrice ⓜ/①
la·vo·ra·to·re/la·vo·ra·tree·che worker
lavoro ⓜ *la·vo·ro job • occupation • work*
forza ① *for·tsa strength • force*
forze ① pl **armate** *for·tse ar·ma·te military*
legale *le·ga·le legal*
legge ① *le·je law*
leggere *le·je·re read*
leggero/a ⓜ/① *le·je·ro/a light (not heavy)*
legna ① **(da ardere)** *le·nya (da ar·de·re) (fire)wood*
legno ⓜ *le·nyo wood*
legume ⓜ *le·goo·me legume*

lei *lay she*
Lei pol *lay you (polite)*
lentamente *len·ta·men·te slowly*
lenti ① pl **a contatto** *len·tee a kon·ta·to contact lenses*
lenticchia ① *len·tee·kya lentil*
lento/a ⓜ/① *len·to/a slow*
lenzuolo ⓜ *len·tswo·lo sheet (bed)*
lesbica ① *lez·bee·ka lesbian*
lettera ① *le·te·ra letter*
letto ⓜ *le·to bed*
— **matrimoniale** *ma·tree·mo·nya·le double bed*
libero/a ⓜ/① *lee·be·ro/a free (not bound) • vacant*
libreria ① *lee·bre·ree·a bookshop*
libretto ⓜ *lee·bre·to booklet*
— **di circolazione** *dee cheer·ko·la·tsyo·ne car owner's title*
libro ⓜ *lee·bro book*
licenza ① *lee·chen·tsa permit*
limetta ① *lee·me·ta lime (fruit) • nail file*
limite ⓜ **di velocità** *lee·mee·te dee ve·lo·chee·ta speed limit*
limonata ① *lee·mo·na·ta lemonade*
limone ⓜ *lee·mo·ne lemon*
linea ① *lee·ne·a line*
— **aerea** *a·e·re·a airline*
lingua ① *leen·gwa tongue • language*
lista ① *lee·sta list*
— **d'attesa** *da·te·za waiting list*
lite ① *lee·te fight*
litigare *lee·tee·ga·re argue*
litro ⓜ *lee·tro litre*
livello ⓜ *lee·ve·lo level (tier)*
livido ⓜ *lee·vee·do bruise*
locale ⓜ *lo·ka·le bar • venue*
locale *lo·ka·le local*
lontano/a ⓜ/① *lon·ta·no/a far*
loro *lo·ro they*
Loro *lo·ro you* pl pol
lozione ① *lo·tsyo·ne lotion*
— **abbronzante** *a·bron·dzan·te tanning lotion*
lubrificante ⓜ *loo·bree·fee·kan·te lubricant*
lucchetto ⓜ *loo·ke·to bike lock • padlock*
luce ① *loo·che light*
lucertola ① *loo·cher·to·la lizard*

lui loo·ee *he*

lumaca ① loo·ma·ka *snail*

luminoso/a ⑩/① loo·meen·o·zo/a *light (not dark)*

luna ① loo·na *moon*
— **di miele** dee mye·le *honeymoon*
— **piena** pye·na *full moon*

lungo/a ⑩/① loon·go/a *long*

luogo ⑩ lwo·go *place (location)*
— **di nascita** dee na·shee·ta *place of birth*

lusso ⑩ loo·so *luxury*

M

ma ma *but*

macchina ① ma·kee·na *car • machine*
— **fotografica** fo·to·gra·fee·ka *camera*

macelleria ① ma·che·le·ree·a *butcher's shop*

madre ① ma·dre *mother*

maestro/a ⑩/① ma·es·tro/a *teacher (primary school or music) • instructor (skiing)*

maglietta ① ma·lye·ta *T-shirt*

maglione ⑩ ma·lyo·ne *jumper • sweater*

magro/a ⑩/① ma·gro/a *thin • lean*

mai mai *never*

maiale ⑩ ma·ya·le *pig • pork*

maionese ① ma·yo·ne·ze *mayonnaise*

male ⑩ ma·le *pain • harm • evil*

mal ⑩ mal
— **di aereo** dee a·e·re·o *travel sickness (air)*
— **di denti** dee den·tee *toothache*
— **di macchina** dee ma·kee·na *travel sickness (car)*
— **di mare** dee ma·re *travel sickness (sea)*
— **di pancia** dee pan·cha *stomach ache*
— **di testa** dee tes·ta *headache*

malato/a ⑩/① ma·la·to/a *ill • sick*

malattia ① ma·la·tee·a *disease*
— **venerea** ve·ne·re·a *venereal disease*

mamma ① ma·ma *mum*

mammografia ① ma·mo·gra·fee·a *mammogram*

manager ⑩ me·nee·je *manager*

mancare man·ka·re *miss • be lacking*

mancia ① man·cha *tip (gratuity)*

mandare man·da·re *send*

mandarino ⑩ man·da·ree·no *mandarin*

mandorla ① man·dor·la *almond*

mangiare man·ja·re *eat*

mango ⑩ man·go *mango*

manifestazione ① ma·nee·fes·ta·tsyo·ne *demonstration (protest)*

mano ① ma·no *hand*

manovale ⑩&① ma·no·va·le *manual worker*

manuale ma·noo·a·le *manual*

manubrio ⑩ ma·noo·bryo *handlebars*

manzo ⑩ man·dzo *beef*

marciapiede ⑩ mar·cha·pye·de *footpath*

mare ⑩ ma·re *sea*

marea ① ma·re·a *tide*

margarina ① mar·ga·ree·na *margarine*

marijuana ① ma·ree·wa·na *marijuana*

marito ⑩ ma·ree·to *husband*

marmellata ① mar·me·la·ta *jam*
— **d'arance** da·ran·che *marmalade*

marmo ⑩ mar·mo *marble*

marrone ⑩/① ma·ro·ne *brown*

martello ⑩ mar·te·lo *hammer*

massaggio ⑩ ma·sa·jo *massage*

materasso ⑩ ma·te·ra·so *mattress*

matita ① ma·tee·ta *pencil*

matrimonio ⑩ ma·tree·mo·nyo *marriage*

mattina ① ma·tee·na *morning*

mazzuolo ⑩ ma·tswo·lo *mallet*

meccanico ⑩&① me·ka·nee·ko *mechanic*

medicina ① me·dee·chee·na *medicine*

medicinale ⑩ me·dee·chee·na·le *drug (medicinal)*

medico ⑩ me·dee·ko *doctor*

meditazione ① me·dee·ta·tsyo·ne *meditation*

mela ① me·la *apple*

melanzana ① me·lan·dza·na *aubergine • eggplant*

melodia ① me·lo·dee·a *tune*

melone ⑩ me·lo·ne *melon*

membro ⑩ mem·bro *member*

mendicante ⑩&① men·dee·kan·te *beggar*

meno me·no *less*

menù ⓜ me·*noo* menu
meraviglioso/a ⓜ/ⓕ me·ra·vee·*lyo*·zo/a
  wonderful
mercato ⓜ mer·*ka*·to market
merletto ⓜ mer·*le*·to lace
mescolare mes·ko·*la*·re mix
mese ⓜ *me*·ze month
messa ⓕ *me*·sa Mass
messaggio ⓜ me·*sa*·jo message
mestiere ⓜ mes·*tye*·re
  craft (trade) • *occupation (work)*
mestruazione ⓕ me·stroo·a·*tsyo*·ne
  menstruation
metallo ⓜ me·*ta*·lo metal
metro ⓜ *me*·tro metre (distance)
metropolitana ⓕ me·tro·po·lee·*ta*·na
  subway
mettere *me*·te·re put
mezzanotte ⓕ me·dza *no*·te midnight
mezzi ⓜ pl **di comunicazione** me·tsee
  dee ko·moo·nee·ka·*tsyo*·ne media
mezzo ⓜ *me*·dzo half
mezzogiorno ⓜ me·dzo·*jor*·no noon
microonda ⓕ mee·kro·on·da microwave
miele ⓜ *mye*·le honey
migliore mee·*lyo*·re better • best
millimetro ⓜ mee·*lee*·me·tro millimetre
minestra ⓕ mee·*nes*·tra soup
minibar ⓜ *mee*·nee·bar
  mini-bar • *bar fridge*
minuto ⓜ mee·*noo*·to minute
minuto/a ⓜ/ⓕ mee·*noo*·to/a tiny
mobili ⓜ pl *mo*·bee·lee furniture
moda ⓕ *mo*·da fashion
modem ⓜ *mo*·dem modem
moderno/a ⓜ/ⓕ mo·*der*·no/a modern
moduli ⓜ pl *mo*·doo·lee paperwork
modulo ⓜ *mo*·doo·lo form (paper)
moglie ⓕ *mo*·lye wife
molestia ⓕ mo·*les*·tya harassment
molto *mol*·to very
molto/a ⓜ/ⓕ *mol*·to/a a lot (of) • many
monastero ⓜ mon·as·*te*·ro monastery
mondo ⓜ *mon*·do world
monete ⓕ pl mo·*ne*·te coins
mononucleosi ⓕ mo·no·noo·*kle*·o·zee
  glandular fever
montagna ⓕ mon·*ta*·nya mountain
monumento ⓜ mo·noo·*men*·to
  monument

morbillo ⓜ mor·*bee*·lo measles
morire mo·*ree*·re die
morso ⓜ *mor*·so bite (dog)
morto/a ⓜ/ⓕ *mor*·to/a dead
mosca ⓕ *mos*·ka fly
moschea ⓕ mos·*ke*·a mosque
mostrare mos·*tra*·re show
moto ⓕ *mo*·to motorbike
motore ⓜ mo·*to*·re engine
motoscafo ⓜ mo·to·*ska*·fo motorboat
mouse ⓜ mows computer mouse
mucca ⓕ *moo*·ka cow
muesli ⓜ *moos*·lee muesli
mughetto ⓜ moo·*ge*·to thrush (medical)
multa ⓕ *mool*·ta fine (payment)
muro ⓜ *moo*·ro wall (outer)
muscolo ⓜ *moo*·sko·lo muscle
museo ⓜ moo·*ze*·o museum
musica ⓕ *moo*·zee·ka music
musicista ⓜ&ⓕ moo·zee·*chee*·sta
  musician
  — di strada dee *stra*·da busker
musulmano/a ⓜ/ⓕ moo·sool·*ma*·no/a
  Muslim
muta ⓕ **di subacqueo** *moo*·ta dee
  soo·ba·*kwe*·o wetsuit
muto/a ⓜ/ⓕ *moo*·to/a mute

N

narrativa ⓕ na·ra·*tee*·va fiction
naso ⓜ *na*·zo nose
Natale ⓜ na·*ta*·le Christmas
natura ⓕ na·*too*·ra nature
nausea ⓕ *now*·ze·a nausea
  — mattutina ma·too·*tee*·na
  morning sickness
nave ⓕ *na*·ve ship • boat
nazionale na·tsyo·*na*·le national
nazionalità ⓕ na·tsyo·na·lee·*ta*
  nationality
nebbioso/a ⓜ/ⓕ ne·*byo*·zo/a foggy
necessario/a ⓜ/ⓕ ne·che·*sa*·ryo/a
  necessary
negozio ⓜ ne·*go*·tsyo shop
  — da campeggio da kam·*pe*·jo
  camping store
  — di abbigliamento dee
  a·bee·lya·*men*·to clothing store

— di articoli sportivi dee ar·*tee*·ko·lee spor·*tee*·vee *sports store*

— di giocattoli dee jo·ka·to·lee *toyshop*

— di scarpe dee *skar*·pe *shoe shop*

— di souvenir dee soo·ve·neer *souvenir shop*

nero/a ⓜ/ⓕ *ne*·ro/a *black*

nessuno/a dei due ⓜ/ⓕ ne·soo·no/a day *doo*·e *neither*

neve ⓕ *ne*·ve *snow*

nido ⓜ *nee*·do *nest • childminding (group)*

niente nyen·te *nothing • none*

nipote ⓜ&ⓕ nee·po·te *grandchild*

no no *no*

noce ⓕ *no*·che *nut • walnut*

— di acagiù dee a·ka·*joo cashew*

nodulo ⓜ *no*·doo·lo *lump*

noi noy *we*

noioso/a ⓜ/ⓕ no·yo·zo/a *boring*

noleggiare no·le·*ja*·re *hire*

nome ⓜ *no*·me *name*

non non no • *not*

— ancora an·*ko*·ra *not yet*

— fumatore foo·ma·*to*·re *non-smoking*

— diretto/a ⓜ/ⓕ dee·*re*·to/a *non-direct*

nonna ⓕ *no*·na *grandmother*

nonno ⓜ *no*·no *grandfather*

nord ⓜ nord *north*

normale nor·*ma*·le *regular*

notizie ⓕ pl no·*tee*·tsye *news*

notte ⓕ *no*·te *night*

nubile ⓕ *noo*·bee·le *single (woman)*

numero ⓜ *noo*·me·ro *number*

— di camera dee *ka*·me·ra *room number*

— di targa dee *tar*·ga *licence plate number*

— di telefono dee te·*le*·fo·no *telephone number*

nuotare nwo·*ta*·re *swim*

nuoto ⓜ *nwo*·to *swimming*

Nuova Zelanda ⓕ *nwo*·va dze·*lan*·da *New Zealand*

nuovo/a ⓜ/ⓕ *nwo*·vo/a *new*

nuvola ⓕ *noo*·vo·la *cloud*

nuvoloso/a ⓜ/ⓕ noo·vo·*lo*·zo/a *cloudy*

O

obiettivo ⓜ o·bye·*tee*·vo *lens • objective*

occhiali ⓜ pl o·*kya*·lee *glasses (spectacles)*

— da sci da shee *goggles (skiing)*

— da sole da so·le *sunglasses*

occhio ⓜ *o*·kyo *eye*

oceano ⓜ o·*che*·a·no *ocean*

odore ⓜ o·*do*·re *smell*

oggetti ⓜ pl o·*je*·tee *articles • things*

— d'artigianato dar·tee·ja·*na*·to *handicrafts*

— di valore dee va·*lo*·re *valuables*

— in ceramica een che·*ra*·mee·ka *pottery*

oggi o·jee *today*

olio ⓜ *o*·lyo *oil*

— d'oliva do·*lee*·va *olive oil*

oliva ⓕ o·*lee*·va *olive*

ombra ⓕ *om*·bra *shadow • shade*

ombrello ⓜ om·*bre*·lo *umbrella*

omeopatia ⓕ o·me·o·pa·*tee*·a *homeopathy*

omosessuale ⓜ&ⓕ o·mo·se·swa·le *homosexual*

onda ⓕ *on*·da *wave*

opera ⓕ o·pe·ra *work (of art)*

— lirica *lee*·ree·ka *opera*

operaio/a ⓜ/ⓕ o·pe·*ra*·yo/a *factory worker*

operatore/operatrice ⓜ/ⓕ o·pe·ra·*to*·re/ o·pe·ra·*tree*·che *operator*

opinione ⓕ o·pee·*nyo*·ne *opinion*

oppure o·*poo*·re *or • otherwise • or else*

ora ⓕ *o*·ra *hour*

orario ⓜ o·*ra*·ryo *timetable*

— di apertura dee a·per·*too*·ra *opening hours*

— ridotto ree·*do*·to *part-time*

orchestra ⓕ or·*kes*·tra *orchestra*

ordinare or·dee·*na*·re *order*

ordinario/a ⓜ/ⓕ or·dee·*na*·ryo/a *ordinary*

ordine ⓜ *or*·dee·ne *order*

orecchini ⓜ pl o·re·*kee*·nee *earrings*

orecchio ⓜ o·*re*·kyo *ear*

originale ⓕ o·ree·jee·*na*·le *original*

oro ⓜ *o*·ro *gold*

orologio ⓜ o·ro·lo·jo clock • watch
orrendo/a ⓜ/ⓕ o·ren·do/a awful
ospedale ⓜ os·pe·da·le hospital
ospitalità ⓕ os·pee·ta·lee·ta hospitality
ossigeno ⓜ o·see·je·no oxygen
osso ⓜ o·so bone
ostello ⓜ della gioventù os·te·lo de·la jo·ven·too youth hostel
osteria ⓕ os·te·ree·a pub
ostrica ⓕ o·stree·ka oyster
ottimo/a ⓜ/ⓕ o·tee·mo/a excellent • great
ovest ⓜ o·vest west

P

pacchetto ⓜ pa·ke·to parcel • packet • package
pace ⓕ pa·che peace
padella ⓕ pa·de·la frying pan
padre ⓜ pa·dre father
padrone/padrona ⓜ/ⓕ di casa pa·dro·ne/pa·dro·na dee ka·za landlord/landlady
paese ⓜ pa·e·ze country (nation)
Paesi Bassi ⓜ pl pa·e·zee ba·see Netherlands
pagamento ⓜ pa·ga·men·to payment
pagare pa·ga·re pay
pagina ⓕ pa·jee·na page
paio ⓜ pa·yo pair (couple)
palazzo ⓜ pa·la·tso palace
palcoscenico ⓜ pal·ko·she·nee·ko stage
palestra ⓕ pa·le·stra gym
palla ⓕ pa·la ball (sports)
pallacanestro ⓕ pa·la·ka·ne·stro basketball
pallamuro ⓕ pa·la·moo·ro handball
pallavolo ⓕ pa·la·vo·lo volleyball
pallone ⓜ pa·lo·ne ball (inflated)
pancetta ⓕ pan·che·ta bacon
pane ⓜ pa·ne bread
— a pasta acida a pas·ta a·chee·da sourdough bread
— di segala dee se·ga·la rye bread
— integrale een·te·gra·le wholemeal bread
— tostato tos·ta·to toast
panetteria ⓕ pa·ne·te·ree·a bakery

panino ⓜ pa·nee·no roll (bread)
panna ⓕ pa·na cream (food)
— acida a·chee·da sour cream
pannolino ⓜ pa·no·lee·no diaper • nappy
pantaloncini ⓜ pl pan·ta·lon·chee·nee shorts
pantaloni ⓜ pl pan·ta·lo·nee pants • trousers
pap test ⓜ pap test pap smear
papà ⓜ pa·pa dad
parabrezza ⓜ pa·ra·bre·dza windscreen
parcheggio ⓜ par·ke·jo carpark
parco ⓜ par·ko park
— nazionale na·tsyo·na·le national park
— giochi jo·kee playground
parlamentare ⓜ&ⓕ par·la·men·ta·re member of parliament
parlamento ⓜ par·la·men·to parliament
parlare par·la·re speak • talk
parola ⓕ pa·ro·la word
parrucchiere ⓕ pa·roo·kye·re beauty salon
parrucchiere/a ⓜ/ⓕ pa·roo·kye·re/a hairdresser
parte ⓕ par·te part
partenza ⓕ par·ten·tsa departure
partire par·tee·re depart • leave
partita ⓕ par·tee·ta game • match
partito ⓜ par·tee·to party (politics)
Pasqua ⓕ pas·kwa Easter
passaggio ⓜ pa·sa·jo pass (sport) • passage
passaporto ⓜ pa·sa·por·to passport
passatempo ⓜ pa·sa·tem·po hobby
passato ⓜ pa·sa·to past
passeggero/a ⓜ/ⓕ pa·se·je·ro/a passenger
passeggiata ⓕ pa·se·ja·ta walk
passo ⓜ pa·so pass (mountain)
pasta ⓕ pas·ta pasta • noodles
pasticceria ⓕ pa·stee·che·ree·a cake shop
pasto ⓜ pas·to meal
— freddo fre·do buffet (meal)
patata ⓕ pa·ta·ta potato
paté ⓜ pa·te pate (food)
patente ⓕ (di guida) pa·ten·te (dee gwee·da) drivers licence

pavimento ⓜ pa·vee·*men*·to *floor*
pazzo/a ⓜ/ⓕ *pa*·tso/a *crazy*
pecora ⓕ *pe*·ko·ra *sheep*
pedale ⓜ pe·*da*·le *pedal*
pedone ⓜ/ⓕ pe·*do*·ne *pedestrian*
pelle ⓕ *pe*·le *skin*
pellicola ⓕ pe·*lee*·ko·la *film (for camera)*
pene ⓜ *pe*·ne *penis*
penicillina ⓕ pe·nee·chee·*lee*·na
  penicillin
penna ⓕ **(a sfera)** *pe*·na (a *sfe*·ra)
  pen (ballpoint)
pensare pen·*sa*·re *think*
pensionato/a ⓜ/ⓕ pen·syo·*na*·to/a
  pensioner • retired
pensione ⓕ pen·*syo*·ne
  guesthouse • boarding house
pentola ⓕ *pen*·to·la *pan*
pepe ⓜ *pe*·pe *pepper*
peperoncino ⓜ pe·pe·ron·*chee*·no *chilli*
peperone ⓜ pe·pe·*ro*·ne *capsicum*
per per *for • to • through • by*
  — esempio e·*zem*·pyo *for example*
  — sempre *sem*·pre *forever*
pera ⓕ *pe*·ra *pear*
percentuale ⓕ per·chen·*twa*·le
  percentage
perché per·*ke* *why • because*
perdere *per*·de·re *lose*
perdonare per·do·*na*·re *forgive*
pericoloso/a ⓜ/ⓕ pe·ree·ko·*lo*·zo/a
  dangerous • unsafe
permanente ⓜ/ⓕ per·ma·*nen*·te
  permanent
permesso ⓜ per·*me*·so
  permission • permit
perso/a ⓜ/ⓕ *per*·so/a *lost*
persona ⓕ per·*so*·na *person*
personale ⓜ/ⓕ per·so·*na*·le *personal*
pesante pe·*zan*·te *heavy*
pesca ⓕ *pe*·ska *fishing • peach*
pesce ⓜ *pe*·she *fish (food)*
pesce/pesci ⓜ sg/pl pe·she/*pe*·shee
  fish (alive)
pescheria ⓕ pe·ske·*ree*·a *fish shop*
peso ⓜ *pe*·zo *weight*
petizione ⓕ pe·tee·*tsyo*·ne *petition*
pettine ⓜ *pe*·tee·ne *comb*
petto ⓜ *pe*·to *chest*

pezzo ⓜ *pe*·tso *piece*
  — di antiquariato dee
  an·tee·kwa·*rya*·to *antique*
  — d'artigianato dar·tee·ja·*na*·to
  craft (product)
piacere pya·*che*·re *like*
pianeta ⓜ pya·*ne*·ta *planet*
piano ⓜ *pya*·no *floor (storey)*
pianta ⓕ *pyan*·ta *map • plant*
piatto ⓜ *pya*·to *plate*
  — fondo *fon*·do *bowl*
piatto/a ⓜ/ⓕ *pya*·to/a *flat*
piazza ⓕ *pya*·tsa *square (town)*
picchetti ⓜ pl pee·*ke*·tee *pegs (tent)*
piccolo/a ⓜ/ⓕ *pee*·ko·lo/a *small*
piccone ⓜ pee·*ko*·ne *pickaxe*
piccozza ⓕ pee·*ko*·tsa *ice axe*
picnic ⓜ *peek*·neek *picnic*
pidocchi ⓜ pl pee·*do*·kee *lice*
piede ⓜ *pye*·de *foot*
pieno/a ⓜ/ⓕ *pye*·no/a *full*
pietra ⓕ *pye*·tra *stone*
pignatta ⓕ pee·*nya*·ta *pot (ceramics)*
pigro/a ⓜ/ⓕ *pee*·gro/a *lazy*
pila ⓕ *pee*·la *battery*
pillola ⓕ *pee*·lo·la *pill • the Pill*
  — anticoncezionale an·tee·kon·che·tsy
  o·na·le *the Pill*
  — del mattino dopo del ma·*tee*·no
  do·po *morning after pill*
ping-pong ⓜ *peeng*·pong *table tennis*
pinzette ⓕ pl peen·*tse*·te *tweezers*
pioggia ⓕ *pyo*·ja *rain*
piombo ⓜ *pyom*·bo *lead*
piscina ⓕ pee·*shee*·na *swimming pool*
pisello ⓜ pee·*ze*·lo *pea*
pista ⓕ *pee*·sta
  trail • track (sports) • racetrack • slope
pistacchio ⓜ pee·*sta*·kyo *pistachio*
pittore/pittrice ⓜ/ⓕ pee·*to*·re/
  pee·*tree*·che *painter*
pittura ⓕ pee·*too*·ra *painting (the art)*
più *pyoo* *more*
plastica ⓕ *pla*·stee·ka *plastic*
un po' oon po *(a) little*
poco/a ⓜ/ⓕ *po*·ko/a *few*
poesia ⓕ po·e·*zee*·a *poetry*
politica ⓕ po·*lee*·tee·ka *politics*
politico ⓜ po·*lee*·tee·ko *politician*

polizia ① po·lee·tsee·a *police (civilian)*
polline ⓜ po·lee·ne *pollen*
pollo ⓜ po·lo *chicken*
polmoni ⓜ pl pol·mo·nee *lungs*
polso ⓜ pol·so *wrist*
polvere ① pol·ve·re *powder*
pomeriggio ⓜ po·me·ree·jo *afternoon*
pomodoro ⓜ po·mo·do·ro *tomato*
pompa ① pom·pa *pump*
pompelmo ⓜ pom·pel·mo *grapefruit*
ponte ⓜ pon·te *bridge*
popolare po·po·la·re *popular*
porro ⓜ po·ro *leek*
porta ① por·ta *door*
portacenere ⓜ por·ta·che·ne·re *ashtray*
portafoglio ⓜ por·ta·fo·lyo *wallet*
portare por·ta·re *bring • carry*
portatile ⓜ por·ta·tee·le *laptop*
portatile por·ta·tee·le *portable*
porto ⓜ por·to *harbour • port*
posate ① pl po·za·te *cutlery*
possibile po·see·bee·le *possible*
posta ① pos·ta *mail*
  — elettronica e·le·tro·nee·ka *email*
  — ordinaria or·dee·na·rya *surface mail*
  — prioritaria pree·o·ree·ta·rya
  express mail
  — raccomandata ① ra·ko·man·da·ta
  registered mail
posteggio ⓜ **di tassi** po·ste·jo dee ta·see
  taxi stand
posto ⓜ pos·to *place • seat*
  — di polizia dee po·lee·tsee·a
  police station
potabile po·ta·bee·le *drinkable*
potere ⓜ po·te·re *power (strength)*
potere po·te·re *can*
povero/a ⓜ/① po·ve·ro/a *poor*
povertà ① po·ver·ta *poverty*
pranzo ⓜ pran·dzo *lunch*
praticare pra·tee·ka·re *play (sport)*
  — il surf eel soorf *surf*
prima colazione ① pree·ma ko·la·tsyo·ne
  breakfast
preferire pre·fe·ree·re *prefer*
preferito/a ⓜ/① pre·fe·ree·to/a *favourite*
pregare pre·ga·re *worship (pray)*
preghiera ① pre·gye·ra *prayer*

prendere pren·de·re *take*
  — in affitto een a·fee·to *rent*
  — in prestito een pres·tee·to *borrow*
prenotare pre·no·ta·re
  book (make a booking)
prenotazione ① pre·no·ta·tsyo·ne
  reservation
preoccupato/a ⓜ/① pre·o·koo·pa·to/a
  worried
preparare pre·pa·ra·re *prepare*
preservativo ⓜ pre·zer·va·tee·vo *condom*
presidente ⓜ/① pre·zee·den·te *president*
pressione ① pre·syo·ne *pressure*
  — del sangue del san·gwe
  blood pressure
presto ① pres·to *early*
prete ⓜ pre·te *priest*
prezioso/a ⓜ/① pre·tsyo·zo/a *valuable*
prezzemolo ⓜ pre·tse·mo·lo *parsley*
prezzo ⓜ pre·tso *price*
  — d'ingresso deen·gre·so
  admission price
prigione ① pree·jo·ne *prison*
prigioniero/a ⓜ/① pree·jo·nye·ro/a
  prisoner
prima pree·ma *before*
  — classe ① kla·se *first class*
  — colazione ① ko·la·tsyo·ne *breakfast*
primavera ① pree·ma·ve·ra
  spring (season)
primo ministro ⓜ/① pree·mo
  mee·nee·stro *prime minister*
primo/a ⓜ/① pree·mo/a *first*
principale preen·chee·pa·le *main*
privato/a ⓜ/① pree·va·to/a *private*
problema ⓜ pro·ble·ma *problem*
  — cardiaco kar·dee·a·ko
  heart condition
produrre pro·doo·re *produce*
profesore/professoressa ⓜ/①
  pro·fe·so·re/pro·fe·so·re·sa
  teacher (general)
profitto ⓜ pro·fee·to *profit*
profondo/a ⓜ/① pro·fon·do/a *deep*
profumo ⓜ pro·foo·mo *perfume*
programma ⓜ pro·gra·ma *program*
proiettore ⓜ pro·ye·to·re *projector*
promessa ① pro·me·sa *promise*
pronto/a ⓜ/① pron·to/a *ready*

pronto soccorso ⓜ *pron·to so·kor·so* first-aid

proprietario/a ⓜ/ⓕ *pro·prye·ta·ryo/a* owner

proroga ⓕ *pro·ro·ga* extension (visa)

prosciutto ⓜ **(cotto)** *pro·shoo·to (ko·to)* ham (boiled)

prossimo/a ⓜ/ⓕ *pro·see·mo/a* next

proteggere *pro·te·je·re* protect

protetto/a ⓜ/ⓕ *pro·te·to/a* protected

protestare *pro·tes·ta·re* protest

provare *pro·va·re* try (attempt)

provviste ⓕ pl *pro·vee·ste* provisions • supplies
— **alimentari** *a·lee·men·ta·ree* food supplies

prugna ⓕ *proo·nya* plum • prune

prurito ⓜ *proo·ree·to* itch

pub ⓜ *poob* pub

pugilato ⓜ *poo·jee·la·to* boxing

pulce ⓕ *pool·che* flea

pulito/a ⓜ/ⓕ *poo·lee·to/a* clean

pulizia ⓕ *poo·lee·tsee·a* cleaning

pullman ⓜ *pool·man* bus (coach)

punteggio ⓜ *poon·te·jo* score

punto ⓜ *poon·to* point

puntura ⓕ *poon·too·ra* bite (insect)

puro/a ⓜ/ⓕ *poo·ro/a* pure

Q

quaderno ⓜ *kwa·der·no* notebook

quadro ⓜ *kwa·dro* painting (canvas)

qualcosa *kwal·ko·za* something

qualcuno/a ⓜ/ⓕ *kwal·koo·no/a* someone

qualità ⓕ *kwa·lee·ta* quality

quando *kwan·do* when

quantità ⓕ *kwan·tee·ta* amount • quantity

quanto/a ⓜ/ⓕ *kwan·to/a* how much

quarantena ⓕ *kwa·ran·te·na* quarantine

quaresima ⓕ *kwa·re·zee·ma* Lent

quartiere ⓜ *kwar·tye·re* suburb

quarto ⓜ *kwar·to* quarter

questo/a ⓜ/ⓕ *kwe·sto/a* this (one)

questura ⓕ *kwes·too·ra* police headquarters

qui *kwee* here

quota ⓕ *kwo·ta* altitude

R

racchetta ⓕ *ra·ke·ta* racquet

raccogliere *ra·ko·lye·re* pick (up)

raccomandare *ra·ko·man·da·re* recommend

raccomandata ⓕ *ra·ko·man·da·ta* registered mail

raccontare *ra·kon·ta·re* tell

racconto ⓜ *ra·kon·to* story

radiatore ⓜ *ra·dya·to·re* radiator

rafano ⓜ *ra·fa·no* horseradish

raffreddore ⓜ *ra·fre·do·re* cold (illness)

ragazza ⓕ *ra·ga·tsa* girl(friend)

ragazzo ⓜ *ra·ga·tso* boy(friend)

ragione ⓕ *ra·jo·ne* reason

ragno ⓜ *ra·nyo* spider

rapido/a ⓜ/ⓕ *ra·pee·do/a* quick

rapinare *ra·pee·na·re* rob

rapporti ⓜ pl **protetti** *ra·por·tee pro·te·tee* safe sex

rapporto ⓜ *ra·por·to* relationship

raro/a ⓜ/ⓕ *ra·ro/a* rare

rasatura ⓕ *ra·za·too·ra* shave

rasoio ⓜ **(elettrico)** *ra·zo·yo (e·le·tree·ko)* razor

ravanello ⓜ *ra·va·ne·lo* radish

razzismo ⓜ *ra·tseez·mo* racism

re ⓜ *re* king

realistico/a ⓜ/ⓕ *re·a·lee·stee·ko/a* realistic

recente *re·chen·te* recent

recinzione ⓕ *re·cheen·tsyo·ne* fence

regalo ⓜ *re·ga·lo* present (gift)
— **di nozze** *dee no·tse* wedding present

reggiseno ⓜ *re·jee·se·no* bra

regina ⓕ *re·jee·na* queen

regione ⓕ *re·jo·ne* region

regista ⓜ&ⓕ *re·jee·sta* director (films)

registrazione ⓕ *re·jee·stra·tsyo·ne* check-in (hotel)

regolare *re·go·la·re* regular

regole ⓕ pl *re·go·le* rules

religione ⓕ *re·lee·jo·ne* religion

religioso/a ⓜ/ⓕ *re·lee·jo·zo/a* religious

reliquia ⓕ *re·lee·kwee·a* relic

remoto/a ⓜ/ⓕ *re·mo·to/a* remote

respirare *res·pee·ra·re* breathe

resto ⓜ *res·to* change (money)

rete ① re·te net
ricco/a ⑩/① ree·ko/a rich (wealthy)
ricetta ① ree·che·ta prescription
ricevere ree·che·ve·re receive
ricevuta ① ree·che·voo·ta receipt
richiedere ree·kye·de·re ask (for something)
riciclabile ree·chee·kla·bee·le recyclable
riciclare ree·chee·kla·re recycle
ricordino ⑩ ree·kor·dee·no souvenir
ridere ree·de·re laugh
rifiutare ree·fyoo·ta·re refuse
rifugiato/a ⑩/① ree·foo·gya·to/a refugee
rifiuti ⑩ pl ree·fyoo·tee rubbish
rilassarsi ree·la·sar·see relax
rimborso ⑩ reem·bor·so refund
ringraziare reen·gra·tsya·re thank
riparare ree·pa·ra·re repair
ripido/a ⑩/① ree·pee·do/a steep
riposare ree·po·za·re rest
riscaldamento ⑩ rees·kal·da·men·to heating
— **centrale** chen·tra·le central heating
rischio ⑩ rees·kyo risk
riscuotere un assegno ree·skwo·te·re oon a·se·nyo cash a cheque
riso ⑩ ree·zo rice
— **integrale** een·te·gra·le brown rice
risposta ① rees·pos·ta answer
ristorante ⑩ rees·to·ran·te restaurant
ritardo ⑩ ree·tar·do delay
ritiro ⑩ **bagagli** ree·tee·ro ba·ga·lyee baggage claim
ritmo ⑩ reet·mo rhythm
ritornare ree·tor·na·re return
ritorno ⑩ ree·tor·no return
rivista ① ree·vee·sta magazine
roba ① ro·ba stuff (belongings) • dope (drugs)
roccia ① ro·cha rock • rock climbing
romantico/a ⑩/① ro·man·tee·ko/a romantic
romanzo ⑩ ro·man·dzo novel
rompere rom·pe·re break
rosa ⑩/① ro·za pink
rossetto ⑩ ro·se·to lipstick
rosso/a ⑩/① ro·so/a red
rotonda ① ro·ton·da roundabout
rotondo/a ⑩/① ro·ton·do/a round

rotto/a ⑩/① ro·to/a broken
roulotte ① roo·lot caravan
rovine ① pl ro·vee·ne ruins
rubare roo·ba·re steal
rubato/a ⑩/① roo·ba·to/a stolen
rubinetto ⑩ roo·bee·ne·to faucet
rugby ⑩ roog·bee rugby
rullino ⑩ roo·lee·no film (roll for camera)
rumoroso/a ⑩/① roo·mo·ro·zo/a noisy
ruota ① rwo·ta wheel
ruscello ⑩ roo·she·lo stream

S

sabato ⑩ sa·ba·to saturday • Sabbath
sabbia ① sa·bya sand
sacchetto ⑩ sa·ke·to bag (shopping)
sacco ⑩ sa·ko sack • bag
— **a pelo** a pe·lo sleeping bag
sala ① sa·la room • hall
— **di transito** dee tran·zee·to transit lounge
— **d'aspetto** das·pe·to waiting room
salame ⑩ sa·la·me salami
salario ⑩ sa·la·ryo wage
saldi ⑩ pl sal·dee sales
saldo ⑩ sal·do balance (account)
sale ⑩ sa·le salt
salire sa·lee·re climb • go up
— **su** su board (a plane, ship)
salmone ⑩ sal·mo·ne salmon
salsa ① sal·sa sauce
salsiccia ① sal·see·cha sausage
saltare sal·ta·re jump
salumeria ① sa·loo·me·ree·a delicatessen
salute ① sa·loo·te health
salva slip ⑩ pl sal·va sleep panty liners
san Silvestro ⑩ san seel·ves·tro New Year's Eve
sandali ⑩ pl san·da·lee sandals
sangue ⑩ san·gwe blood
santo/a ⑩/① san·to/a saint
santuario ⑩ san·too·a·ryo shrine
sapere sa·pe·re know (how to)
sapone ⑩ sa·po·ne soap
sardine ① pl sar·dee·ne sardines
sarto/a ⑩/① sar·to/a tailor
sauna ① sow·na sauna
sbagliato/a ⑩/① sba·lya·to/a wrong

sbaglio ⓜ *sba·lyo* mistake

scacchi ⓜ pl *ska·kee* chess

scala ⓕ **mobile** *ska·la mo·bee·le* escalator

scalare *ska·la·re* climb

scale ⓕ pl *ska·le* stairway

scanner ⓜ *ska·ner* scanner

scarafaggio ⓜ *ska·ra·fa·jo* cockroach

scarpe ⓕ pl *skar·pe* shoes

scarpette ⓕ pl *skar·pe·te* boots (soccer)

scarponi ⓜ pl *skar·po·nee* boots (hiking, ski)

scatola ⓕ *ska·to·la* box • carton • can • tin

scatoletta ⓕ *ska·to·le·ta* tin • can

scheda ⓕ **telefonica** *ske·da te·le·fo·nee·ka* phone card

scherma ⓕ *sker·ma* fencing (sport)

scherzo ⓜ *sker·tso* joke

schiena ⓕ *skye·na* back (body)

sci ⓜ shee skiing • ski(s)
— **acquatico** *a·kwa·tee·ko* waterskiing

sciare *shee·a·re* ski

sciarpa ⓕ *shar·pa* scarf

scienza ⓕ *shen·tsa* science

sciopero ⓜ *sho·pe·ro* strike

sciovia ⓕ *shee·o·vee·a* ski-lift

sciroppo ⓜ *shee·ro·po* syrup
— **per la tosse** per la *to·se* cough medicine

scogliera ⓕ *sko·lye·ra* cliff

scommessa ⓕ *sko·me·sa* bet

scomodo/a ⓜ/ⓕ *sko·mo·do/a* uncomfortable

sconosciuto/a ⓜ/ⓕ *sko·no·shoo·to/a* stranger

sconto ⓜ *skon·to* discount

scorie ⓕ pl *sko·rye* waste (rubbish)
— **radioattive** *ra·dyo·a·tee·ve* nuclear waste
— **tossiche** *to·see·che* toxic waste

scottatura ⓕ *sko·ta·too·ra* sunburn

Scozia ⓕ *sko·tsya* Scotland

scrittore/scrittrice ⓜ/ⓕ *skree·to·re/ skree·tree·che* writer

scrivere *skree·ve·re* write

scultura ⓕ *skool·too·ra* sculpture

scuola ⓕ *skwo·la* school
— **superiore** *soo·pe·ryo·re* high school

scuro/a ⓜ/ⓕ *skoo·ro/a* dark

se se if

seccato/a ⓜ/ⓕ *se·ka·to/a* cross (angry)

secchio ⓜ *se·kyo* bucket

secco/a ⓜ/ⓕ *se·ko/a* dry

seconda classe ⓕ *se·kon·da kla·se* second class

di seconda mano ⓜ/ⓕ dee *se·kon·da ma·no* second-hand

secondo ⓜ *se·kon·do* second

secondo/a ⓜ/ⓕ *se·kon·do/a* second

sedere *se·de·re* sit

sedia ⓕ *se·dya* chair
— **a rotelle** a *ro·te·le* wheelchair

sedile ⓜ *se·dee·le* seat (chair)

seggiolino ⓜ *se·jo·lee·no* child seat

seggiovia ⓕ *se·jo·vee·a* chairlift (skiing)

segnale ⓜ *se·nya·le* signal • dial tone
— **acustico** *a·koos·tee·ko* dial tone

segnare *se·nya·re* score

segno ⓜ *se·nyo* sign

segretario/a ⓜ/ⓕ *se·gre·ta·ryo/a* secretary

seguire *se·gwee·re* follow

sella ⓕ *se·la* saddle

semaforo ⓜ *se·ma·fo·ro* traffic lights

semplice ⓜ/ⓕ *sem·plee·che* simple

sempre *sem·pre* always

senape ⓕ *se·na·pe* mustard

seno ⓜ *se·no* breast

sensuale ⓜ/ⓕ *sen·soo·a·le* sensual

sentiero ⓜ *sen·tye·ro* path • track • trail
— **di montagna** dee mon·*ta·nya* mountain path

sentimenti ⓜ pl *sen·tee·men·tee* feelings

sentire *sen·tee·re* feel • hear

senza *sen·tsa* without
— **piombo** *pyom·bo* unleaded

senzatetto ⓜ&ⓕ *sen·tsa·te·to* homeless

separato/a ⓜ/ⓕ *se·pa·ra·to/a* separate

sera ⓕ *se·ra* evening

serie ⓕ **(televisiva)** *se·ree·e (te·le·vee·see·va)* (TV) series

serio/a ⓜ/ⓕ *se·ryo/a* serious

serpente ⓜ *ser·pen·te* snake

serratura ⓕ *se·ra·too·ra* lock (door)

servizi ⓜ pl **igienici** *ser·vee·tse ee·je·nee·chee* toilets

servizio ⓜ ser·vee·tsyo
  service • service-charge
  — militare mee·lee·*ta*·re
  military service
sessismo ⓜ se·*seez*·mo *sexism*
sesso ⓜ se·so *sex*
seta ① se·ta *silk*
settimana ① se·tee·*ma*·na *week*
  — santa *san*·ta *Holy Week*
sfogo ⓜ *sfo*·go *rash*
  — da pannolino da pa·no·*lee*·no
  nappy rash
sfruttamento ⓜ sfroo·ta·*men*·to
  exploitation
shampoo ⓜ *sham*·poo *shampoo*
si *see yes*
sicuro/a ⓜ/① see·*koo*·ro/a *safe*
sidro ⓜ *see*·dro *cider*
sieropositivo/a ⓜ/①
  sye·ro·po·zee·*tee*·vo/a *HIV positive*
sigaretta ① see·ga·*re*·ta *cigarette*
sigaro ⓜ *see*·ga·ro *cigar*
simile ⓜ/① *see*·mee·le *similar*
simpatico/a ⓜ/① seem·*pa*·tee·ko/a
  nice (person)
sinagoga ① see·na·go·ga *synagogue*
sindaco ⓜ *seen*·da·ko *mayor*
sinistra ① see·*nee*·stra *left (direction)*
sintetico/a ⓜ/① seen·*te*·tee·ko/a
  synthetic
siringa ① see·*reen*·ga *syringe*
slitta ① *slee*·ta *sleigh • toboggan*
soccorso ⓜ so·*kor*·so *help • aid*
socialista ⓜ&① so·cha·*lee*·sta *socialist*
socio/a ⓜ/① *so*·cho/a *member*
soffice ⓜ/① *so*·fee·che *soft*
sognare so·*nya*·re *dream*
sogno ⓜ *so*·nyo *dream*
soldato ⓜ sol·*da*·to *soldier*
soldi ⓜ pl *sol*·dee *money • cash*
sole ⓜ *so*·le *sun*
soleggiato/a ⓜ/① so·le·*ja*·to/a *sunny*
solo *so*·lo *only*
  — andata ① an·*da*·ta *one-way*
sonniferi ⓜ pl so·*nee*·fe·ree *sleeping pills*
sonno ⓜ *so*·no *sleep • sleepiness*
sopra *so*·pra *above • over*
soprannome ⓜ so·pra·*no*·me *nickname*
sordo/a ⓜ/① *sor*·do/a *deaf*

sorella ① so·*re*·la *sister*
sorpresa ① sor·*pre*·sa *surprise*
sorridere so·ree·*de*·re *smile*
sostenitore/sostenitrice ⓜ/①
  sos·te·nee·*to*·re/sos·te·nee·*tree*·che
  supporter
sotto *so*·to *below*
sottoaceti ⓜ pl so·to·a·*che*·tee *pickles*
sottotitoli ⓜ pl so·to·*tee*·to·lee *subtitles*
spacciatore/spacciatrice ⓜ/①
  spa·cha·*to*·re/spa·cha·*tree*·che
  drug dealer
Spagna ① *spa*·nya *Spain*
spago ⓜ *spa*·go *string*
spalla ① *spa*·la *shoulder*
spazio ⓜ *spa*·tsyo *space*
spazzatura ① spa·tsa·*too*·ra
  rubbish • garbage
spazzolino ⓜ **da denti** spa·tso·*lee*·no da
  den·tee *toothbrush*
specchio ⓜ *spe*·kyo *mirror*
speciale spe·*cha*·le *special*
specialista ⓜ&① spe·cha·*lee*·sta
  specialist
specie ① *spe*·che *species • type*
  — in via di estinzione een vee·a dee
  es·teen·*tsyo*·ne *endangered species*
  — protetta pro·*te*·ta *protected species*
spermicida ① sper·mee·*chee*·da
  spermicide
spesso *spe*·so *often*
spesso/a ⓜ/① *spe*·so/a *thick*
spettacolo ⓜ spe·*ta*·ko·lo
  show • performance
spiaggia ① *spya*·ja *beach*
spiccioli ⓜ pl *spee*·cho·lee *loose change*
spina ① *spee*·na *plug (electricity)*
  — multipla *mool*·tee·pla *adaptor*
spinaci ⓜ pl spee·*na*·chee *spinach*
spingere *speen*·je·re *push*
spirale ① spee·*ra*·le *IUD*
spogliatoio ⓜ spo·lya·*to*·yo
  change room (sport)
sporco/a ⓜ/① *spor*·ko/a *dirty*
sport ⓜ *sport sport*
sportivo/a ⓜ/① spor·*tee*·vo/a
  sportsperson
sposalizio ⓜ spo·za·*lee*·tsyo *wedding*
sposare spo·*za*·re *marry*

sposato/a ⓜ/ⓕ spo·za·to/a *married*
spremuta ⓕ spre·moo·ta
fruit juice (fresh)
— **d'arancia** da·ran·cha
orange juice (fresh)
spuntino ⓜ spoon·tee·no *snack*
squadra ⓕ skwa·dra *team*
stadio ⓜ sta·dyo *stadium*
stagione ⓕ sta·jo·ne *season*
stampante ⓕ stam·pan·te
printer (computer)
stanco/a ⓜ/ⓕ stan·ko/a *tired*
stanza ⓕ stan·tsa *room*
stasera ⓕ sta·se·ra *tonight*
Stati Uniti d'America ⓜ pl sta·tee
oo·nee·tee da·me·ree·ka *USA*
stato ⓜ **civile** sta·to chee·vee·le
marital status
statua ⓕ sta·too·a *statue*
stazione ⓕ sta·tsyo·ne *(train) station*
— **d'autobus** dow·to·boos *bus station*
— **della metropolitana** de·la
me·tro·po·lee·ta·na *metro station*
— **di servizio** dee ser·vee·tsyo
petrol station • service station
— **ferroviaria** fe·ro·vyar·ya *train station*
stelle ⓕ pl ste·le *stars*
stendersi sten·der·see *lie (not stand)*
sterlina ⓕ ster·lee·na *pound (money)*
stesso/a ⓜ/ⓕ ste·so/a *same*
stile ⓜ stee·le *style*
stipendio ⓜ stee·pen·dyo *salary*
stitichezza ⓕ stee·tee·ke·tsa *constipation*
stivali ⓜ pl stee·va·lee *boots*
stoffa ⓕ sto·fa *fabric*
stomaco ⓜ sto·ma·ko *stomach*
stordito/a ⓜ/ⓕ stor·dee·to/a *dizzy*
storia ⓕ sto·rya *history • story*
storico/a ⓜ/ⓕ sto·ree·ko/a *historical*
storta ⓕ stor·ta *sprain*
strada ⓕ stra·da *road • street*
straniero/a ⓜ/ⓕ stra·nye·ro/a *foreign*
strano/a ⓜ/ⓕ stra·no/a *strange*
strato **d'ozono** stra·to do·dzo·no
ozone layer
stretto/a ⓜ/ⓕ stre·to/a *tight*
studente/studentessa ⓜ/ⓕ stoo·den·te/
stoo·den·te·sa *student*

stufa ⓕ stoo·fa *heater • stove*
— **a gas** a gaz *gas stove*
stupido/a ⓜ/ⓕ stoo·pee·do/a *stupid*
stupro ⓜ stoo·pro *rape*
stuzzicadenti ⓜ stoo·tsee·ka·den·te
toothpick
su soo *on • up*
succo ⓜ soo·ko *juice*
— **d'arancia** da·ran·cha
orange juice (bottled)
— **di frutta** dee froo·ta
fruit juice (bottled)
sud ⓜ sood *south*
sugo ⓜ soo·go *sauce*
suocera ⓕ swo·che·ra *mother-in-law*
suocero ⓜ swo·che·ro *father-in-law*
suonare (la chitarra) swo·na·re (la
kee·ta·ra) *play (guitar)*
suora ⓕ swo·ra *nun*
supermercato ⓜ soo·per·mer·ka·to
supermarket
superstizione ⓕ soo·per·stee·tsyo·ne
superstition
surf ⓜ **da neve** soorf da ne·ve
snow boarding
surgelati ⓜ pl soor·je·la·tee
frozen foods
sussidio ⓜ **di disoccupazione**
soo·see·dyo dee dee·zo·koo·pa·tsyo·ne
unemployment benefit
sveglia ⓕ sve·lya *alarm clock*
svegliarsi sve·lyar·see *wake up*
Svizzera ⓕ svee·tse·ra *Switzerland*

T

tabaccheria ⓕ ta·ba·ke·ree·a *tobacconist*
tabacco ⓜ ta·ba·ko *tobacco*
tabellone ⓜ **segnapunti** ta·be·lo·ne
se·nya·poon·tee *scoreboard*
tacchino ⓜ ta·kee·no *turkey*
tachimetro ⓜ ta·kee·me·tro *speedometer*
taglia ⓕ ta·lya *size (clothes)*
tagliare ta·lya·re *cut*
tagliaunghie ⓕ ta·lya·oon·gye
nail clippers
taglio ⓜ **di capelli** ta·lyo dee ka·pe·lee
haircut
tamponi ⓜ pl tam·po·nee *tampons*

tappa ① *ta·pa*
  leg (in race or journey) • *stage (in race)*
tappeto ⓜ *ta·pe·to mat* • *rug*
tappi ⓜ pl **per le orecchie** *ta·pee per le o·re·kye earplugs*
tappo ⓜ *ta·po plug (bath)*
tardi *tar·dee late (adj)*
targa ① *tar·ga number plate*
tariffa ① **postale** *ta·ree·fa pos·ta·le postage*
tasca ① *tas·ka pocket*
tassa ① *ta·sa tax*
tassì ⓜ *ta·see taxi*
tasso ⓜ **di cambio** *ta·so dee kam·byo exchange rate*
tastiera ① *tas·tye·ra keyboard*
tavola ① *ta·vo·la table*
  — **da surf** da soorf *surfboard*
tazza ① *ta·tsa cup*
tè ⓜ *te tea*
teatro ⓜ *te·a·tro theatre*
  — **dell'opera** del·o·per·a *opera house*
telecomando ⓜ *te·le·ko·man·do remote control*
telefonare *te·le·fo·na·re telephone*
telefonata ① *te·le·fo·na·ta phone call*
telefono ⓜ *te·le·fo·no telephone*
  — **cellulare** che·loo·la·re *mobile/cell phone*
  — **diretto** dee·re·to *direct-dial*
  — **pubblico** poo·blee·ko *public telephone*
telegramma ⓜ *te·le·gra·ma telegram*
telenovela ① *te·le·no·ve·la soap opera*
teleobiettivo ⓜ *te·le·o·bye·tee·vo telephoto lens*
telescopio ⓜ *te·le·sko·pyo telescope*
televisione ① *te·le·vee·zyo·ne television*
temperatura ① *tem·pe·ra·too·ra temperature (weather)*
temperino ⓜ *tem·pe·ree·no penknife*
tempio ⓜ *tem·pyo temple*
tempo ⓜ *tem·po time* • *weather*
  — **pieno** pye·no *full-time*
temporale ⓜ *tem·po·ra·le storm*
tenda ① *ten·da tent*
tensione ① **premestruale** *ten·syo·ne pre·me·stroo·a·le premenstrual tension*
Terra ① *te·ra Earth*

terra ① *te·ra land*
terremoto ⓜ *te·re·mo·to earthquake*
terribile ⓜ/① *te·ree·bee·le terrible*
terzo/a ⓜ/① *ter·tso/a third*
tessera ① *te·se·ra pass (document)*
test ⓜ **di gravidanza** *test dee gra·vee·dan·tsa pregnancy test kit*
testa ① *tes·ta head*
tiepido/a ⓜ/① *tye·pee·do/a warm*
tifoso/a ⓜ/① *tee·fo·zo/a fan (person)* • *supporter*
timido/a ⓜ/① *tee·mee·do/a shy*
tipico/a ⓜ/① *tee·pee·ko/a typical*
tipo ⓜ *tee·po type*
tirare *tee·ra·re pull*
titolo ⓜ *tee·to·lo title*
titoli ⓜ pl **di studio** *tee·to·lee dee stoo·dee·o qualifications*
toboga ⓜ *to·bo·ga toboggan* • *sledge*
toccare *to·ka·re touch*
tofu ⓜ *to·foo tofu*
tomba ① *tom·ba grave*
tonno ⓜ *to·no tuna*
topo ⓜ *to·po mouse (rodent)* • *rat*
torcia ① **elettrica** *tor·cha e·le·tree·ka torch (flashlight)*
torre ① *to·re tower*
torta ① *tor·ta cake* • *pie*
tossico/a ⓜ/① *to·see·ko/a toxic*
tossicodipendenza ① *to·see·ko·dee·pen·den·tsa drug addiction*
tossire *to·see·re cough*
tostapane ⓜ *tos·ta·pa·ne toaster*
tovaglia ① *to·va·lya tablecloth*
tovagliolo ⓜ *to·va·lyo·lo napkin*
tradurre *tra·doo·re translate*
traffico ⓜ *tra·fee·ko traffic*
traghetto ⓜ *tra·ge·to ferry*
tram ⓜ *tram tram*
tramezzino ⓜ *tra·me·dzee·no sandwich*
tramonto ⓜ *tra·mon·to sunset*
tranquillo/a ⓜ/① *tran·kwee·lo/a quiet*
trasporto ⓜ *tras·por·to transport*
travestito ⓜ *tra·ves·tee·to drag queen*
treno ⓜ *tre·no train*
triste *tree·ste sad*
troppo (caro/a) *tro·po ka·ro/a too (expensive)*
troppo/a ⓜ/① *tro·po/a too much* • *too many*

trovare tro·va·re find
trucco ⓜ troo·ko make-up
tu too you (inf)
tubo ⓜ **di scappamento** too·bo dee ska·pa·men·to exhaust (car)
tuffi ⓜ pl too·fee diving (in pool)
turista ⓜ&ⓕ too·ree·sta tourist
tutti/e ⓜ/ⓕ too·tee/too·te all (plural)
tutto ⓜ too·to everything
tutto/a ⓜ/ⓕ too·to/a all (singular)
TV ⓕ tee·voo TV

U

ubriaco/a ⓜ/ⓕ oo·bree·a·ko/a drunk
uccello ⓜ oo·che·lo bird
ufficio ⓜ oo·fee·cho office
  — **del turismo** del too·reez·mo tourist office
  — **oggetti smarriti** o·je·tee sma·ree·tee lost property office
  — **postale** pos·ta·le post office
ultimo/a ⓜ/ⓕ ool·tee·mo/a last
un po' oon po (a) little
una volta ⓕ oo·na vol·ta once
università ⓕ oo·nee·ver·see·ta university
universo ⓜ oo·nee·ver·so universe
uomo ⓜ wo·mo man
  — **d'affari** da·fa·ree businessman
uovo ⓜ wo·vo egg
urgente ⓜ/ⓕ oor·jen·te urgent
urlare oor·la·re shout
usare oo·za·re use
usa e getta oo·za e je·ta disposable
uscire con oo·shee·re kon go out with • date
uscita ⓕ oo·shee·ta exit
utile oo·tee·le useful
uva ⓕ pl oo·va grapes
  — **passa** pa·sa raisin

V

vacanza ⓕ va·kan·tsa holiday • vacation
vacanze ⓕ pl va·kan·tse holidays
vaccinazione ⓕ va·chee·na·tsyo·ne vaccination
vagina ⓕ va·jee·na vagina

vagone ⓜ va·go·ne carriage • wagon
  — **letto** le·to sleeping car
valigetta ⓕ va·lee·je·ta briefcase
  — **del pronto soccorso** del pron·to so·kor·so first-aid kit
valigia ⓕ va·lee·ja suitcase
valle ⓕ va·le valley
valore ⓜ va·lo·re value (price)
vanga ⓕ van·ga spade
vecchio/a ⓜ/ⓕ ve·kyo/a old
vedere ve·de·re see
vedovo/a ⓜ/ⓕ ve·do·vo/a widower/widow
veduta ⓕ ve·doo·ta lookout
vegetariano/a ⓜ/ⓕ ve·je·ta·rya·no/a vegetarian
velenoso/a ⓜ/ⓕ ve·le·no·zo/a poisonous
veloce ve·lo·che fast
velocità ⓕ ve·lo·chee·ta speed
vendere ven·de·re sell
vendita ⓕ ven·dee·ta sale
venire ve·nee·re come
ventilatore ⓜ ven·tee·la·to·re fan (machine)
vento ⓜ ven·to wind
verde ver·de green
verdura ⓕ ver·doo·ra vegetable
vero/a ⓜ/ⓕ ve·ro/a true
vescica ⓕ ve·shee·ka blister
vetro ⓜ ve·tro glass
via ⓕ vee·a way
  — **aerea** a·e·re·a airmail
viaggiare vee·a·ja·re travel
viaggio ⓜ vee·a·jo trip
  — **d'affari** da·fa·ree business trip
viale ⓜ vee·a·le avenue
vicino/a ⓜ/ⓕ vee·chee·no/a close • nearby
vicino (a) vee·chee·no (a) near (to)
vicolo ⓜ vee·ko·lo lane
videocamera ⓕ vee·de·o·ka·me·ra videocamera
videonastro ⓜ vee·de·o·nas·tro video tape
videoregistratore ⓜ vee·de·o·re·jee·stra·to·re video
vigna ⓕ vee·nya vineyard • wine cellar
vigneto ⓜ vee·nye·to vineyard
villaggio ⓜ vee·la·jo village

vincere vee·che·re *win*
vincitore/vincitrice ⓜ/ⓕ veen·chee·to·re/
veen·chee·*tree*·che *winner*
vino ⓜ vee·no *wine*
  — bianco byan·ko *white wine*
  — rosso ro·so *red wine*
  — spumante spoo·*man*·te
  sparkling wine
viola vee·o·la *purple*
virus ⓜ vee·roos *virus*
visita ⓕ vee·zee·ta
  visit • tour • medical examination
  — guidata gwee·da·ta *guided tour*
vista ⓕ vee·sta *view*
visto ⓜ vee·sto *visa*
vita ⓕ vee·ta *life*
vitamine ⓕ pl vee·ta·mee·ne *vitamins*
vitello ⓜ vee·te·lo *veal*
vitto ⓜ vee·to *food*
vivere vee·ve·re *live*
vocabolarietto ⓜ vo·ka·bo·la·rye·to
  phrasebook
vocabolario ⓜ vo·ka·bo·la·ryo *dictionary*
voce ⓕ vo·che *voice*

volare vo·la·re *fly*
volere vo·le·re *want*
volo ⓜ vo·lo *flight*
volta ⓕ vol·ta *time • turn*
volume ⓜ vo·loo·me *volume*
vomitare vo·mee·ta·re *vomit*
votare vo·ta·re *vote*
vuoto/a ⓜ/ⓕ vwo·to/a *empty*

Y

yogurt ⓜ yo·goort *yogurt*

Z

zaino ⓜ dzai·no *backpack • knapsack*
zanzara ⓕ tsan·tsa·ra *mosquito*
zenzero ⓜ dzen·dze·ro *ginger*
zia ⓕ tsee·a *aunt*
zoom ⓜ zoom *zoom lens*
zucca ⓕ tsoo·ka *pumpkin*
zucchero ⓜ tsoo·ke·ro *sugar*
zucchini ⓜ pl tsoo·kee·nee
  courgette • zucchini

FINDER

The topics covered in this book are listed below in Italian. If you're having trouble understanding Italian, show this page to the person you're talking to so they can look up the relevant section.

What kind of traveller are you?

A. You're eating chicken for dinner *again* because it's the only word you know.

B. When no one understands what you say, you step closer and shout louder.

C. When the barman doesn't understand your order, you point frantically at the beer.

D. You're surrounded by locals, swapping jokes, email addresses and experiences – other travellers want to borrow your phrasebook or audio guide.

If you answered A, B, or C, you NEED Lonely Planet's language products ...

- **Lonely Planet Phrasebooks** – for every phrase you need in every language you want

- **Lonely Planet Language & Culture** – get behind the scenes of English as it's spoken around the world – learn and laugh

- **Lonely Planet Fast Talk & Fast Talk Audio** – essential phrases for short trips and weekends away – read, listen and talk like a local

- **Lonely Planet Small Talk** – 10 essential languages for city breaks

- **Lonely Planet Real Talk** – downloadable language audio guides from lonelyplanet.com to your MP3 player

... and this is why

- **Talk to everyone everywhere**
  Over 120 languages, more than any other publisher

- **The right words at the right time**
  Quick-reference colour sections, two-way dictionary, easy pronunciation, every possible subject – and audio to support it

Lonely Planet Offices

Australia
90 Maribyrnong St, Footscray,
Victoria 3011
☎ 03 8379 8000
fax 03 8379 8111
✉ talk2us@lonelyplanet.com.au

USA
150 Linden St, Oakland,
CA 94607
☎ 510 893 8555
fax 510 893 8572
✉ info@lonelyplanet.com

UK
72-82 Rosebery Ave,
London EC1R 4RW
☎ 020 7841 9000
fax 020 7841 9001
✉ go@lonelyplanet.co.uk

lonelyplanet.com